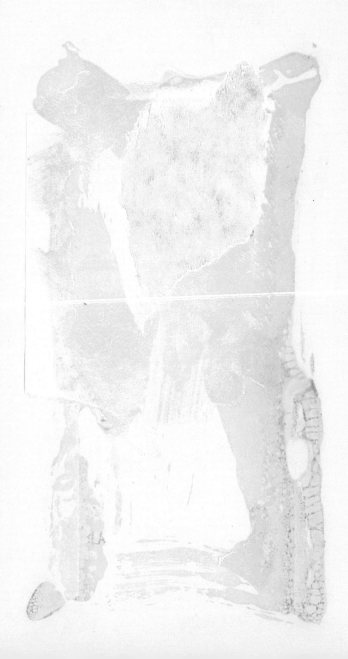

Autobiography of Brook Farm

EDITED BY

HENRY W. SAMS

CHAIRMAN OF DEPARTMENT OF ENGLISH

PENNSYLVANIA STATE UNIVERSITY

⁓⁓⁓ *Autobiography of*

Brook Farm ⁓⁓⁓

GLOUCESTER, MASS.

PETER SMITH

1974

LIBRARY OF CONGRESS
CATALOG CARD NO.: 58-7829

Reprinted, 1974, by Permission of
Prentice-Hall, Inc.
Englewood Cliffs, N. J. 07632

ISBN: 0-8446-4056-5

Introduction

All the materials collected in this volume pertain to the history of Brook Farm. In so far as is practicable, they are arranged in the order in which they were written. When the date of composition cannot be precisely fixed, the date of publication is used instead. The earliest items predate by several months the beginning of associative residency at the Farm. The latest were written during the early years of the twentieth century, when even the youngest of the boys and girls of Brook Farm had grown old.

Each item is headed by a bibliographical note. In addition, the page from which each word of text has been taken is indicated by page numbers within the text. For example, the first item in the book is reprinted from Zoltan Haraszti, *The Idyll of Brook Farm* (Boston: Public Library, 1937), pp. 12-13. Within the text of this item the marking [13] occurs, indicating that the portion of the text which precedes it appears on page 12 of Haraszti's booklet; the portion which follows, on page 13.

Throughout the book every effort has been made to present the texts exactly as they are on the pages from which they are quoted. Typographical conventions change from time to time; for this reason punctuation in these texts does not always conform with the practices recommended for current use. Nathaniel Hawthorne, especially in the privacy of his notebooks, was sometimes a hasty speller; therefore, he may be found writing *chrystal* for *crystal*, and *cloathing* for *clothing*. Nor was Hawthorne alone in misdemeanors of this kind. When blunders in the text are so conspicuous as to make their authenticity suspect, the Latin *sic*, in brackets, has been inserted, meaning "thus it is in the original." At times, too, a word necessary to the sense of a passage is left out of the original text. When this happens, the missing word is supplied in brackets—either by the present editor or by one of the editors from whom he quotes.

The materials of the book are divided into Parts. Each Part is headed by a Preface designed to lead toward profitable lines of enquiry.

The readings in this book are not, of course, *all* the evidence on Brook Farm. They are a selection. However, they include enough information to support a detailed study of Brook Farm.

An exhaustive biography of Brook Farm would require information that could not be included here. For example, it would require a broad view of economic history, particularly of the severe economic depression of the 1830's. It would require detailed reference to the history of religious and philosophical thought in New England. It would require consideration of art, music, literature, and education both in America and abroad. And it would certainly benefit by descriptions of some of the many other "associations" and "phalanxes" contemporary with Brook Farm—they dotted the country from New England to Wisconsin—and of Charles Fourier himself, the acknowledged philosophical leader of associationists.

None of this information is included in this volume. It is an *autobiography*. The picture it provides is small, particular, and local—a microscopic image of "association." For this reason readers are well advised rather to seek sharpness of detail than vastness of scope.

The volume is furnished with a thoroughgoing index. A reader who wishes to concern himself with an individual person—Hawthorne, Dana, Isaac Hecker—or with a single topic—pigs, sports, or the Phalanstery—can quickly find the data for his project.

After thorough consideration of the facts, one comes at last to a judgment of Brook Farm. There is no standard appraisal of it. One eminent critic has called it "madness." Others equally eminent refer to its "gayety, beauty, and loving-kindness." In a sense it failed. The plan collapsed. In another sense it succeeded. But whatever judgment one may feel drawn toward, the story of Brook Farm remains a bright moment of history, with value for later times.

A number of the papers and letters included in this book, although not unknown to students in American Literature, are here printed for the first time.

Most important among these are nine letters of Nathaniel Hawthorne from holographs in the Huntington Library. I am indebted to Professor Randall Stewart and Professor Norman Pearson for supplying true copies of these letters, and especially to Professor Pearson for his courtesy in permitting me to print them here in advance of his forthcoming edition of Hawthorne's letters.

Professor Pearson also put me in the way of using the unpublished Brook Farm correspondence in the possession of the Abernethy Library of Middlebury College, Middlebury, Vermont. For this, too, I am indebted to him. I am grateful also to Miss Mary Noel, Curator of the Abernethy Library for her generous and intelligent assistance.

Finally, I am happy to express my thanks to my colleague, Mrs. Wilma R. Ebbitt, whose criticism of the manuscript was of inestimable help.

HENRY W. SAMS

Contents

Autobiography of Brook Farm

BROOK FARM, BOSTON, AND VICINITY

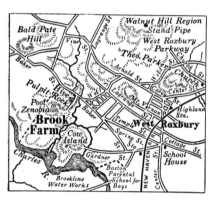

Two maps based on maps printed
in Donald G. Mitchell, *American
Lands and Letters* (New York:
Charles Scribner's Sons, 1904), I,
155.

BROOK FARM, WEST ROXBURY,
AND VICINITY

PART ONE

From the Beginning

to the Earliest

Articles of Association

༄ 1840–1841

Editor's Preface

The early stages of the story of Brook Farm are the least well documented stages. Evidences of the nature of George Ripley's plan were scarce even to his contemporaries. Elizabeth Peabody was impatient with him for his refusal to write out a prospectus, or at least an announcement, for the world at large.

Even so, the initiative which brought Brook Farm into existence was clearly George Ripley's. During the early months the Community was more often referred to simply as Ripley's Farm than by the name under which it afterwards became famous.

Ripley has little to say to us about his community. With a minimum of theoretical talk, he started it going.

Here at the outset he enjoyed the interest, if not in every instance the wholehearted support, of a remarkable group of men and women well known in the vicinity of Boston and Concord. Of this group, those who have left some record of their thoughts about Ripley's Farm are as follows: Ralph Waldo Emerson, whose reputation was already great enough to suggest the possibility of the fame which he ultimately won; Margaret Fuller, a young woman of extraordinary erudition; Sophia Ripley, wife of George Ripley, and if not a metaphysical, yet a tart and excellently informed writer of letters; Elizabeth Peabody, bookseller, bluestocking, and a friend of all thoughtful persons; Nathaniel Hawthorne, as yet unknown to fame, but dedicated to writing and to his prospective bride, Sophia Peabody; and Charles A. Dana, fresh from his studies at Harvard—young, enthusiastic, and vigorous.

These are the persons who tell us about the beginnings of Brook Farm. The books and papers in which their comments are preserved are listed at the end of this introductory note. Like the *dramatis personae* at the beginning of a play, the books are listed in the order in which they appear on ensuing pages.

As one reads through these early records, he learns that each of those who wrote about the Farm saw Ripley's experiment in a light different from all the others. It is interesting to ask, as one reads, just what each of them expected, or hoped for, from the community at the Farm. How was each of them related to the Farm? Which ones intended to live there? When, why, and under what circumstances did each one go there? How did each one appraise what he saw?

When the first Articles of Association were finally written out by Charles Dana, some degree of unanimity must have been arrived at, at least by those who actually lived at the Farm. And yet, some of those who had begun the experiment in high spirits had already begun to question it. Criticisms were already taking shape. Why, for example, did Emerson refuse at the outset to join an enterprise which clearly had won his interest and respect? What fault had he to find with so wholesome an undertaking?

And above all, who were these people of the Farm? What did they want their lives to be? How did they set about fulfilling their ideals?

History is the record of men. We may look at them singly, and then again in groups. As our understanding grows, details arrange themselves, individuals emerge, feature by feature, until finally they stand clearly before us almost as in life. The sounds, colors, and movements of the community gradually become familiar. We can see into the past, and through it into the permanent nature of things.

Oddly enough there is no final summary of history. Just as Elizabeth Peabody and Margaret Fuller, sitting with the Ripleys and discussing the Farm, heard different intonations and formed different opinions, so historians read the same facts differently. There is no single clue, no pat "secret," in any of the evidence that remains. Each statement, note, and record must be studied, reflected upon, absorbed.

And at last, when we know enough, the true history—true so far as we can understand it—takes form and substance in our minds.

Books

Zoltan Haraszti. *The Idyll of Brook Farm.* Boston: Public Library, 1937.

Journals of Ralph Waldo Emerson. Edited by E. W. Emerson and W. E. Forbes. 10 volumes. Boston: Houghton Mifflin Company, 1911.

T. W. Higginson. *Margaret Fuller Ossoli*. Boston: Houghton Mifflin Company, 1884.

O. B. Frothingham. *George Ripley*. Boston: Houghton Mifflin Company, 1882.

The Letters of Ralph Waldo Emerson. Edited by Ralph L. Rusk. 6 volumes. New York: Columbia, 1939.

Nathaniel Hawthorne, holograph letters in the possession of the Huntington Library, San Marino, California. Nine letters printed here are based on true copies made by Professor Randall Stewart and Professor Norman Pearson. An edition of Hawthorne's letters by Professor Pearson is now in preparation.

"Rev. George Ripley" and "The Community at West Roxbury, Mass.," two articles from the *Monthly Miscellany of Religion and Letters*, May 1841 (pp. 293-295) and August 1841 (pp. 113-118). Photostatic copies were supplied the editor by the Columbia University Library.

Manning Hawthorne. "Hawthorne and Utopian Socialism," *New England Quarterly*, XII (1939), 727-729.

Nathaniel Hawthorne. *The American Notebooks*. Edited by Randall Stewart. New Haven: Yale, 1932.

no. 1 ～

Letter from Mrs. George Ripley, Brook Farm, August 1, 1840, to John S. Dwight, here reprinted from Zoltan Haraszti, *The Idyll of Brook Farm* (Boston: Public Library, 1937), pp. 12-13.

Our farm is a sweet spot, which I will not describe, for I trust we shall see you here before the season is past. I am not at all disappointed in my expectations from seclusion, for even my lonely hours have been [13] bright ones, and in this tranquil retreat I have found that entire separation from worldly care and rest to the spirit which I knew was in waiting for me somewhere. We are nearly two miles from any creature, but one or two quiet farmers' families, and do not see so many persons here in a month as we do in one morning at home. Birds and trees, sloping green hills and hay fields as far as the eye can reach—and a brook clear running, at the foot of a green bank covered with shrubbery opposite our window, sings us to our rest with its quiet tune, and chants its morning song to the rising sun. Many dreamy days have been my portion here—roaming about the meads, or lying half asleep under the nut trees on the green knoll near by—or jogging along on my white pony for miles and miles through the green lanes and small roads which abound in our neighborhood—where you meet no well-dressed gentlemen and ladies taking their afternoon airing, and hardly a solitary hay-cart or foot passenger. Even George lies for hours on green banks, reading Burns, and whistling to the birds, who sing to him. Neither are we entirely recluse. Long walks and short rides in various directions bring us to various friends, and the still priestess of Nature in Newton, as well as the brilliant sybil on the plains, are often our hostesses, and sometimes our guests. Last evening William R., Theodore and myself walked over to Margaret's to meet the Farrars and heard Mrs. Cumming play and sing. . . .

no. 2 ~

Entry in the *Journals* of Ralph Waldo Emerson, September 26, 1840. Here reprinted from *Journals of Ralph Waldo Emerson*, edited by E. W. Emerson and W. E. Forbes (Boston: Houghton Mifflin Company, 1911), V, 465.

Perhaps it is folly, this scheming to bring the good and like-minded together into families, into a colony. Better that they should disperse and so leaven the whole lump of society.

no. 3 ~

Entry in the *Journals* of Ralph Waldo Emerson for October 17, 1840. Here reprinted from *Journals of Ralph Waldo Emerson*, edited by E. W. Emerson and W. E. Forbes (Boston: Houghton Mifflin Company, 1911), V, 473-474.

Yesterday George and Sophia Ripley, Margaret Fuller and Alcott discussed here the Social Plans. I wished to be convinced, to be thawed, to be made nobly mad by the kindlings before my eye of a new dawn of human piety. But this scheme was arithmetic and comfort: this was a hint borrowed from the Tremont House and United States Hotel; a rage in our poverty and politics to live rich and gentlemanlike, an anchor to leeward against a change of weather; a prudent forecast on the probable issue of the great questions of Pauperism and Poverty. And not once could I be inflamed, but sat aloof and thoughtless; my voice faltered and fell. It was not the cave of persecution which is the palace of spiritual power, but only a room in the Astor House hired for the Transcendentalists. I do not wish to remove from my present prison to a prison a little larger. I wish to break all [474] prisons. I have not yet conquered my own house. It irks and repents me. Shall I raise the siege of this hencoop, and march baffled away to a pretended siege of Babylon? It seems to me that so to do were to dodge the problem I am set to solve, and to hide my impotency in the thick of a crowd. I can see too, afar,—that I should not find myself more than now,—no, not so much, in that select, but not by me selected, fraternity. Moreover, to join this body would be to traverse all my long trumpeted theory, and the instinct which spoke from it, that one man is a counterpoise to a city,—that a man is stronger than a city, that his solitude is more prevalent and beneficent than the concert of crowds.

no. 4 ～

From a letter from Margaret Fuller, October 28, 1840, here reprinted from T. W. Higginson, *Margaret Fuller Ossoli* (Boston: Houghton Mifflin Company, 1884), p. 180.

In the town I saw the Ripleys. Mr. R. more and more wrapt in his new project. He is too sanguine, and does not take time to let things ripen in his mind; yet his aim is worthy, and with his courage and clear mind his experiment will not, I think, to him at least, be a failure. I will not throw any cold water, yet I would wish him the aid of some equal and faithful friend in the beginning, the rather that his own mind, though that of a captain, is not that of a conqueror. I feel more hopeful as he builds less wide, but cannot feel that I have anything to do at present, except to look on and see the coral insects at work.

Ballou was with him to-night; he seems a downright person, clear as to his own purposes, and not unwilling to permit others the pursuit of theirs.

no. 5 ～

A letter from George Ripley to Ralph Waldo Emerson. Here reprinted from O. B. Frothingham, *George Ripley* (Boston: Houghton Mifflin Company, 1882), pp. 307-312.

Boston, *November* 9, 1840

MY DEAR SIR,—Our conversation in Concord was of such a general nature, that I do not feel as if you were in complete possession of the idea of the Association which I wish to see established. As we have now a prospect of carrying it into effect, at an early period, I wish to submit the plan more distinctly to your judgment, that you may decide whether it is one that can have the benefit of your aid and coöperation.

Our objects, as you know, are to insure a more natural union between intellectual and manual labor than now exists; to combine the thinker and the worker, as far as possible, in the same individual; to guarantee the highest mental freedom, by providing all with labor, adapted to their tastes and talents, and [308] securing to them the fruits of their industry; to do away the necessity of menial services, by opening the benefits of education and the profits of labor to all; and thus to prepare a society of liberal, intelligent, and cultivated persons, whose relations with each other would permit a more simple and wholesome life, than can be led amidst the pressure of our competitive institutions.

To accomplish these objects, we propose to take a small tract of land, which, under skillful husbandry, uniting the garden and the farm, will be adequate to the subsistence of the families; and to connect with this a school or college, in which the most complete instruction shall be given, from the first rudiments to the highest culture. Our farm would be a place for improving the race of men that lived on it; thought would preside over the operations of labor, and labor would contribute to the expansion of thought; we should have industry without drudgery, and true equality without its vulgarity.

An offer has been made to us of a beautiful estate, on very reasonable terms, on the borders of Newton, West Roxbury, and Dedham. I am very familiar with the premises, having resided on them a part of last summer, and we might search the country in vain for anything more eligible. Our proposal now is for three or four families to take possession on the first of April next, to attend to the cultivation of the farm and the erection of buildings, to prepare for the coming of as many more in the autumn, and thus to commence the institution in the simplest manner, and [309] with the smallest number, with which it can go into operation at all. It would thus be not less than two or three years, before we should be joined by all who mean to be with us; we should not fall to pieces by our own weight; we should grow up slowly and strong; and the attractiveness of our experiment would win to us all whose society we should want.

The step now to be taken at once is the procuring of funds for the necessary capital. According to the present modification of our plan, a much less sum will be required than that spoken of in our discussions at Concord. We thought then $50,000 would be needed; I find now, after a careful estimate, that $30,000 will purchase the estate and buildings for ten families, and give the required surplus for carrying on the operations for one year.

We propose to raise this sum by a subscription to a joint stock company, among the friends of the institution, the payment of a fixed interest being guaranteed to the subscribers, and the subscription itself secured by the real estate. No man then will be in danger of losing; he will receive as fair an interest as he would from any investment, while at the same time he is contributing towards an institution, in which[,] while the true use of money is retained, its abuses are done away. The sum required cannot come from rich capitalists; their instinct would protest against such an application of their coins; it must be obtained from those who sympathize with our ideas, and who are willing to aid their realization with their money, if not by their personal coopera-[310]tion. There are some of this description on whom I think we can rely; among ourselves we can produce perhaps $10,000; the remainder must be subscribed for by those who wish us well, whether they mean to unite with us or not.

I can imagine no plan which is suited to carry into effect so many divine ideas as this. If wisely executed, it will be a light over this country and this age. If not the sunrise, it will be the morning star. As a practical man, I see clearly that we must have some such arrangement, or all changes less radical will be nugatory. I believe in the divinity of labor; I wish to "harvest my flesh and blood from the land;" but to do this, I must either be insulated and work to disadvantage, or avail myself of the services of hirelings, who are not of my order, and whom I can scarce make friends; for I must have another to drive the plough, which I hold. I cannot empty a cask of lime upon my grass alone. I wish to see a society of educated friends, working, thinking, and living together, with no strife, except that of each to contribute the most to the benefit of all.

Personally, my tastes and habits would lead me in another direction. I have a passion for being independent of the world, and of every man in it. This I could do easily on the estate which is now offered, and which I could rent at a rate, that with my other resources, would place me in a very agreeable condition, as far as my personal interests were involved. I should have a city of God, on a small scale of my own; and please God, I should hope one day to [311] drive my own cart to market and sell greens. But I feel bound to sacrifice this private feeling, in the hope of a great social good. I shall be anxious to hear from you. Your decision will do much towards settling the question with me, whether the time has come for the fulfillment of a high hope, or whether the work belongs to a future generation. All omens now are favorable; a singular union of diverse talents is ready for the enterprise; everything indicates that we ought to arise and build; and if we let slip this occasion, the unsleeping Nemesis will deprive us of the boon we seek. For myself, I am sure that I can never give so much thought to it again; my mind must act on other objects, and I shall acquiesce in the course of fate, with grief that so fair a light is put out. A small pittance of the wealth which has been thrown away on ignoble objects, during this wild contest for political supremacy, would lay the cornerstone of a house, which would ere long become the desire of nations.

I almost forgot to say that our friends, the "Practical Christians," insist on making their "Standard,"—a written document,—a prescribed test. This cuts them off. Perhaps we are better without them. They are good men; they have salt, which we needed with our spice; but we might have proved too liberal, too comprehensive, too much attached to the graces of culture, to suit their ideas. Instead of them, we have the offer of ten or twelve "Practical Men," from Mr. S. G. May, who himself is deeply interested in the proposal, and would like one day to [312] share in its concerns. Pray write me with as much frankness as I have used towards you, and believe me ever your friend and faithful servant,

GEORGE RIPLEY

P. S. I ought to add, that in the present stage of the enterprise no proposal is considered as binding. We wish only to know what can probably be relied on, provided always, that no pledge will be accepted until the articles of association are agreed on by all parties.

I recollect you said that if you were sure of compeers of the right stamp you might embark yourself in the adventure: as to this, let me suggest the inquiry, whether our Association should not be composed of various classes of men? If we have friends whom we love and who love us, I think we should be content to join with others, with whom our personal sympathy is not strong, but whose general ideas coincide with ours, and whose gifts and abilities would make their services important. For instance, I should like to have a good washerwoman in my parish admitted into the plot. She is certainly not a Minerva or a Venus; but we might educate her two children to wisdom and varied accomplishments, who otherwise will be doomed to drudge through life. The same is true of some farmers and mechanics, whom we should like with us.

no. 6 〜

Letter from Samuel Osgood, Nashua, November 21, 1840, to John Sullivan Dwight, here reprinted from Zoltan Haraszti, *The Idyll of Brook Farm* (Boston: Public Library, 1937), p. 14.

I was in Boston last week, and saw Ripley and our other friends. What exciting times these are. Do you hear of the New Harmony, which is probably about to be established by him, Emerson, etc.? Really one is almost tempted to join them for better or for worse. However, it is well to wait for a knowledge of their plans before undertaking to praise or blame them. I am reading Brisbane's book on the reorganization of Society. I understand, however, that our new-light Socialists eschew Brisbane's dictum. I hope we shall soon see their projected Utopia realized.

no. 7 〜

From a letter from R. W. Emerson, Concord, December 2, 1840, to William Emerson, here reprinted from *The Letters of Ralph Waldo Emerson*, edited by Ralph L. Rusk (New York: Columbia, 1939), II, 364-365.

. . . [365] We are absorbed here at home in discussions of George Ripley's Community. I forget if I have mentioned it to you. He is very anxious to enrol me in his company, & that I should subscribe money to its funds. I am very discontented with many of my present ways & bent on mending them; but not as favorably disposed to his Community of 10 or 12 families as to a more private reform. G. R. wishes to raise $30,000.; to buy a farm of 200 acres in Spring St, Roxbury. for 12000—build $12000. worth of cottages thereon & remove himself with pioneers to the premises on 1 April next. The families who shall come are to do their own work which a studied cooperation is to make easier & simpler. The farm & such mechanical operations as are practised is to give subsistence to the company. A school or college in which the learneder clerks are to teach, it is presumed, will pay a profit—and out of many means the interest at 5 per cent of the capital is to be paid. If I should go there I get rid of menial labor: I learn to work on a farm under skilful direction: I am provided with many means & opportunities of such literary labor as I may wish. Can I not get the same advantages at home without pulling down my house? Ah my dear brother that is the very question we now consider. . . .

Your affectionate brother
WALDO

no. 8 ~~

Letter from R. W. Emerson, Concord, December 15, 1840, to George Ripley, here reprinted—without editorial indications of Emerson's revisions—from *The Letters of Ralph Waldo Emerson*, edited by Ralph L. Rusk (New York: Columbia, 1939), II, 368-371.

MY DEAR SIR,

It is quite time I made an answer to your proposition that I should join you in your new enterprise. The design appears to [369] me so noble & humane, proceeding, as I plainly see, from a manly & expanding heart & mind that it makes me & all men its friends & debtors. It becomes a matter of conscience to entertain it friendly & to examine what it has for us.

I have decided not to join it & yet very slowly & I may almost say penitentially. I am greatly relieved by learning that your coadjutors are now so many that you will no longer ascribe that importance to the defection of individuals which you hinted in your letter to me . . . might . . . attach to mine.

The ground of my decision is almost purely personal to myself. I have some remains of skepticism in regard to the general practicability of the plan, but these have not much weighed with me. That which determines me is the conviction that the Community is not good for me. Whilst I see it may hold out many inducements for others it has little to offer me which with resolution I cannot procure for myself. It seems to me that it would not be worth my while to make the difficult exchange of my property in Concord for a share in the new Household. I am in many respects suitably placed . . . in an agreeable neighborhood, in a town which I have many reasons to love & which has respected my freedom so far that I may presume it will indulge me farther if I need it. Here I have friends & kindred. Here I have builded & planted: & here I have greater facilities to prosecute such practical enterprizes as I may cherish, than I could probably find by any removal. I cannot accuse my townsmen or my social position of my domestic grievances:—only my own sloth & conformity. It seems to me a circuitous & operose way of relieving myself of any irksome circumstances, to put on your community the task of my emancipation which I ought to take on myself. [370]

The principal particulars in which I wish to mend my domestic life are in acquiring habits of regular manual labor, and in ameliorating or abolishing in my house the condition of hired menial service. I should like to come one step nearer to nature than this usage permits. But surely I need not sell my house & remove my family to Newton in order to make the experiment of labor & self help. I am already in the act of trying some domestic & social experiments which my present position favors. And I think that my present position has even greater advantages than yours would offer me for testing my improvements in those small private parties into which men are all set off already throughout the world.

. . . —But I own I almost shrink from making any statement of my objections to our ways of living because I see how slowly I shall mend them. My own health & habits & those of my wife & my mother are not of that robustness which should give any pledge of enterprize & ability in reform. And whenever I am engaged in literary composition I find myself not inclined to insist with heat on new methods. Yet I think that all I shall solidly do, I must do alone. I do not think I should gain anything—I who have little skill to converse with people—by a plan of so many parts and which I comprehend so slowly & imperfectly as the proposed Association.

If the community is not good for me neither am I good for it. I do not look on myself as a valuable member to any community which is not either very large or very small & select. I fear that yours would not find me as profitable & pleasant an associate as I should wish to be and as so important a project seems imperatively to require in all its constituents. Moreover I am so ignorant & uncertain in my improvements that I would fain hide my attempts & failures in solitude where they shall perplex none or very few beside myself. The result of our secretest improvements will certainly have as much renown as shall be due to them.

In regard to the plan as far as it respects the formation of a School or College, I have more hesitation, inasmuch as . . . a concentration of scholars in one place seems to me to have certain great advantages. Perhaps as the school emerges to more distinct consideration out of the Farm, I shall yet find it attractive. And yet I am very apt to relapse into the same skepticism as to modes & arrangements, the same magnify[371]ing of the men—the men alone. According to your ability &

mine, you & I do now keep school for all comers, & the energy of our thought & will measures our influence. In the community we shall utter not a word more—not a word less.

Whilst I refuse to be an active member of your company I must yet declare that of all the . . . philanthropic projects of which I have heard yours is the most pleasing to me and if it is prosecuted in the same spirit in which it is begun, I shall regard it with lively sympathy & with a sort of gratitude.

Yours affectionately
R W EMERSON

no. 9 ⤸

> Letter from Nathaniel Hawthorne to Sophia Peabody, here reprinted from a true copy of the holograph letter now at the Huntington Library, San Marino, California. The true copy, made by Professor Randall Stewart of Vanderbilt University and Professor Norman Pearson of Yale University, appears here through their generosity—Professor Pearson supplied it for use in advance of his forthcoming edition of Hawthorne's letters—and by permission of the Huntington Library.

Oak Hill, April 13th, 1841

OWNEST LOVE,

Here is thy poor husband in a polar Paradise! I know not how to interpret this aspect of Nature—whether it be of good or evil omen to our enterprise. But I reflect that the Plymouth pilgrims arrived in the midst of storm and stept ashore upon mountain snow-drifts; and nevertheless they prospered, and became a great people—and doubtless it will be the same with us. I laud my stars, however, that thou wilt not have thy first impressions of our future home from such a day as this. Thou wouldst shiver all thy life afterwards, and never realize that there could be bright skies, and green hills and meadows, and trees heavy with foliage, where now the whole scene is a great snow-bank, and the sky full of snow likewise. Through faith, I persist in believing that spring and summer will come in due season; but the unregenerated man shivers within me, and suggests a doubt whether I may not have wandered within the precincts of the Arctic circle, and chosen my heritage among everlasting snows. Dearest, provide thyself with a good stock of furs; and if thou canst obtain the skin of a polar bear, thou wilt find it a very suitable summer dress for this region. Thou must not hope ever to walk abroad, except upon snow-shoes, nor to find any warmth, save in thy husband's heart.

Belovedest, I have not yet taken my first lesson in agriculture, as thou mayest well suppose—except that I went to see our cows foddered, yesterday afternoon. We have eight of our own; and the number is now increased by a transcendental heifer, belonging to Miss Margaret Fuller. She is very fractious, I believe, and apt to kick over the milk pail. Thou knowest best, whether, in these traits of character, she resembles her mistress. Thy husband intends to convert himself into a milk-maid, this evening; but I pray heaven that Mr. Ripley may be moved to assign him the kindliest cow in the herd—otherwise he will perform his duty with fear and trembling.

Ownest wife, I like my brethren in affliction very well; and couldst thou see us sitting round our table, at meal-times, before the great kitchen-fire, thou wouldst call it a cheerful sight. Mrs. Barker is a most comfortable woman to behold; she looks as if her ample person were stuffed full of tenderness—indeed, as if she were all one great, kind heart. Wert thou but here, I should ask for nothing more—not even for sunshine and summer weather; for thou wouldst be both, to thy husband. And how is that cough of thine, my belovedest? Hast thou thought of me, in my perils and wanderings? Thou must not think how I longed for thee, when I crept into my cold bed last night,—my bosom remembered thee,—and refused to be comforted without thy kisses. I trust that thou dost muse upon me with hope and joy, not with repining. Think that I am gone before, to prepare a home for my Dove, and will return for her, all in good time.

Thy husband has the best chamber in the house, I believe; and though not quite so good as the apartment I have left, it will do very well. I have hung up thy two pictures; and they give me a glimpse of summer and of thee. The vase I intended to have brought in my arms; but could not very conveniently do it yesterday; so that it still remains at Mrs. Hillards, together with my carpet. I shall bring them the next opportunity.

Now farewell, for the present, most beloved. I have been writing this in my chamber; but the fire is getting low, and the house is old and cold; so that the warmth of my whole person has retreated to my heart, which burns with love for thee. I must run down to the kitchen or parlor hearth, where thy image shall sit beside me—yea be pressed to my breast. At bed-time, thou shalt have a few lines more. Now I think of it, dearest, wilt thou give Mrs. Ripley a copy of Grandfather's Chair and Liberty Tree; she wants them for some boys here. I have several copies of Famous Old People.

14

April 14th. 10 A.M. Sweetest, I did not milk the cows last night, because Mr. Ripley was afraid to trust them to my hands, or me to their horns—I know not which. But this morning, I have done wonders. Before breakfast, I went out to the barn, and began to chop hay for the cattle; and with such "righteous vehemence" (as Mr. Ripley says) did I labor, that, in the space of ten minutes, I broke the machine. Then I brought wood and replenished the fires; and finally sat down to breakfast and ate up a huge mound of buckwheat cakes. After breakfast, Mr. Ripley put a four-pronged instrument into my hands, which he gave me to understand was called a pitch-fork; and he and Mr. Farley being armed with similar weapons, we all three commenced a gallant attack upon a heap of manure. This affair being concluded, and thy husband having purified himself, he sits down to finish this letter to his most beloved wife. Dearest, I will never consent that thou come within a half a mile of me, after such an encounter as that of this morning. Pray Heaven that this letter retain none of the fragrance with which the writer was imbued. As for thy husband himself, he is peculiarly partial to the odor; but that whimsical little nose of thine might chance to quarrel with it.

Belovedest, Miss Fuller's cow hooks the other cows, and has made herself ruler of the herd, and behaves in a very tyrannical manner. Sweetest, I know not when I shall see thee; but I trust it will not be longer than till the end of next week. I love thee! I love thee! I would thou wert with me; for then would my labor be joyful—and even now, it is not sorrowful. Dearest, I shall make an excellent husbandman. I feel the original Adam reviving within me.

Miss Sophia A. Peabody,
 13 West-street,
  Boston.

no. 10

Letter from Elizabeth Palmer Peabody, Boston, April 26, 1841, to John Sullivan Dwight, Northampton, here reprinted from Zoltan Haraszti, *The Idyll of Brook Farm* (Boston: Public Library, 1937), pp. 14 and 17. Pages 15 and 16 are occupied by a picture.

The Ripleys have been three weeks yesterday at their place—that is George, with occasional visits of two or three days from Sophia or Frank Farley. William Allen and Elise Barker went the first fortnight and they cleaned the stable, arranged the house, ploughed and planted, going through the hardest and most disagreeable work they will ever have to do. They also every day milk their cows, and such is the effect [17] of regular feeding that already they give ⅓ more milk than at first. In a fortnight Hawthorne and Mr. Warren Burton joined them, and Hawthorne has taken hold with the greatest spirit and proves a fine workman. But Frank Farley is the crown of all. He knows how to do every species of work, from cooking and other kinds of domestic labour through all the processes of farming and dealing with live stock; and solaces his leisure hours with the fine arts—for he draws—and reads aloud with histrionic beauty. . . .

While they are so few, and the community plan is not in full operation, it is unavoidable that they must work very hard; but they do it with great spirit, and their health and courage rises to meet the case. William Channing is, I believe, to join them in June as well as George Bradford. They have young Newcomb from Providence, Margaret Fuller's brother Lloyd fitting for College, and one or two more children who also help. Miss Ripley keeps her town school in the country next house to them for the summer. . .

What is altogether desirable is that they buy the farm and go to build, and get all their hands and heads assembled. Ripley still relucts from printing even a prospectus, but has determined on the 11th of May to have a meeting which will be holden at our house on account of our large party to which is invited a company of persons—combining supposable interest in the plan with solid cash in their purses or influence over the purses of others—and to these is to be shown what this school is, its moral, intellectual, practical aspect, its relation to the life of its professors; and then it is to be shown that without ten thousand dollars capital can be raised in addition to what money the associates bring, this same school cannot go into immediate operation. By an article which operates as a bonus for those who take a share as well as send a pupil, they think they can raise this in such a way as that while it benefits the community it benefits the other party too. They hope to raise this 10 or 12 thousand dollars instanter and proceed to build—and so all gather together in the fall.

no. 11 ～

"Rev. George Ripley," an article in *The Monthly Miscellany of Religion and Letters*, May 1841, pp. 293-295, here reprinted from photostatic copies supplied by the Columbia University Library.

REV. GEORGE RIPLEY.—It is with sincere regret, and with a sense of personal loss, that we notice Mr. Ripley's retirement from the ministry in this city [Boston]. For nearly fifteen years he has been the faithful pastor of the Purchase street Society, and an active and efficient cooperator with his brethren in attempts to promote the intellectual and spiritual elevation of the community. In choosing another sphere of occupation he has acted from a sense of duty, and although we wish he could have seen it to be his duty to remain among us, we hope he will be abundantly prospered and will accomplish all his purposes of usefulness in his new employment. His plans for the future are connected with the education of the young of both sexes. His immediate object, as we understand, is the gathering of a cooperative association for the purposes of practical education. We can discover nothing chimerical or "Transcendental" in this scheme. On the contrary, it seems to us both practical and practicable. It proposes to unite the advantages of physical and intellectual development for the young, and of mental culture and healthful and economical habits for older persons, under social [294] relations which it is thought will be peculiarly favorable to these ends. By a partial combination of their several resources many individuals may obtain facilities of improvement and enjoyment beyond what any of them could separately command, while private tastes and domestic associations will be carefully respected. The union of persons of different philosophical and theological views in this enterprise is a security against the existence, and should be protection against the imputation, of any sectarian design. A sentence or two from an article in the "New England Farmer" may exhibit more clearly the nature of the proposed institution.

"An association has been formed by several gentlemen in this city and vicinity, for the purpose of establishing a 'Practical Institute of Agriculture and Education.' The design of this institution is to furnish the means of a liberal education to those who are not intended for the learned professions. The principles of science, which lie at the foundation of the practical arts of life, will form the chief objects of attention, while the study of the languages will occupy a subordinate sphere. It is intended to combine the study of scientific agriculture with its practical operations, to illustrate the great improvements of modern husbandry by actual experiment; to increase the attachment of the farmer to the cultivation of the soil, by showing the dignity of the pursuit, and the knowledge and ability which it demands, and thus to prepare young men, who propose to make agriculture the business of their lives, for the intelligent discharge of the duties of their calling. It is contemplated, we also understand, to connect with the institution a department for classical learning, in which pupils will be prepared for admission to any of the New England colleges, or be instructed in a course similar to that which is pursued by under-graduates, while at the same time they will have an opportunity to study the sciences on which agriculture is founded, and to engage in its practical details to such extent as may be desired."

The site chosen for the institution is in Newton, on a pleasant, but little travelled, road leading from West Roxbury, about eight miles from Boston.

We are glad to learn that Mr. Ripley does not intend to relinquish preaching, but will render such services in the supply of pulpits as may be consistent with his residence at Newton.—The Purchase street Society, upon accepting his resignation, unanimously passed the following resolutions:—

"*Resolved*, That the thanks of this religious society be rendered to their pastor, Rev. George Ripley, for his long-tried and faithful services, as well in the pulpit, as in his parochial walks.

"*Resolved*, That having the entire confidence in the integrity, moral worth, and religious character of our much esteemed pastor, we take this occasion at parting, to say, that we can recommend him to the Christian world as a Christian minister, every way worthy, and every way qualified to preach the Gospel; and viewing the separation between pastor and people about to take place, and the time fast approaching when that [295] friendly and familiar voice will be no longer heard within these walls, we cannot permit the present period to pass without expressing our sincere and deep regret that circumstances make it necessary to induce our beloved pastor to ask his discharge; and assuring him, that although time and chance may separate us, he has our best wishes in all future time, that his lot may be that of happiness and usefulness, and in whatever sphere of labor he may be called that he may be richly and abundantly blessed."

no. 12 ❧

Letter from Nathaniel Hawthorne to Louisa Hawthorne, here reprinted from a true copy of the holograph letter now at the Huntington Library, San Marino, California. The true copy, made by Professor Randall Stewart of Vanderbilt University and Professor Norman Pearson of Yale University, appears here through their generosity—Professor Pearson supplied it for use in advance of his forthcoming edition of Hawthorne's letters—and by permission of the Huntington Library.

Brook Farm, West Roxbury,
May 3ᵈ, 1841

[To: Louisa Hawthorne.]

As the weather precludes all possibility of ploughing, hoeing, sowing, and other such operations, I bethink me that you may have no objection to hear something of my whereabout and whatabout. You are to know then, that I took up my abode here on the 12th ultimo, in the midst of a snow-storm, which kept us all idle for a day or two. At the first glimpse of fair weather, Mr. Ripley summoned us into the cow-yard, and introduced me to an instrument with four prongs, commonly called a dung-fork. With this tool, I have already assisted to load twenty or thirty carts of manure, and shall take part in loading nearly three hundred more. Besides, I have planted potatoes and pease, cut straw and hay for the cattle, and done various other mighty works. This very morning, I milked three cows; and I milk two or three every night and morning. The weather has been so unfavorable, that we have worked comparatively little in the fields; but, nevertheless, I have gained strength wonderfully—grown quite a giant, in fact—and can do a day's work without the slightest inconvenience. In short, I am transformed into a complete farmer.

This is one of the most beautiful places I ever saw in my life, and as secluded as if it were a hundred miles from any city or village. There are woods, in which we can ramble all day, without meeting anybody, or scarcely seeing a house. Our house stands apart from the main road; so that we are not troubled even with passengers looking at us. Once in a while, we have a transcendental visitor, such as Mr. Alcott; but, generally, we pass whole days without seeing a single face, save those of the brethren. At this present time, our effective force consists of Mr. Ripley, Mr. Farley, (a farmer from the far west,) Rev. Warren Burton (author of various celebrated works) [,] three young men and boys, who are under Mr. Ripley's care, and William Allen, his hired man, who has the chief direction of our agricultural labors. In the female part of the establishment there is Mrs. Ripley, and two women folks. The whole fraternity eat together; and such a delectable way of life has never been seen on earth, since the days of the early Christians. We get up at half-past four, breakfast at half-past six, dine at half[-]past twelve, and go to bed at nine.

The thin frock, which you made for me, is considered a most splendid article; and I should not wonder if it were to become the summer uniform of the community. I have a thick frock, likewise; but it is rather deficient in grace, though extremely warm and comfortable. I wear a tremendous pair of cow-hide boots, with soles two inches thick. Of course, when I come to see you, I shall wear my farmer's dress.

We shall be very much occupied during most of this month, plough-ing and planting; so that I doubt whether you will see me for two or three weeks. You have the portrait by this time, I suppose; so you can very well dispense with the original. When you write to me (which I beg you will do soon) direct your letter to West Roxbury, as there are two Post Offices in the town. I would write more; but William Allen is going to the village, and must have this letter; so good-bye.

NATH HAWTHORNE,
Ploughman.

Miss Maria L. Hawthorne,
    Salem
    Massachusetts

no. 13 ∾

Letter from Mrs. George Ripley, Brook Farm, May 6, 1841, to John Sullivan Dwight, here reprinted from Zoltan Haraszti, *The Idyll of Brook Farm* (Boston: Public Library, 1937), pp. 17-18.

We feel established and perfectly at home in the country, and our relations to each other are so natural and true that they seem to have [18] existed always. The number assembled around the table in our large middle kitchen is thirteen and will soon number sixteen. My sister opens her house with eight or nine more next week. You will be inter-ested to hear of the merits of our head man, William Allen, who is wise and refined, industrious and amiable, and knows how to do everything. Mr. Farley is beyond praise, always on the alert, practised in all kinds of labour, the hardest worker in the field, the irresistible wit at table, the refined gentleman in the parlour and everywhere . . . Hawthorne is one to reverence, to admire with that deep admiration so refreshing to the soul. He is our prince—prince in everything—yet despising no labour and very athletic and able-bodied in the barnyard and field. Mr. Burton does well and (entre nous) if he does not add to the charms of our social circle, does not interfere with them. A brother of Jane Tuckerman's, a young lad of 14, training to labor is a perpetual pleasure to us; a very active and intelligent young man of 16, a drover who loves music first, to drive oxen next, and read Coleridge to rest him-self; Lloyd Fuller, who has all the Fuller faults (entre nous again) without their merits, but who serves to show us how a refractory member can be kept in check by the influence of the rest. The Miss Slades are going with us for the present, and there is a little boy whom we are training, who plays Orson to our little Valentine, and it has been one of my best pleasures to see him gradually surrendering himself to the influences of culture. The very expression of his countenance is changing. A bright girl from Maine helps me in the house work, which is light compared to my city labors: and I expect daily Mr. Benton's little girl, and a niece of ours from the country to aid us still further. Mr. Bradford joins us at the end of the month, and Charles Newcomb is only waiting for the first pleasant day to come. I intend to gather a class immediately and resume my old vocation. All of us are agreeably disappointed in our physical power, particularly George who does a harder day's work each day than the last, and feels better than ever before . . .

no. *14* ～

Letter from Margaret Fuller to R. W. Emerson, here reprinted from T. W. Higginson, *Margaret Fuller Ossoli* (Boston: Houghton Mifflin Company, 1884), pp. 181-182.

Cambridge, 10th May, 1841.

Your letter, my dear friend, was received just as I was on the wing to pass a few days with the fledglings of Community; and I have only this evening returned to answer it. I will come on Saturday afternoon next if no cross accident mar the horizon of my hopes, and the visible heavens drop not down Niagaras. All that I have to say may best be reserved till I come; it is necessary that I should be economical, for I have of late [182] been as gentle, as dull, and as silent as the most fussy old bachelor could desire his housekeeper to be. You said, however, I could come and live there, if I had not a mind to talk, so I am not afraid, but will come, hoping there may be a flow after this ebb, which has almost restored the health of your affectionate

MARGARET.

no. *15* ～

Letter from Nathaniel Hawthorne to Sophia Peabody, here reprinted from a true copy of the holograph letter now at the

Huntington Library, San Marino, California. The true copy, made by Professor Randall Stewart of Vanderbilt University and Professor Norman Pearson of Yale University, appears here through their generosity—Professor Pearson supplied it for use in advance of his forthcoming edition of Hawthorne's letters—and by permission of the Huntington Library.

Brook Farm, June 1st, 1841—nearly 6 A.M.

VERY DEAREST,

I have been too busy to write thee a long letter by [before] this opportunity; for I think this present life of mine gives me an antipathy to pen and ink, even more than my Custom House experience did. I could not live without the idea of thee, nor without spiritual communion with thee; but, in the midst of toil, or after a hard day's work in the gold mine, my soul obstinately refuses to be poured out on paper. That abominable gold mine! Thank God, we anticipate getting rid of its treasures, in the course of the next two or three days. Of all hateful places, that is the worst; and I shall never comfort myself for having spent so many days of blessed sunshine there. It is my opinion, dearest, that a man's soul may be buried and perish under a dungheap or in a furrow of the field, just as well as under a pile of money. Well; that giant, Mr. George Bradford, will probably be here to-day; so that there will be no danger of thy husband being under the necessity of laboring more than he likes, hereafter. Meantime, my health is perfect, and my spirits buoyant, even in the gold mine.

And how art thou belovedest? Two or three centuries have passed since I saw thee; and then thou wast pale and languid. Thou didst comfort thee [me] in that little note of thine; but still I cannot help longing to be informed of thy present welfare. Thou art not a prudent little Dove, and wast naughty to come on such a day as thou didst; and it seems to me that Mrs. Ripley does not know how to take care of thee at all. Art thou quite well now.

Dearest wife, I intend to come and see thee either on Thursday or Friday—perhaps my visit may be deferred till Saturday, if the gold mine should hold out so long. I yearn for thee unspeakably. Good bye now; for the breakfast horn has sounded, sometime since. God bless thee, ownest.

THY LOVINGEST HUSBAND.

Miss Sophia A. Peabody,
    13 West-street,
       Boston.

no. 16 ~

Letter from Elizabeth Palmer Peabody, Boston, June 24, 1841, to
John Sullivan Dwight, here reprinted from Zoltan Haraszti, *The
Idyll of Brook Farm* (Boston: Public Library, 1937), pp. 18-19.

With respect to the Community, I do not see how it is to step out of its
swaddling clothes, unless Mr. Ripley makes known in some regular
way, or allows some friend to do so, the plan in detail and in connection
with the Ideal. He enjoys the 'work' so much that he does not clearly
see that his plan is not in the way of being demonstrated any farther
than that it is being made evident that gentlemen, if they will work as
many hours as boors, will succeed even better in cultivating a farm.
[19] But I trust something will be done soon of a magnetic character—
to find the steel which is scattered in the great heap of leads which make
up our society. I am more and more interested in it, as I see the evils
arising out of the present corrupt, or petrified, organization.

no. 17 ~

Letter from Nathaniel Hawthorne, Boston, July 18, 1841, to David
Mack, here reprinted from Manning Hawthorne, "Hawthorne and
Utopian Socialism," *The New England Quarterly*, XII (1939),
727-729.

To David Mack, Esq.
My dear Sir:—

Your letter has this moment been put in my hands. I truly thank you
for it and wish to lose no time in correcting some misapprehensions
which have been caused by your judging of my feelings through the
medium of third persons—and partly from my brief and imperfect
communications to you last Sunday.

I have never felt that I was called upon by Mr. Ripley to devote so
much of my time to manual labor, as has been done, since my residence
at Brook Farm; nor do I believe that others have felt constraint of that
kind from him personally. We have never looked upon him as a master,
or an employer, but as a fellow laborer on the same terms with ourselves, with no more right to bid us perform any one act of labor than
we have to bid him. Our constraint has been entirely that of circumstances which were as much beyond his control as our own; and as

there is no way of escaping this constraint except by leaving the farm at once—and that step none of us were prepared to take because (though attributing less importance to the success of this immediate enterprise than Mr. Ripley does) we still felt that its failure would be very inauspicious to the prospects of this community. For my own part there are private and personal motives which, without the influence of those shared by us all, would still make me wish to bear all the drudgery of this one summer's labor were it much more onerous than I have found it. It is true that I do not infrequently regret that the summer is passing with so little enjoyment of nature and my own thoughts and with the sacrifice of some objects that I had hoped to accomplish. Such were the regrets to which I alluded last Sunday, but Mr. Ripley cannot be held responsible for the disagreeable circumstances which cause them.

I recollect speaking very despondently, perhaps despairingly, of the prospects of the situation. My views in this respect vary somewhat with the state of my spirits but I confess that of late my hopes are never very sanguine. I form my judgment, however, not from anything that has passed within the precincts of Brook Farm but from external circumstances—from the improbability [728] that adequate funds will be raised or that any feasible plan can be suggested for proceeding without a very considerable capital. I likewise perceive that there would be some very knotty points to be discussed, even had we capital enough to buy an estate. These considerations have somewhat lessened the heartiness and cheerfulness with which I formerly went forth to the fields and perhaps have interposed a medium of misunderstanding between Mr. Ripley and us all. His zeal will not permit him to doubt of eventual success; and he perceives, or imagines, a more intimate connection between our present farming operations and our ultimate enterprise than is visible to my perceptions. But as I said before the two things are sufficiently connected to make me desirous of giving my best efforts to the promotion of the former.

You will see, I think, from what I have now stated, that there was no pressing necessity for me, or my fellow laborers, to dishearten Mr. Ripley by expressing dissatisfaction with our present mode of life. It is our wish to give his experiment a full and fair trial; and if his many hopes are to be frustrated we should be loth to give him reason to attribute the failure to lack of energy and persaverance [*sic*] in his associates. Nevertheless, we did, several days since, (he and myself, I mean) have a conversation on this subject; and he is now fully possessed of my feelings in respect to personal labor.

Probably you have not heard of Mr. Burton's departure from Brook Farm. It occurred night before last. It is an unfortunate event in all its aspects. You will probably learn some of the circumstances which led to it from Mr. Ripley, who, I doubt not, will render all justice to Mr. Burton so far as his position may enable him to form a correct judgment. It is a subject not easily to be discussed in a letter; but I hope at some future time to communicate my views of the matter viva voce. Leave this paragraph out, if you think best.

I have written this letter in great haste so that very probably it may fail to satisfy your mind on the subjects involved. I shall be happy, whenever an opportunity occurs, to talk at large and with all frankness about the interests which we have in common. [729] This, however, cannot be done for a week or two, as I am about to accompany Mr. Farley, to the sea shore—at his own and Mr. Ripley's request. His health is such that this step is deemed essential.

I remain yours sincerely,
NATH. HAWTHORNE

no. 18 ∾

"The Community at West Roxbury, Mass.," an article in *The Monthly Miscellany of Religion and Letters*, August 1841, pp. 113-118, here reprinted from photostatic copies supplied by the Columbia University Library.

THE COMMUNITY AT WEST ROXBURY, MASS.—Some curiosity having been excited respecting the Establishment of Agriculture and Education at West Roxbury, we have asked and received leave to print the following extract from a letter written by a friend—not a member of the new Community—to a lady in England.

* * * "And what hinders,—say these associates,—that we should have an organization of society on Christian ideas, if those who have [114] these ideas only come out from the world, and communicate and live: —live wholly,—live in the body by a constant increase of health, live in the spirit by a complete unfolding of heart, intellect, and moral nature?"

On consideration it was seen, that the labour of society might be lessened by machinery and cooperation of numbers, while the desirable fruits of labour would not be in the least sacrificed; that there was no need of any drudge in society, provided there was no drone; that a diffusion of bodily labour would be equally a means of health to those who do not work at all, and to those who work too much; that there need be no want, if there were indulged no superfluity; no perpetual sacrifice by many of the higher pleasures of life, were there a reasonable and righteous sacrifice by some of mere bodily luxuries.

This insight could hardly exist without stimulating the conscience, and the question arising,—how *dare* I be a drone when others are drudges? How dare I sacrifice not only my own, but others' health, in sequestrating myself from my share of bodily labour, or neglecting a due mental cultivation? How dare I have superfluities, when others are in want? How dare I oppose the unfolding of the spiritual progress of my whole race, by all the force of my personal selfishness and indolence? In short, is it not the sin against the Holy Ghost, with this new-found insight, to hesitate to enter immediately upon the immortal life?

The associates were not previously acquainted with each other. The protest of Mr. R—— against a situation in life, which, taking society as it is, is undoubtedly one of the most disinterested, had excited inquiry among other earnest livers, in the most dissimilar external situations,— scholars, candidates for the ministry, teachers, mechanics, farmers, young men and young women with no especial vocation; and this inquiry led to mutual understanding. They said to one another:—"We belong together, let us unite and realize our principles. Some of us have bodily strength and skill of labour, some of us have scientific education, some of us have knowledge of domestic arts; each of us wishes to be enriched with the power of the other, be it manual, intellectual, or moral. Let us put together our means and buy a farm, and cultivate it. Let us go together and teach one another our various knowledges and skills; and above all, let us teach our children according to their genius, and according to the genius of humanity, neglecting all those customs and prejudices which have no life in them."

But here the question came up of the disadvantages. Surely *community* has its advantages, but let us not sacrifice individuality. Every man must be wholly himself before he can be a desirable associate. Private property and personal isolation have their indispensable good influences; this was acknowledged. But why not have an organization [115] in which both these principles shall be combined? In a family, these two poles of society act. Individuality and the intensest social action are united there. Why may they not be in God's great family? They planned then that every one should retain some property,—enough to be so far independent that each one could leave the Association, if it were necessary or desirable, and not be cast penniless on the world. This is effected by an arrangement of which I will endeavour to give you a general outline.

Every man and woman who has any money puts it in, and it is understood each shall have five percent interest. They also put themselves in as labourers; whose labour is worth the same number of cents an hour, whatever is the office or service. For it is not supposed that money is the only or chief compensation for labour. There are compensations of a different kind, which this community provides by its constitution; —freedom to work in the vocation adapted to your disposition and genius; freedom from care respecting the temporal future of your children, or your own age; in short, freedom to *live,* which our "merchant princes" seldom redeem from the calls of business, with their incomes of ten thousand a year; how much less the majority of society! With two thirds of the stock of money put in, the Community as such would buy a farm, stock it, provide it with implements of agriculture, build a sufficient number of houses on a very simple scale and one large house for general purposes, and furnish a ware-house with all such merchandise as is necessary for comfortable subsistence, purchased at such advantage as the quantity they would want makes possible, and sold at cost. The Community as such also provides gratuitously for all the individual members houses, medical attendance, nursing, education in all departments, amusements; and to all persons over seventy and under ten years of age, and to all persons who are sick, free board, unless their five percent interest can support them. But every capable person must pay board, calculated at cost; and it is believed that the board will not amount to the labour, and therefore that it will not be necessary, after they have fairly got under weigh, for a well gifted person to bring any other contribution than his labour, even though he have the usual number of helpless dependents; which, by the way, children over ten years of age are not considered, for they will be credited at half price by the hour for their light labours until they are twenty, when they will in ordinary cases have accumulated three or four hundred dollars, to be paid to them at that time. This, with a perfect education, would be a very good beginning of life for a young person who should incline to leave the Community and seek his or her fortune in the world at large. [116]

It seems to me that here we see brought about, in the most peaceable manner in the world, that very rectification of things which Mr. Brownson in his Article on the Labouring Classes is understood to declare will require a bloody revolution, a war such as the world has not heard of; viz., that no child shall be born richer or poorer than another, except by inward gift of God, but all shall inherit from society a good education and an independent place. Then might there not be good hope that these gifts of God would be used, as Jesus used his, purely for disinterested purposes; the energy now thrown into the brute law of self-preservation, becoming love of God and man?

It is calculated that, once in operation, the Community will have annually an overplus of money, instead of the population's pressing upon the means of subsistence, as is the common fact in the society of competition. This overplus is to be divided among the associates according to their labour, and they can throw it back again into the common fund to increase the common advantages, according to personal disposition, since all the necessaries of life are secured to them at all events. You see that private property, so necessary to secure personal isolation at will, is reconciled with community of labour. Persons who enter upon this scheme will indeed forego forever the hope of great individual accumulation, but, as a vast overpayment for this, infancy and old age are to be maintained sacred, sickness provided for, and "carking care" taken forever out of life.

Family integrity is also to be sacred. Any married couple with their children may live together, eat together, and have a paramount right to each other; or they may go to the commons. Social intercourse is to be so free as to be under individual choice, as it is not now. Rooms for intercourse are to be open every evening, which can be used for religious exercises, religious teaching, scientific and literary lectures, benevolent associations, or mere conversation, or amusements—such as dancing, music, (and I hope dramatic exhibitions, but I do not know, for I never heard that subject mentioned.) All are to go freely to these rooms, but any are to stay at home when they please, and no questions asked. This facility and universality of intercourse will preclude all excuse for invading people's leisure. The principle they wish to establish is, that every man has a primary right to decide for himself as to what are his social duties, as well as all other duties; nor be appropriated without his own consent.

The "governmental" machinery is to be very simple. The Directions of Agriculture, of Domestic Labour, of Education, &c. are at certain times to state in general meeting what is to be done; and the people are to volunteer to the several departments for certain hours, which [117] they shall specify,—being credited so much the hour at the general rate of labour. If any thing is left undone, it is to be restated, and if none volunteer, the Community as such is to hire it done, until persons are found who have taste or genius for this department, or who, for the sake of society or the education of their children, are desirous to become associates on the condition of doing these duties. The associates vote about the admission of new members, in order that none should enter who are not in sympathy with the idea; and they pledge themselves to take care of each other. The associates may also vote out any member for moral turpitude proved, or for idleness; but things will so work, that ungenial or unworthy members will doubtless take themselves off before it is put to vote.

These associates have some money among them, though not more than half enough to commence their operations. But in point of personal power,—although they have bodily power, and habits of labour too, among them, abundantly sufficient for the work of the place, as they are proving this summer by working (a few of them) as hired men to one of their number who has taken the farm for a year on his own responsibility,—they are richest in intellectual power. Consequently on this account, as well as because it is the natural business of a true society to be doing the work of education, they will receive children to be educated with their children, and be paid for it; but only so many as can be domesticated in their families, and as will enter into all the labours like the children of the Community, according as these are desirable for the development of their bodies and minds.

Here is the germ of the true University. Moral education will not be here *exparte* life. It will be the life of the Community pervading the life of the members. They lay out to have science and literature and art taught in all branches. Scientific agriculture will naturally take the lead, but boys are to be fitted, from the first, for our colleges; and in the end, all that is taught in our colleges will be involved in the course of instruction. Female education will also be there more complete than it has ever been, because they will be able to combine the retirement of private education with all that is desirable of public education. They begin also with infancy. The infant education will be divided among such women as come forward to do this work; and the parents will have the liberty of choosing among these those whose genius they think most adapted to their children, or of keeping their children under their own sole care. The number of teachers will also make it so easy for each, that there will be no danger of the genius of instruction becoming wearied down by confinement and fagging.

How can education growing so naturally out of life be otherwise [118] than perpetually advancing? The Faculty is neither dependent on government patronage, nor on popular favour. The Instructors stand on the soil, having earned their subsistence, and with the leisure and intellectual power they redeem from slavery to the means of subsistence they offer to carry on the great work of man—human education. I feel that the spectacle of this Community will stand in society as the Constitution of the United States does among the nations, and for more; for the Constitution is but a human instrument, while this Community is a divine life.

I have said that they have begun agricultural labour in a private sort of way already. They have also commenced their school operations upon the very few whom Mr. and Mrs. R—— could take into their small house; and they have received applications in behalf of many more pupils whom they cannot accommodate. But if they had their thirty thousand dollars now, they would buy the farm they have hired, and put up the buildings for the accommodation of all their families, and go into operation as a Community this autumn, or next spring at latest. And I have not the slightest doubt that, were a knowledge of the idea and details of the plan, even so far as this letter gives, widely diffused, there would be found many a person in this broad land who would rejoice to buy the stock, and take the interest in the education of his children. One or two subscribers would be enough.

My letter is so long, I must defer to another time the account of the school in more detail, and of the individuals who are to compose the association. You see I have lost entirely my horror of *community*,— now that I have found it can be so restricted, as to leave personal liberty and family integrity sacred. If it succeeds, two of the most important problems of human life will be settled, viz. the reconciliation of labour with cultivation and elegance of mind and manners, and the independence of the Faculty of education. I think too it can be proved the true church;—but of that another time.

no. 19 ～

Letter from Nathaniel Hawthorne to Sophia Peabody, here reprinted from a true copy of the holograph letter now at the Huntington Library, San Marino, California. The true copy, made by Professor Randall Stewart of Vanderbilt University and Professor Norman Pearson of Yale University, appears here through their generosity—Professor Pearson supplied it for use in advance of his forthcoming edition of Hawthorne's letters—and by permission of the Huntington Library.

Brook Farm, Aug. 12th, 1841.

DEAREST UNUTTERABLY, Mrs. Ripley is going to Boston this morning, to Miss Slade's wedding; so I sit down to write a word to thee, not knowing whither to direct it. My heart searches for thee, but wanders about vaguely, and is strangely dissatisfied. Where art thou? I fear that thou didst spend yesterday in the unmitigated east-wind of the sea-coast. Perhaps thou art shivering, at this moment, and yearning for the warmth of thy husband's breast.

Dearest, I would that I were with thee. It seems as if all evil things had more power over thee, when I am away. Then thou art exposed to noxious winds, and to pestilence, and to deathlike weariness; and, moreover, nobody knows how to take care of thee but thy husband. Everybody else thinks it of importance that thou shouldst paint and sculpture; but it would be no trouble to me, if thou shouldst never touch clay or canvass again. It is not what thou dost, but what thou art, that I concern myself about. And if thy mighty works are to be wrought only by the anguish of thy head, and weariness of thy frame, and sinking of thy heart, then do I never desire to see another. And this should be the feeling of all thy friends. Especially ought it to be thine, for thy husband's sake.

Belovedest, I am very well, and not at all weary; for yesterday's rain gave us a holyday; and moreover the labors of the farm are not so pressing as they have been. And—joyful thought!—in a little more than a fortnight, thy husband will free from his bondage—free to think of his Dove—free to enjoy Nature—free to think and feel! I do think that a greater weight will then be removed from me, than when Christian's burthen fell off at the foot of the cross. Even my Custom House experience was not such a thraldom and weariness; my mind and heart were freer. Oh, belovedest, labor is the curse of this world, and nobody can meddle with it, without becoming proportionably brutified. Dost thou think it a praiseworthy matter, that I spent five golden months in providing food for cows and horses? Dearest, it is not so. Thank God, my soul is not utterly buried under a dungheap. I shall yet rescue it, somewhat defiled, to be sure, but not utterly unsusceptible of purification.

Farewell now, truest wife. It is time this letter were sealed. Love me; for I love thee infinitely, and pray for thee, and rejoice in thee, and am troubled for thee—for I know not where thou art, nor how thou dost.

Wilt thou accept a thousand kisses?

THINE OWNEST.

Miss Sophia A. Peabody,
Care of Mr. Daniel Newhall,
Lynn, Mass.

no. 20 ~

Letter from Nathaniel Hawthorne to Sophia Peabody, here reprinted from a true copy of the holograph letter now at the Huntington Library, San Marino, California. The true copy, made by
Professor Randall Stewart of Vanderbilt University and Professor
Norman Pearson of Yale University, appears here through their
generosity—Professor Pearson supplied it for use in advance of his
forthcoming edition of Hawthorne's letters—and by permission of
the Huntington Library.

Brook Farm, Aug. 22ᵈ, 1841.

MOST DEAR WIFE, it seems a long time since I have written to thee. Dost
thou love me at all? I should have been reprehensible in not writing,
the last time Mr. and Mrs. Ripley went to town; but I had an indis-
pensible [*sic*] engagement in the bean-field—whither, indeed, I was
glad to betake myself, in order to escape a parting scene with poor Mr.
Farley. He was quite out of his wits, the night before, and thy husband
sat up with him till long past midnight. The farm is pleasanter now that
he is gone; for his unappeasable wretchedness threw a gloom over
everything. Since I last wrote to thee, we have done haying; and the
remainder of my bondage will probably be light. It will be a long time,
however, before I shall know how to make a good use of leisure, either
as regards enjoyment or literary occupation.

Belovedest, my bosom yearns for thee. Methinks it is an age since
thou hast been in my arms. When am I to see thee again? The first of
September comes a week from Tuesday next; but I think I shall ante-
date the month, and compel it to begin on Sunday. Wilt thou consent?
Then, on Saturday afternoon, (for I will pray Mr. Ripley to give me up
so much time, for the sake of my past diligence) I will come to thee,
dearest wife, and remain in the city till Monday evening. Thence I
shall go to Salem, and spend a week there, longer or shorter according
to the intensity of the occasion for my presence. I do long to see our
mother and sisters; and I should not wonder if they felt some slight
desire to see me. I received a letter from Louisa, a week or two since,
scolding me most pathetically for my long absence. Indeed, I have
been rather naughty in this respect; but I knew that it would be unsatisfactory to them and myself, if I came only for a single day—and
that has been the longest space that I could command.

Dearest wife, it is extremely doubtful whether Mr. Ripley will succeed in locating his community on this farm. He can bring Mr. Ellis

to no terms; and the more they talk about the matter, the farther they appear to be from a settlement. Thou and I must form other plans for ourselves; for I can see few or no signs that Providence purposes to give us a home here. I am weary, weary, thrice weary of waiting so many ages. Yet what can be done? Whatever may be thy husband's gifts, he has not hitherto shown a single one that may avail to gather gold. I confess that I have strong hopes of good from this arrangement with Monroe; but when I look at the scanty avails of my past literary efforts, I do not feel authorized to expect much from the future. Well; we shall see. Other persons have bought large estates and built splendid mansions with such little books as I mean to write; so perhaps it is not unreasonable to hope that mine may enable me to build a little cottage— or, at least, to buy or hire one. But I am becoming more and more convinced, that we must not lean upon the community. What ever is to be done, must be done by thy husband's own individual strength. Most beloved, I shall not remain here through the winter, unless with an absolute certainty that there will be a home ready for us in the spring. Otherwise I shall return to Boston,—still, however, considering myself an associate of the community; so that we may take advantage of any more favorable aspect of affairs. Dearest, how much depends on those little books! Methinks, if anything could draw out my whole strength, it should be the motives that now press upon me. Yet, after all, I must keep these considerations out of my mind, because an external pressure always disturbs, instead of assisting me.

Dearest, I have written the above in not so good spirits as sometimes; but now that I have so ungenerously thrown my despondency on thee, my heart begins to throb more lightly. I doubt not that God has great good [in] store for us; for He would not have given us so much, unless He were preparing to give us a great deal more. I love thee! Thou lovest me! What present bliss! What sure and certain hope!

THINE OWNEST HUSBAND.

Miss Sophia A. Peabody,
    13 West-street
        Boston.

no. 21 〜

Letter from Nathaniel Hawthorne to Sophia Peabody, here reprinted from a true copy of the holograph letter now at the Huntington Library, San Marino, California. The true copy, made by Professor Randall Stewart of Vanderbilt University and Professor

Norman Pearson of Yale University, appears here through their generosity—Professor Pearson supplied it for use in advance of his forthcoming edition of Hawthorne's letters—and by permission of the Huntington Library.

Salem, Sept 3ᵈ 1841—4 °clock P.M.

Most beloved.—Thou dost not expect a letter from thy husband; and yet, perhaps, thou wilt not be absolutely displeased should one come to thee tomorrow. At all events, I feel moved to write; though the haze and sleepiness, which always settles upon me here, will certainly be perceptible in every line. But what a letter didst thou write to me! Thou lovest like a celestial being, (as truly thou art) and dost express thy love in heavenly language;—it is like one angel writing to another angel; but alas! the letter has miscarried, and has been delivered to a most unworthy mortal. Now wilt thou exclaim against thy husband's naughtiness! And truly he is very naughty. Well then; the letter was meant for him, and could not possibly belong to any other being, mortal or immortal. I will trust that thy idea of me is truer than my own consciousness of myself.

Dearest, I have been out only once, in the day time, since my arrival. How immediately and irrecoverably (if thou didst not keep me out of the abyss) should I relapse into the way of life in which I spent my youth! If it were not for my Dove, this present world would see no more of me forever. The sunshine would never fall on me, no more than on a ghost. Once in a while, people might discern my figure gliding stealthily through the dim evening—that would be all. I should be only a shadow of the night; it is thou that givest me reality, and makest all things real for me. If, in the interval since I quitted this lonely old chamber, I had found no woman (and thou wast the only possible one) to impart reality and significance to life, I should have come back hither ere now, with the feeling that all was a dream and a mockery. Dost thou rejoice that thou hast saved me from such a fate? Yes; it is a miracle worthy even of thee, to have converted a life of shadows into the deepest truth, by thy magic touch.

Belovedest, I have not yet made acquaintance with Miss Polly Metis. Mr. Foote was not in his office when I called there; so that my introduction to the erudite Polly was unavoidably deferred. I went to the Athenaeum this forenoon, and turned over a good many dusty books. When we dwell together, I intend that my Dove shall do all the reading that may be necessary, in the concoction of my various histories; and she shall repeat the substance of her researches to me, when our heads are on the pillow. Thus will knowledge fall upon me like heavenly dew.

Sweetest, it seems very long already since I saw thee; but thou hast been all the time in my thoughts; so that my being has been continuous. Therefore, in one sense, it does not seem as if we had been parted at all. But really I should judge it to be twenty years since I left Brook Farm; and I take this to be one proof that my life there was an unnatural and unsuitable, and therefore an unreal one. It already looks like a dream behind me. The real Me was never an associate of the community; there has been a spectral Appearance there, sounding the horn at daybreak, and milking the cows, and hoeing potatoes, and raking hay, toiling and sweating in the sun, and doing me the honor to assume my name. But be not thou deceived, Dove of my heart. This Spectre was not thy husband. Nevertheless, it is somewhat remarkable that thy husband's hands have, during this past summer, grown very brown and rough; insomuch that many people persist in believing that he, after all, was the aforesaid spectral horn-sounder, cow-milker, potato-hoer, and hay raker. But such a people do not know a reality from a shadow.

Enough of nonsense. Belovedest, I know not exactly how soon I shall return to the Farm. Perhaps not sooner than a fortnight from tomorrow; but, in that case, I shall pay thee an intermediate visit of one day. Wilt thou expect me on Friday or Saturday next, from ten to twelve °clock on each day,—not earlier nor later . . .[1]

Miss Sophia A. Peabody,
  Care of Dr. N. Peabody,
    Boston, Mass.

no. 22 ～

Letter from Nathaniel Hawthorne to Sophia Peabody, here reprinted from a true copy of the holograph letter now at the Huntington Library, San Marino, California. The true copy, made by Professor Randall Stewart of Vanderbilt University and Professor Norman Pearson of Yale University, appears here through their generosity—Professor Pearson supplied it for use in advance of his forthcoming edition of Hawthorne's letters—and by permission of the Huntington Library.

Brook Farm, Sept 22ᵈ, 1841– P.M.

DEAREST LOVE, here is thy husband again, slowly adapting himself to the life of this queer community, whence he seems to have been absent

---

[1] At this point two or three lines have been excised from the manuscript, including the signature. Professor Pearson's note.

half a life time—so utterly has he grown apart from the spirit and manners of the place. Thou knowest not how much I wanted thee, to give me a home-feeling in the spot—to keep a feeling of coldness and strangeness from creeping into my heart and making me shiver. Nevertheless, I was most kindly received; and the fields and woods looked very pleasant, in the bright sunshine of the day before yesterday. I had a friendlier disposition towards the farm, now that I am no longer obliged to toil in its stubborn furrows. Yesterday and to-day, however, the weather has been intolerable—cold, chill, sullen, so that it is impossible to be on kindly terms with mother Nature. Would I were with thee, mine own warmest and truest-hearted wife! I never shiver, while encircled in thine arms.

Belovedest, I doubt whether I shall succeed in writing another volume of Grandfather's Library, while I remain at the farm. I have not the sense of perfect seclusion, which has always been essential to my power of producing anything. It is true, nobody intrudes into my room; but still I cannot be quiet. Nothing here is settled—everything is but beginning to arrange itself—and though thy husband would seem to have little to do with aught beside his own thoughts, still he cannot but partake of the ferment around him. My mind will not be abstracted. I must observe, and think, and feel, and content myself with catching glimpses of things which may be wrought out hereafter. Perhaps it will be quite as well that I find myself unable to set seriously about literary occupation for the present. It will be good to have a longer interval between my labor of the body and that of the mind. I shall work to the better purpose, after the beginning of November. Meantime, I shall see these people and their enterprise under a new point of view, and perhaps be able to determine whether thou and I have any call to cast in our lot among them.

Sweetest, our letters have not yet been brought from the Post Office; so that I have known nothing of thee since our parting kiss. Surely we were very happy—and never had I so much peace and joy as in brooding over thine image, as thou wast revealed to me in our last interview. I love thee with all the heart I have—and more. Now farewell, most dear. Mrs. Ripley is to be the bearer of this letter; and I reserve the last page for tomorrow morning. Perhaps I shall have a blessed word from thee, ere then.

Septr. 23^d—Before breakfast—Sweetest wife, thou hast not written to me. Nevertheless, I do not conclude thee to be sick, but will believe that thou hast been busy in creating Laura Bridgman. What a faithful and attentive husband thou hast! For once he has anticipated thee in writing.

Belovedest, I do wish the weather would put off this sulky mood. Had it not been for the warmth and brightness of Monday, when I arrived here, I should have supposed that all sunshine had left Brook Farm forever. I have no disposition to take long walks, in such a state of the sky; nor have I any buoyancy of spirit. Thy husband is a very dull person, just at this time. I suspect he wants thee. It is his purpose, I believe, either to walk or ride to Boston, about the end of next week, and give thee a kiss—after which he will return quietly and contentedly to the farm. Oh what joy, when he will see thee every day!

We had some tableaux last night. They were were [*sic*] very stupid, (as, indeed, was the case with all I have ever seen) but do not thou tell Mrs. Ripley so. She is a good woman, and I like her better than I did—her husband keeps his old place in my judgment. Farewell, thou gentlest Dove—thou perfectest woman—thou desirablest wife.

THINE OWNEST HUSBAND.

Miss Sophia A. Peabody,
    Boston,
      Mass.

no. 23 ❦

Letter from Nathaniel Hawthorne to Sophia Peabody, here reprinted from a true copy of the holograph letter now at the Huntington Library, San Marino, California. The true copy, made by Professor Randall Stewart of Vanderbilt University and Professor Norman Pearson of Yale University, appears here through their generosity—Professor Pearson supplied it for use in advance of his forthcoming edition of Hawthorne's letters—and by permission of the Huntington Library.

Brook Farm, Septr 25th, 1841.—½ past 7. A.M.

OWNEST DOVE, it was but just now that I thought of sending thee a few lines by Mr. Ripley; for this penning of epistles is but a wretched resource, when I want thee on my very bosom. What shall I do? What shall I do? To talk to thee in this way does not bring thee nearer; it only compels me to separate myself from thee, and put thee at a distance. Of all humbugs, pretending to alleviate mortal woes, writing is the greatest.

Yet thy two letters were a great comfort to me—so great, that they could not possibly have been dispensed with. Dearest, I did not write thee what Mr. and Mrs. Ripley said to me, because they have said nothing which I did not know before. The ground, upon which I must judge of the expediency of our abiding here, is not what they may say, but what actually is, or is likely to be; and of this I doubt whether either of them is capable of forming a correct opinion. Would that thou couldst be here—or could have been here all summer—in order to help me think what is to be done. But one thing is certain—I cannot and will not spend the winter here. The time would be absolutely thrown away, so far as regards any literary labor to be performed,—and then to suffer this famished yearning for thee, all winter long! It is impossible.

Dearest, do not thou wear thyself out with working on that bust. If it cause thee so much as a single head-ache, I shall wish that Laura Bridgman were at Jericho. Even if thou shouldst not feel thyself wearied at the time, I fear that the whole burthen of toil will fall upon thee when all is accomplished. It is no matter if Laura should go home without being sculptured—no matter if she goes to her grave without it. I dread to have thee feel an outward necessity for such a task; for this intrusion of an outward necessity into labors of the imagination and intellect is, to me, very painful.

Oh, what weather! It seems to me as if every place were sunny, save Brook Farm. Nevertheless, I had rather a pleasant walk to a distant meadow, a day or two ago; and we found white and purple grapes, in great abundance, ripe, and gushing with rich juice when the hand pressed their clusters. Didst thou know what treasures of wild grapes there are in this land. If we dwell here, we will make our own wine— of which, I know, my Dove will want a great quantity.

Good bye, sweetest. If thou canst continue to send me a glimpse of sunshine, I will be the gratefullest husband on earth. I love thee inextinguishably. Thou hast no place to put all the love that I feel for thee.

THINE OWNEST HUSBAND.

Miss Sophia A. Peabody,
    Boston,
    Mass.

no. 24 ～

Passages from Nathaniel Hawthorne, *American Notebook, September 26, 1841 to May 14, 1852;* here reprinted from *The American Notebooks,* edited by Randall Stewart (New Haven: Yale, 1932), pp. 75-76. (Professor Stewart's notes have been omitted.)

Sept 26th, 1841

A walk this morning along the Needham road. A clear, breezy morning, after nearly a week of cloudy and showery weather. The grass is much more fresh and vivid than it was last month, and trees still retain much of their verdure; though here and there there is a shrub or bough arrayed in scarlet and gold. Along the road, in the midst of the beaten track, I saw mushrooms or toadstools, which had sprung, probably, during the night.

The houses in this vicinity are many of them quite antique, with long sloping roofs, commencing at a few feet from the ground, and ending in a lofty peak. Some of them have huge old elms, overshadowing the yard. You may see the family sleigh near the door, having stood there all through the summer sunshine, and perhaps with weeds sprouting up through the crevices of its bottom, the growth of the months since snow departed. Old barns, patched, and supported by timbers leaned against the sides, and stained with the dung of past ages.

Sept 26th, *continued.*

A walk in the forenoon, along the edge of the meadow towards Cow Island. Large trees, almost a wood, principally of pine, with the green pasture glades intermixed, and cattle feeding. They cease grazing when an intruder appears, and look at him with long and wary observation. Then bend their necks to the pasture again. Where the firm ground of the pasture ceases, the meadow begins—loose, spongy, yielding to the tread, sometimes permitting the foot to sink into black mud, or perhaps over ankles in water. Cattle paths, somewhat firmer than the general surface, traverse the dense shrubbery which here overgrows the meadow. This shrubbery consists of small birch, elders, maples, and other trees, with here and there white pines of larger growth. The whole is tangled and wild, thick-set, so that it is necessary to part the rustling stems and branches, and go crashing through. There are creeping plants of various sorts, which clamber up the trees; and some of them have changed color in the slight frosts which already [have] befallen these low grounds; so that you see a spiral wreath of scarlet leaves twining up to the tip-top of a green tree, intermingling its bright hues with the verdure, as if all were of one piece. Sometimes, instead of scarlet, the spiral wreath is of a golden yellow.

Within the verge of the meadow, mostly near the firm shore of pasture ground, I found several grapevines, hung with abundance of large purple grapes. The vines had caught hold of maples and alders, and climbed to the top, curling round about and interwreathing their twisted folds in so intimate a manner, that it was not easy to tell the parasite from the supporting tree or shrub. Sometimes the same vine had enveloped several shrubs, and caused a strange tangled confusion, converting all these poor plants to the purposes of its own support, and hindering their growing to their own benefit and convenience. The broad vine-leaves, some of them yellow or yellowish-tinged, were seen apparently growing on the same stems with the sil-[76]ver maple leaves, and those of the other shrubs, thus married against their will by this conjugal twine; and the purple clusters of grapes hung down from above and in the midst, so that a [man] might might [*sic*] gather grapes, if not of thorns, yet of as alien bushes. One vine had ascended almost to the tip-top of a large white pine tree, spreading its leaves and hanging its purple clusters among all its boughs—still climbing and clambering, as if it would not be content till it crowned the very summit of the tree with a wreath of its own foliage and a cluster of grapes. I mounted high into the tree, and ate grapes there, while the vine wreathed still high [*sic*] into the depths of the tree, above my head. The grapes were sour, being not yet fully ripe; some of them, however, were sweet and pleasant. The vine embraces the tree like a serpent.

[*Ibid.* pp. 76-78.]

Sept 27th

A ride to Brighton yesterday morning, it being the day of the weekly cattle fair. William Allen and myself went in a wagon, carrying a calf, to be sold at the fair. The calf had not had his breakfast, as his mother had preceded him to Brighton; and he kept expressing his hunger and discomfort by loud, sonorous baa-s, especially when we passed any cattle in the fields or on the road. The cows, grazing within hearing expressed great interest, and some of them came galloping to the road-side to behold the calf. Little children, also, on their way to school, stopt to laugh and point at poor little Bossie. He was a prettily behaved urchin, and kept thrusting his hairy muzzle between William and myself, apparently wishing to be stroked and patted. It was an ugly thought, that his confidence in human nature, and Nature in general, was to be so ill rewarded as by cutting his throat, and selling him in quarters. This, I suppose, has been his fate before now.

It was a beautiful morning, clear as chrystal [*sic*], with an invigorating, but not disagreeable coolness. The general aspect of the country was as green as summer;—greener indeed than mid or latter summer—and there were occasional interminglings of the brilliant hues of Autumn, which made the scenery more beautiful, both visibly and in sentiment. We saw no absolutely mean or poor-looking abodes along the road. There were warm and comfortable farm-houses, ancient, with the porch, the sloping roof, the antique peak, the clustered chimneys, of old times; and modern cottages, smart and tasteful; and villas, with terraces before them, and dense shade, and wooden urns on pillars, and other such tokens of gentility. Pleasant groves of oak and walnut, also, there were, sometimes stretching along vallies [*sic*], sometimes ascending a hill and cloathing [*sic*] it all round, so as to make it a great clump of verdure. Frequently, we passed people with cows, oxen, sheep or pigs, for Brighton fair.

On arriving at Brighton, we found the village thronged with people, horses, and vehicles. Probably there is no place in New England where the character of our agricultural population may be so well studied. Almost all the farmers, within a reasonable distance, make it a point, I suppose, to attend Brighton fair pretty frequently, if not on business, yet as amateurs. Then there are all the cattle-people and butchers who supply the Boston market, and dealers from far and near; and [77] every man who has a cow or yoke of oxen, whether to sell or buy, goes to Brighton on Monday. There were a thousand or two of cattle in the extensive pens, belonging to the tavern keeper, besides many standing about. You could hardly stir a step without running upon the horns of one dilemma or the other, in the shape of ox, cow, bull, or ram. The yeomen appeared to be more in their element than I ever saw them anywhere else, except, indeed, at labor—more than at musterings and such gatherings of amusement. And yet this was a sort of festal day, too, as well as a day of business. Most of the people were of a bulky make, with much bone and muscle, and some good store of fat, like people who lived on flesh-diet—with mottled faces, too, hard and red, as if they adhered to the old fashion of spirit-drinking;—great round-paunched country squires were there too, sitting under the porch of the tavern, or waddling about, whip in hand, discussing the points of the cattle. There, also, were gentlemen farmers, neatly, trimly, and fashionably dressed in handsome surtouts, and pantaloons strapt under their boots. Yeomen, too, in their black or blue sunday suits, cut by country tailors, and awkwardly worn. Others (like myself) had on the blue stuff frocks which they wear in the fields—the most comfortable garment that ever man invented. Country loafers, too, were among the throng—men who looked wistfully at the liquors in the bar, and waited for some friend to invite them to drink—poor shabby, out at elbowed devils. Also, dandies from the city, stayed and buckramed, who had come to see the humors of Brighton fair. All these, and other varieties of mankind, either thronged the spacious bar-room of the hotel, drinking, smoking, talking, bargaining; or walked about among the cattle-pens, looking with knowing eyes at the horned people. The owners of the cattle stood near at hand, waiting for offers; there was something indescribable in their aspect that showed them to be the owners, though they intermixed among the crowd. The cattle, brought from a hundred separate farms, or rather a thousand, seemed to agree very well together, not quarrelling in the least. They almost all had a history, no doubt, if they could but have told it—the cows had each given their milk to support families—had roamed the pastures, and come home to the barn-yard—had been looked upon as a sort of member of the domestic circle, and was known by a name, as Brindle or Cherry. The oxen, with their necks bent by the heavy yoke, had toiled in the plough-field and in haying time, for many years, and knew their master's stall as well as the master himself did his own table. Even the young steers, and the little calves, had something of domestic sacredness about them; for children had watched their growth, and petted them, and played with them. And here they all were, old and young, gathered from their thousand homes to Brighton fair; whence the great chance was that they would go to the slaughter-house, and thence be transmitted, in sirloins, joints, and such pieces, to the tables of the Boston people.

William Allen had come to buy four little pigs, to take the places of our four, who have now grown large, and are to be fatted and killed within a few weeks. There were several hundreds, in pens appropriated to their use, grunting discordantly, and apparently in no very good humor with their companions or the world at large. Most, or many, of these pigs had been imported from the state of [78] New York. The drovers set out with a large number, and peddle them along the road, till they arrive at Brighton with the remainder. William selected four, and bought them at five cents per pound. These poor little porkers were forthwith seized by the tails, their legs tied, and they thrown into our wagon, where they kept up a continual grunt and squeal, till we got home. Two of them were yellowish, or light gold colored; the other two black and white speckled; and all four of very piggish aspect and deportment. One of them snapt at William's finger most spitefully, and bit it to the bone.

All the scene of the fair was very characteristic and peculiar—cheerful and lively, too, in the bright, warm sun. I must see it again; for it ought to be studied.

[*Ibid.* pp. 78-79.]

Sept 28th, 1841

A picnic party in the woods, yesterday, in honor of Frank Dana's birth-day, he being six years old. I strolled into the woods, after dinner, with Mr. Bradford; and in a lonesome glade, we met the apparition of an Indian chief, dressed in appropriate costume of blanket, feathers, and paint, and armed with a musket. Almost at the same time, a young gipsey [*sic*] fortune teller came from among the trees, and proposed to tell my fortune; which while she was doing, the goddess Diana (known on earth as Miss Ellen Slade) let fly an arrow and hit me smartly in the hand. This fortune teller and goddess were a fine contrast, Diana being a blonde, fair, quiet, with a moderate composure; and the gipsey [*sic*] (Ora Gannet) a bright, vivacious, dark-haired, rich-complexioned damsel—both of them very pretty; at least, pretty enough to make fifteen years enchanting. Accompanied by these denizens of the wild wood, we went onward, and came to a company of fantastic figures, arranged in a ring for a dance or game. There was a Swiss girl, an Indian squaw, a negro of the Jim Crow order, one or two foresters; and several people in Christian attire; besides children of all ages. Then followed childish games, in which the grown people took part with mirth enough—while I, whose nature it is to be a mere spectator both of sport and serious business, lay under the trees and looked on. Meanwhile, Mr. Emerson and Miss Fuller, who had arrived an hour or two before, came forth into the little glade where we were assembled. Here followed much talk.

The ceremonies of the day concluded with a cold collation of cakes and fruit. All was pleasant enough; "an excellent piece of work; would't were done!" It has left a fantastic impression on my memory, this intermingling of wild and fabulous characters with real and homely ones, in the secluded nook of the woods. I remember them with the sunlight breaking through overshadowing branches, and they appearing' and disappearing confusedly—perhaps starting out of the earth; as if the every day laws of Nature were suspended for this par- ticular occasion. There are the children, too, laughing and sporting about, as if they were at home among such strange shapes—and anon bursting into loud uproar of lamentation, when the rude gambols of the merry-makers chanced to overturn them. And apart, with a shrewd Yankee observation of the scene, stands our friend Orange, a thickset, sturdy figure, in his blue frock, enjoying the fun well enough, yet [79] rather laughing with a perception of its nonsensicallness [*sic*], than at all entering into the spirit of the thing.

This morning I have been helping to gather apples. The principal farm labors, at this time, are ploughing for winter rye, and breaking up the green sward for next year's crop of potatoes; gathering squashes—and not much else, except such year round employments as milking. The crop of rye, to be sure, is in process of being threshed, at odd intervals.

I ought to have mentioned, among the diverse and incongruous guests of the picnic party, our two Spanish boys from Manilla [*sic*] —Lucas with his heavy features and almost mulatto complexion; and Jose, slighter, with rather a feminine face—not a gay-girlish one, but grave, reserved, eying you sometimes with an earnest, but secret ex- pression, and causing you to question what sort of person he is. Make up the group with good, homely, sensible Mrs. Pratt, and her hus- band, every way fitted to her—pattern specimens of New England matrimony.

no. 25 ❧

Letter from Nathaniel Hawthorne to Sophia Peabody, here re- printed from a true copy of the holograph letter now at the Hunt- ington Library, San Marino, California. The true copy, made by Professor Randall Stewart of Vanderbilt University and Professor Norman Pearson of Yale University, appears here through their generosity—Professor Pearson supplied it for use in advance of his forthcoming edition of Hawthorne's letters—and by permission of the Huntington Library.

Brook Farm, Septr 29th, 1841.—A.M.

OWNEST WIFE, I love thee most exceedingly—never so much before; though I am sure I have loved thee through a past eternity. How dost thou do? Dost thou remember that, the day after tomorrow, thou art to meet thy husband? Does thy heart thrill at the thought?

Dearest love, thy husband was elected to two high offices, last night—viz, to be a Trustee of the Brook Farm estate, and Chairman of the Committee of Finance!!!! Now dost thou not blush to have formed so much lower an opinion of my business talents, than is entertained by other discerning people? From the nature of my office, I shall have the chief direction of all the money affairs of the community—the making of bargains—the supervision of receipts and expenditures &c. &c. &c. Thou didst not think of this, when thou didst pronounce me unfit to make a bargain with that petty knave of a publisher. A prophet has no honor among them of his own kindred, nor a financier in the judgment of his wife.

Belovedest, my accession to these august offices does not at all decide the question of my remaining here permanently. I told Mr. Ripley, that I could not spend the winter at the farm, and that it was quite uncertain whether I returned in the spring.

Now, farewell, most dear and sweet wife. Of course, thou canst not expect that a man in eminent public station will have much time to devote to correspondence with a Dove. I will remember thee in the intervals of business, and love thee in all my leisure moments. Will not this satisfy thee?

God bless thee, mine ownest—my treasure—thou gold and diamond of my soul!—my only desirablest—my possession forever—my enough and to spare, yet never, never to be spared! Sweetest, if it should be very stormy on Saturday, expect me not—but the first fair day thereafter.

I put all my love into one kiss, and have twice as much left as before.

THY TRUEST HUSBAND.

Miss Sophia A. Peabody,
    Care of Dr. N. Peabody,
        Boston,
            Mass.

no. 26 ～

The earliest articles of association at Brook Farm, here reprinted fom O. B. Frothingham, *George Ripley* (Boston: Houghton Mifflin Company, 1882), pp. 112-117.

ARTICLES OF ASSOCIATION OF THE SUBSCRIBERS TO THE BROOK FARM INSTITUTE OF AGRICULTURE AND EDUCATION.

Articles of Association made and executed this twenty-ninth day of September, one thousand eight hundred and forty-one, by and between the several persons and their assigns, who have given their signatures to this instrument and by it associated themselves together for the purpose and objects hereinafter set forth:—

Art. I. The name and style of this Association shall be The Subscribers to the Brook Farm Institute of Agriculture and Education; and all persons who shall hold one or more shares of the stock of the Association shall be members; and every member shall be entitled to one vote on all matters relating to the funds of the Association.

Art. II. The object of the Association is to purchase such estates as may be required for the establishment and continuance of an agricultural, literary, and scientific school or college, to provide such lands and houses, animals, libraries and apparatus, as may be found expedient or advantageous to the main purpose of the Association.

Art. III. The whole property of the Association, real and personal, shall be vested in and held by Four Trustees to be elected annually by the Association.

Art. IV. No shareholder shall be liable to any assessment whatever on the shares held by him, nor shall he be held responsible individually in his private [113] property on account of this Association; nor shall the Trustees, or any officer or agent of the Association, have any authority to do anything which shall impose personal responsibility on any shareholder by making any contracts or incurring any debts for which the shareholders shall be individually or personally responsible.

Art. V. All conveyances to be taken for lands or other real estate purchased by the Association in pursuance of these articles shall be made to the Trustees, their successors in office or survivors as joint tenants, and not as tenants in common.

Art. VI. The Association guarantees to each shareholder the interest of five per cent. annually on the amount of stock held by him in the Association, and this interest may be paid in certificates of stock and credited on the books of the Association; provided, however, that each shareholder may, at the time of the annual settlement, draw on the funds of the Association, not otherwise appropriated, to an amount not exceeding that of the interest credited in his favor.

Art. VII. The shareholders on their part, for themselves, their heirs and assigns, do renounce all claim on any profits accruing to the Association for the use of their capital invested in the stock of the Association, except five per cent. interest on the amount of stock held by them, payable in the manner described in the preceding article.

Art. VIII. Every subscriber may receive the tuition of one pupil

46

for every share held by him, instead [114] of five per cent. interest, as stated above, or tuition to an amount not exceeding twenty per cent. interest on his investment.

ART. IX. No share shall be transferred from one person to another without the consent of the Trustees, nor shall any such transfer be valid without their signature.

ART. X. Every shareholder may withdraw his amount of stock and whatever interest is due thereon, by giving twelve months' notice to the Trustees of the Association.

ART. IX. The capital stock of the Association, now consisting of Twelve Thousand Dollars, shall be divided into shares of Five Hundred Dollars each, and may be increased to any amount at the pleasure of the Association.

ART. XII. These articles, it is understood and agreed on, are intended for the safe, legal, and orderly holding and management of such property real and personal as shall further the purposes of the "Brook Farm Institute of Agriculture and Education," to which Institute this Association of subscribers is subordinate and auxiliary.

SUBSCRIPTION.

We, the undersigned, do hereby agree to pay the sum attached to our names, to be invested in the Brook Farm Institute of Agriculture and Education, according to the conditions described in the foregoing Articles of Association.

Date, 1841 [115]

NAMES.	SHARES.	SUMS.
Geo. Ripley	No. 1, 2, and 3	$1,500
Nath. Hawthorne	" 18 and 19	1,000
Minot Pratt	" 4, 5, and 6	1,500
Charles A. Dana	" 10, 11, and 12	1,500
William B. Allen	" 7, 8, and 9	1,500
Sophia W. Ripley	" 16 and 17	1,000
Maria T. Pratt	" 20 and 21	1,000
Sarah F. Stearns	" 22 and 23	1,000
Marianne Ripley	" 13, 14, and 15	1,500
Charles O. Whitmore	" 24	500

OFFICERS.

At a meeting of the Brook Farm Institute of Agriculture and Education, held on Wednesday, September 29, 1841, the following persons were appointed to office as follows:—

General Direction.
Geo. Ripley,   Minot Pratt,
Wm. B. Allen.

Direction of Finance.
Nath. Hawthorne,   Chas. A. Dana,
Wm. B. Allen.

Direction of Agriculture.
Wm. B. Allen,   Minot Pratt,
Geo. Ripley.

Direction of Education.
Sophia W. Ripley,   Charles A. Dana,
Marianne Ripley.

Charles A. Dana was appointed Recording Secre-[116]tary, and Minot Pratt, Treasurer; and the meeting adjourned.

CHAS. ANDERSON DANA, *Secretary.*

At a meeting of the Brook Farm Institute of Agriculture and Education on Saturday last, October 30, 1841, the following votes were passed:—

Voted, 1. To transfer the Institution recently carried on by George Ripley to the Brook Farm Institute of Agriculture and Education from and after November 1, 1841, according to the conditions stated in the instrument of this date, and signed by George Ripley, William B. Allen, and Charles A. Dana.

2. To transfer the establishment recently carried on by Marianne Ripley to the Brook Farm Institute, from and after November 1, 1841, according to the conditions stated in the instrument referred to in the above vote.

3. That, in the annual settlement with individual members, each member shall be allowed board in proportion to the time employed for the Association; that is, one year's board for one year's labor; one half year's board for one half year's labor; and if no labor is done, the whole board shall be charged.

4. That the price of board charged to the Associates shall be $4.00 per week, until otherwise ordered, including house-rent, fuel, light, and washing.

5. That three hundred days' labor shall be considered equal to one year's labor, and shall entitle a person to one share of the annual dividend, and no allowance shall be made for a greater amount of labor.

6. That sixty hours shall be considered equal to [117] six days' labor for the months of May, June, July, August, September, and October, inclusive; forty-eight hours, from November to April, inclusive.

7. That for children of the associates, over ten years of age, board shall be charged at half the established rate.

8. That the price of board and tuition shall be $4.00 a week for boys, and $5.00 a week for girls over twelve years of age; and $3.50 a week for children under that age, exclusive of washing and separate fire.   CHAS. ANDERSON DANA, *Secretary*.

PART TWO

From Association
to Phalanx

~~~ 1841–1844

Editor's Preface

Any division of historical materials into parts is arbitrary. It is fair to say that some divisions are "better" than others, but none is absolute and final. Oftentimes such a division reflects a purpose in the mind of the person who makes it. He divides his material in order to emphasize his own particular views.

The division of this book into parts was made after the editor had decided to arrange all the pieces of evidence in chronological order. The points of division were selected to emphasize the organizational aspects of the history of Brook Farm. What were the public rules of life at the Farm? How did they change from year to year?

Students who find themselves hampered by this emphasis may wish to contrive a new division of their own. For example, Part One might be the "Hawthorne Period"; Part Two might be the "Dwight Period"; and Part Three could be called "The Period of Divided Counsel." Other students might prefer to sort all materials into two bundles, early and late, perhaps with such titles as (1) "Brook Farm: Private Retreat," and (2) "Brook Farm: Public Cause." For each new interpretation of the Brook Farm story there is an appropriate arrangement of materials.— Make your own.

The division which is used in this book is a fairly good one. There is no necessity for changing it unless it proves troublesome. It has one quality that all divisions should have: each part is different from all the others in some important way.

Part Two in this division is different from Part One in a number of ways, one of them is the appearance of a new stridency in the word "association."—What is association in this special sense? Several new names appear among our informants in Part Two, and two of them—Albert Brisbane and Osborne Macdaniel—are first heard as advocates of association. Brisbane was in fact a professional newspaper man who devoted his efforts and his column to this idea. He also wrote for the *Phalanx*, a journal whose cause was identical with his own. Students should be careful to notice the role of this little magazine, and of its successor, *The Harbinger*, throughout the later history of the Farm. Another important journal is *The Dial*, in which Elizabeth Peabody herself wrote and published the statement she had failed to get from Ripley.

Another new voice is that of the eccentric Charles Lane, an Englishman noted for his vigorous devotion to slender causes. He was a violent vegetarian, among other things. In fact, he disapproved, on economic and moral grounds, of the use of domestic animals for any purpose. He was quick to criticize all institutions that might be suspected of resting on a foundation of mere custom. For example, marriage. Is a perfect association possible so long as each man persists in maintaining a domestic hearth?

Among the voices familiar from Part One, that of Nathaniel Hawthorne is most interesting here, for it is with a new intonation that he speaks. And he speaks of things different from those which claimed his attention before. In Part Two are answers to the questions raised by Hawthorne's sojourn at the Farm. Why did he go there? Why did he leave? What kind of young man must he have been?

And finally, in Part Two there is a new set of articles of association, this time presented as a "Constitution." Close comparison of the constitution of 1844 with the "Articles" of 1841 discloses important developments. Precisely what these developments were, and the degree to which they fix the direction of change, which is the essential history of Brook Farm, are hard questions. Their final answers belong to the last stages of a conscientious study of the facts.

Additional Books

Elizabeth P. Peabody. "Plan of the West Roxbury Community," *The Dial*, II (January, 1842), 361-372.

Lindsay Swift, *Brook Farm, Its Members, Scholars, and Visitors.* New York: The Macmillan Company, 1900.

Unpublished letters in the possession of the Abernethy Library of American Literature, Middlebury College, Middlebury, Vermont.

Photostatic copies and typewritten transcriptions were supplied by Miss Mary Noel, Curator of the Abernethy Library.

F. B. Sanborn. *A. Bronson Alcott, His Life and Philosophy*. 2 volumes. Boston: Roberts, 1893.

Phalanx or Journal of Social Science, Devoted to the Cause of Association and Social Reform, Volume I, twenty-three numbers published at New York; Number 1, on Thursday, October 5, 1843 and the last, Number 23—containing an announcement of its discontinuation and of the projected beginning of *The Harbinger*—on Wednesday, May 28, 1845. (Because of their special identification with the interests of Brook Farm, *Phalanx* and *The Harbinger* are more fully described than other periodicals included in this and in subsequent lists.)

Charles Lane. "Brook Farm," *The Dial*, IV (January, 1844), 351-357.

Constitution of the Brook Farm Association for Industry and Education, West Roxbury, Mass. With an Introductory Statement. Boston: I. R. Butts, Printer, No. 2 School Street, 1844.

no. 27 ❧

Nathaniel Hawthorne, *American Notebook, September 26, 1841 to May 14, 1852;* here reprinted from *The American Notebooks*, edited by Randall Stewart (New Haven: Yale, 1932), pp. 79-80. (Professor Stewart's notes have been omitted.)

Octr 1st, 1841, Friday

I have been looking at our four swine, not of the last lot, but those in process of fatting. They lie among the clean rye straw in their stye [*sic*], nestling close together; for they seem to be a sensitive beast to the cold; and this is a clear, bright, chrystal [*sic*], north-west windy, cool morning. So there lie these four black swine, as deep among the straw as they can burrow, the very symbols of slothful ease and sensual comfort. They [seem] to be actually oppressed and over-burthened with comfort. They are quick to notice any one's approach to the stye [*sic*], and utter a low grunt—not drawing a breath for that particular purpose, but grunting with their ordinary breath—at the same time turning an observant, though dull and sluggish eye upon the visitor. They seem to be involved and buried in their own corporeal substance, and to look dimly forth at the outer world. They breathe not easily, and yet not with difficulty or discomfort; for the very unreadiness and oppression with which their breath comes, appears to make them sensible of the deep sensual satisfaction which they feel. Swill, the remnant of their last meal, remains in their trough, denoting that their food is more abundant than even a hog can demand. Anon, they fall asleep, drawing short and heavy breaths, which heave their huge sides up and down; but at the slightest noise, they sluggishly unclose their eyes, and give another gentle grunt. They also grunt among themselves, apparently without any external cause, but merely to express their swinish sympathy. I suppose it is the knowledge that these four grunters are doomed to die within two or three weeks, that gives them a sort of awfulness in my conception; it makes me contrast their present gross substance of fleshly life with the nothingness speedily to come.

Meantime, the four newly bought pigs are running about the cow-yard, lean, active, shrewd, investigating everything, as their nature is. When I throw apples among them, they scramble with one another for the prize; and the successful one scampers away to eat it at leisure. They thrust their snouts into the mud, and pick a grain of corn out of the filth. Nothing within their sphere do they leave unex-[80]amined —grunting all the time, with infinite variety of expression. Their language seems to be the most copious of that of any quadruped; and, indeed, there is something deeply and indefinably interesting in the swinish race. They appear the more a mystery, the longer you gaze at them; it seems as if there was an important meaning to them, if you could but find out. One interesting trait in swine, is their perfect independence of character. They care not for man, and will not adapt themselves to his notions, as other beasts do; but are true to themselves, and act out their hoggish nature.

[*Ibid*. p. 80.]

Octr 7th.

Since Saturday last (it being now Thursday) I have been in Boston and Salem; and there has been a violent storm and rain during the whole time. This morning shone as bright as if it meant to make up for all the dismalness of the past days. Our brook, which in the summer was no longer a running stream, but stood in pools along its pebbly course, is now full from one grassy verge to another, and hurries along with a murmuring rush. It will continue to swell, I suppose; and in the winter and spring, it will flood all the broad meadows through which it flows—

. . . . . .

[*Ibid*. pp. 80-82.]

Octr 8th, 1841.

Another gloomy day, lowering with portents of rain close at hand. I have walked up in the pasture, this morning, and looked about me a little. The woods present a very diversified appearance, just now, with perhaps more varieties of tint, though less marked ones, than they are destined to wear at a somewhat later pe-[81]riod. There are some strong yellow hues, and some deep red; there are innumerable shades of green; some few having the depth of summer; others, partially changed towards yellow, look fresh[l]y verdant, the delicate tinge of early summer, or of May. Then there is the solemn and dark green of the pines. The effect is, that every tree in the wood, and every bush among the shrubbery, seems to have a separate existence, since, confusedly intermingled, each wears its peculiar hue, instead of being lost in the universal verdure of the summer. And yet there is a one-ness of effect, likewise, when we choose to look at a whole sweep of woodland, or swamp shrubbery, instead of analyzing its component trees. Scattered over the pasture, which the late rains have kept toler-ably green, there are spots, or islands, of a dusky red—a deep, sub-stantial hue, very well fit to be close to the ground, while the yellow, and light fantastic shades of green, soar upward to the sky. These red spots are the blue-berry bushes. The sweet fern is changed mostly to a russet hue, but still retains its wild and delightful fragrance, when pressed by the hand. Wild china asters are scattered about, but begin-ning to wither. A little while ago, mushrooms or toad-stools were very numerous, along the wood-paths, and by the road sides, especially after rain. Some were of spotless white, some yellow, some scarlet. They are always mysteries, and objects of interest, to me, springing, as they do, so suddenly from no root or seed, and growing nobody can tell why. I think, too, these are rather a pretty object—little fairy tables, centre tables, standing on one leg. But their growth appears to be checked now; and they are of a brown hue, and decayed.

The farm business, to-day, is to dig potatoes. I worked a little at it. The process is first to grasp all the stems of a hill, and pull them up. A great many of the potatoes are thus pulled; clinging to the stems, and to one another, in curious shapes, long red things, and little round ones, imbedded in the earth which clings to the roots. These being plucked off, the rest of the potatoes are dug out of the hill with a hoe; —the tops being flung into a heap for the cow yard. On my way home, I paused to inspect the squash field. Some of the squashes lay in heaps, as they were gathered, presenting much variety of shape and hue—as golden yellow, like great lumps of gold, dark green, striped and variegated &c; and some were round, and some lay curling their long necks, nestling, as it were, and seeming as if they had life. Some are regularly scalloped, and would make handsome patterns for dishes.

· · · · · · · ·

[*Ibid*. pp. 82-84.]

Octr 9th, Saturday.

Still dismal weather. Our household, being composed in great measure of children and young people, is generally a cheerful one enough, even in gloomy weather. For a week past, we have been especially gladdened with a little seamstress from Boston, about seventeen years old, but of such a petite figure that, at first view, one would take her to be hardly in her teens. She is very vivacious and smart, laughing, singing, and talking, all the time—talking sensibly, but still taking the view of matters that a city girl naturally would. If she were larger than she is, and of less pleasing aspect, I think she might be intolerable; but being so small, and with a white skin, healthy as a wild flower, she is really very agreeable; and to look at her face is like being shone upon by a ray of the sun. She never walks, but bounds and dances along; and this motion, in her small person, does not give the idea of violence. It is like a bird, hopping from twig to twig, and chirping merrily all the time. Sometimes she is a little vulgar; but even that works well enough into her character, and accords with it. On continued observation and acquaintance, you discover that she is not a little girl, but really a little woman, with all the prerogatives and liabilities of a woman. This gives a new aspect to her character; while her girlish impression still continues, and is strangely combined with the sense that this frolicsome little maiden has the material for that sober character, a wife. She romps with the boys, runs races with them in the yard, and up and down the stairs, and is heard scolding laughingly at their rough play. She asks William Allen to put her "on top of that horse;" whereupon he puts his large brown hands about her waist, and, swinging her to-and-fro, places her on horseback. By the bye, William threatened to rivet two horseshoes round her neck, for having clambered, with the other girls and boys, upon a load of hay; whereby the said load lost its balance, and slided off the cart. She strings the seed-berries of roses together, making a scarlet necklace of them, which she wears about her neck. She gathers everlasting flowers, to wear in her [hair?] or bonnet, arranging them with the skill of a dress-maker. In the evening, she sits singing by the hour together, with the musical part of the establishment—often breaking into laughter, whereto she is [83] incited by the tricks of the boys. The last thing you hear of her, she is tripping up stairs, to bed, talking lightsomely or sing-ing; and you meet her in the morning, the very image of lightsome morn itself, smiling briskly at you, so that one takes her for a promise of cheerfulness through the day. Be it said, among all the rest, there is a perfect maiden modesty in her deportment; though I doubt whether the boys, in their rompings with her, do not feel that she has past out of her childhood.

This lightsome little maid has left us this morning; and the last thing I saw of her was her vivacious face, peeping through the curtain of the carryall, and nodding a brisk farewell to the family, who were shouting their adieus at the door. With her other merits, she is an ex-cellent daughter, and, I believe, supports her mother by the labor of her hands. It would be difficult to conceive, beforehand, how much can be added to the enjoyment of a household by mere sunniness of temper and smartness of disposition; for her intellect is very ordinary, and she never says anything worth hearing, or even laughing at, in itself. But she herself is an expression, well worth studying.

October 9th, *continued.*

A walk, this afternoon, to Cow Island. The clouds had broken away, towards noon, and let forth a few sunbeams; and more and more blue sky continued to appear, till at last it was really warm and sunny—indeed, rather too warm, in the sheltered hollows; though it is de-lightful to be too warm now, after so much stormy chillness. Oh, the beauty of grassy slopes, and the hollow ways of paths, winding between hills, and the intervals between the road and a woodlot; and all such places, where Summer lingers and sits down, strewing dande-lions of gold, and blue asters, as her parting gifts, and memorials! I went to a grape vine, which I have already visited several times, and found some clusters of grapes still remaining, and now perfectly ripe. Coming within view of the river, I saw several wild ducks, under the shadow of the opposite shore, which was high, and covered with a grove of pines. I should not have discovered the ducks, had they not risen, and skimmed the surface of the glassy river, breaking its dark water with a bright streak, and sweeping round gradually rose high enough to fly away. I likewise started a partridge, just within the

verge of the woods; and in another [place] a large squirrel ran across
the woodpath, from one shelter of trees to the other. Small birds in
flocks were flitting about the fields, seeking and finding I know not
what sort of food. There are little fish also darting in shoals through
the pools and depths of the brooks, which are now replenished to their
brims, and beyond, and rush towards the river with a swift, amber-
colored current.

. . . .

[*Ibid.* pp. 84-85.]

October 10th, Sunday.

I visited my grape vine, this afternoon, and ate the last of its clusters.
This vine climbs around a young maple tree, which has now assumed
the yellow leaf. The vine leaves are more decayed than those of the
maple. Thence to Cow Island, a solemn and thoughtful walk. Returned from the island by another path, of the width of a pair of
wagon wheels, passing through a grove of hard-wood trees, the lightsome hues of which make the walk more cheerful than among the
pines. The roots of oak trees emerged from the soil, and contorted
themselves across the path. The sunshine, also, broke across in spots,
and in other spots the shadow was [85] deep; but still there was intermingling enough of sunshine and bright hues to keep off the gloom
from the whole path.

. . . .

[*Ibid.* pp. 84-85.]

October 12th.—Tuesday.

The cawing of the crow resounds among the woods, at this season.
A sentinel is aware of your approach a great way off, and gives the
alarm to his comrades loud and eagerly—Caw—caw—caw—. Immediately,
the whole conclave replies in the same word; and you behold them
rising above the trees, flapping darkly, and winging their way to deeper
solitudes. Sometimes, however, they remain on a tree, till you come
near enough to discern their sable gravity of aspect, each occupying a
separate bough, or perhaps the blasted tip-top of a pine tree. As you
approach, one after another, with loud cawing, flaps his wings and
throws himself upon the air.

There is hardly a more striking feature in the landscape, now-a-
days, than the red patches of blueberry bushes, as seen on a long sloping

hill side, like islands among the grass, with trees growing on them; or crowning the summit of a bare, brown hill with their somewhat russet liveliness—or circling round the base of an earth-embedded rock. At a distance, this hue clothing spots and patches of the earth looks more like a picture—yet such a picture as I never saw painted—than anything else. Being a strong, substantial hue, too, it serves well to be the ground-work of the picture, while the fantastic lightness of the yellow, and yellowish-green, tree-tops, is flung up towards the sky.

The oaks are now beginning to look sere, and their leaves have withered borders. It is pleasant to notice the wide circle of greener grass, beneath the circumference of an overshadowing oak. Passing an orchard, you hear an uneasy rustling in the trees, not as if they were struggling with the wind. Scattered about, are barrels to contain the apples; and perhaps a great heap of golden or scarlet apples is collected in one place.

[*Ibid.* pp. 85-87.]

October 13th.—Wednesday.

A good view from an upland swell of our pasture across the valley of the river Charles. There is the meadow, as level as a floor and carpeted with green, perhaps two miles from the rising ground on this side of the river, to that on the opposite side. The river winds through the midst of this level space, without any banks at [86] all; for it fills its bed almost to the brim, and bathes the meadow grass on either side. A tuft of shrubbery, at broken intervals, is scattered along its border; and thus the river meanders sluggishly along, without other life than what it gains from gleaming in the sun. Now, into this broad, flat meadow, as into a lake, capes and headlands put themselves forth, and shores of firm woodland border it, all covered with variegated foliage, making the contrast so much the stronger of their height and rough outline with the unvaried plane of the meadow. And beyond the river, far away, rises a long gradual swell of country, covered with an apparently dense growth of foliage, for miles, till the horizon terminates it; and here and there a house or two rises among the contiguity of trees. Every where, the trees have their autumnal hue, so that the whole landscape is red, russet, orange, and yellow, blending at a distance into a rich tint of brown orange, or thereabout—except the green meadow, so definitely hemmed in by the higher ground.

. . . .

No language can give an idea of the beauty and glory of the trees, just at this time. It would be easy, by a process of word-daubing, to set down a confused idea of gorgeous colors, like a bunch of tangled skeins of bright silk; but there is nothing, in the reality, of the glare which would thus be conveyed. And yet the splendor both of individual trees and of whole scenes, is unsurpassable. The oaks are now far advanced in their change of hue; and, in certain positions relatively to the sun, they appear lighted up and gleaming with a most magnificent deep gold, varying, according as portions of the foliage are in shadow or sunlight. On the sides which receive the direct sunshine, the effect is altogether rich; and in other points of view, it is equally beautiful, if less brilliant. This hue of the oak is more magnificent than the lighter yellow of the maples and walnuts. The whole landscape is now covered with this indescribable magnificence; you discern it on the [87] uplands, afar off; and Blue Hill in Milton, at the distance of several miles, actually seemed to glisten with rich, dark light—no, not glisten, nor gleam; but perhaps a subdued glow will do something towards the expression of it.

Met few people this morning—a grown girl, in company with a little boy, gathering barberries in a secluded lane—a portly autumnal gentleman, wrapped in a great coat, who asked the way to Mr. Joseph Goddard's—a fish-cart from the city, the driver of which sounded his horn along the lonesome way.

[*Ibid.* pp. 87-88.]

October 18th, Monday.

. · . . . . .

I passed through a very pleasant wood-path, yesterday, quite shut in and sheltered by trees that had not yet thrown off their yellow foliage. The sun shone strongly in among these trees, and quite kindled them; so that the path seemed the brighter for their shade, than if it had been quite exposed to the sun. [88]

In the village grave-yard, which lies contiguous to the street, I saw a man digging a grave; and one inhabitant after another turned aside from the street to look into the grave, and talk with the digger. I heard him laugh, with the hereditary mirthfulness of men of that occupation.

In a hollow of the woods, yesterday afternoon, I lay a long while watching a squirrel, who was capering about among the trees (oaks

and white-pines, so close together that their branches intermingled)
over my head. The squirrel seemed not to approve of my presence;
for he frequently uttered a sharp, quick, angry noise, like that of a
scissor-grinder's wheel. Sometimes I could see him sitting on an im-
pending bough, with his tail over his back, looking down pryingly
upon me; it seems to be a natural posture with him to sit on his hind
legs, holding up his forepaws. Anon, with a peculiarly quick start, he
would scamper along the branch, and be lost to sight in another part
of the tree, whence his shrill chatter would again be heard. Then I
would see him rapidly descending the trunk, and running along the
ground; and a moment afterwards, casting my eyes upward, I beheld
him flitting like a bird among the high interweaving branches, at the
summit of the trees, directly over my head. Afterwhile, he apparently
became accustomed to my presence, and set about some business of
his. He descended the trunk of a tree to the ground, took up a piece
of a decayed bough of a tree (a great burthen for such a small per-
sonage) and, with this in his mouth, again climbed the tree, and
passed from the branches of that to those of another, and thus onward and onward, till he was out of sight. Shortly afterwards he returned for another burthen; and this he repeated several times. I suppose he was building a nest—at least, I know not what else could have
been his object. Never was there such an active, cheerful, choleric,
continually-in-motion fellow, as this little red squirrel—talking to himself, chattering at me, and as sociable in his own person as if he had
half a dozen companions, instead of being alone in the lonesome wood.
Indeed, he flitted about so quickly, and showed himself in different
places so suddenly, that I was in some doubt whether there were not
two or three of him.

[*Ibid*. pp. 88-89.]

October 22ᵈ. Friday.

A continual succession of unpleasant Novembry days; and Autumn
has made rapid progress in the work of decay. It is now somewhat
of a rare good fortune to find a verdant grassy spot, on some slope, or
in a hollow; and even such seldom seen cases are bestrewn with dried
brown leaves;—which, however, methinks, make the short fresh grass
look greener around them. Dry leaves are now plentiful everywhere,
save where there are none but pine-trees; they rustle beneath the tread
—and there is nothing more autumnal than that sound. Nevertheless, in
a walk [89] this afternoon I have seen two oak trees which retained

almost the verdure of summer. They grew close to the huge Pulpit Rock, so that portions of their trunks appeared to grasp the rough surface; and they were rooted beneath it; and ascending high into the air, they overshadowed the gray crag with fresh foliage. Other oaks, here and there, have a few green leaves or boughs, among their rustling and russet shade.

.   .   .   .

Yesterday, I found two mushrooms in the woods, evidently of the preceding night growth. Also, I saw a mosquito, frost-pinched, and so wretched that I felt avenged for all the injuries which his tribe inflicted me upon [sic] last summer—and so did not molest this lone survivor.

Walnuts, in their green rinds, are falling from the trees; and so are chesnut-burrs [sic].

I found a maple leaf to-day, yellow all over, except its extremest point, which was a bright scarlet. It looked as if a drop of blood were hanging from it. The first change of the maple is to scarlet—next to yellow. Then it withers, wilts, and drops off—as most of them have already done.

[*Ibid.* pp. 89-90.]

Octr 27th. [The last entry that Hawthorne made at Brook Farm.]

Fringed gentians, found the last, probably, that will be seen this year, growing on the margin of the brook.

The device of a sun-dial for a monument over a grave—with some suitable motto.

To symbolize moral or spiritual disease by disease of the body;— thus, when a person committed any sin, it might cause a sore to appear on the body;—this to be wrought out.

A man with the right perception of things—a feeling within him of what is true [90] and what is false. It might be symbolized by the talisman, with which, in fairy tales, an adventurer was enabled to distinguish enchantments from realities.

no. 28 ❧

A letter from George Ripley to Ralph Waldo Emerson. Here reprinted from O. B. Frothingham, *George Ripley* (Boston: Houghton Mifflin Company, 1882), pp. 312-314.

Brook Farm, *December* 17, 1841

MY DEAR SIR,—I feel so sure of your sympathy in the ideas which our little company are trying to [313] illustrate, that I do not hesitate to bespeak your attention to our prospects.

We are now in full operation as a family of workers, teachers, and students; we feel the deepest inward convictions that for us our mode of life is the true one, and no attraction would tempt any one of us to exchange it for that which we have quitted lately. A rare Providence seems to have smiled on us in the materials which have been drawn together on this spot; and so many powers are at work with us and for us, that I cannot doubt we are destined to succeed in giving visible expression to some of the laws of social life, that as yet have been kept in the background.

We are all of us here full of joy and hope; we have overcome great obstacles; our foundation, I trust, is wisely laid. We seem to have every element of success, except the hindrances that arise from our poverty. Some of our friends have put us in possession of the means of owning the estate we live on; and our personal resources are sufficient, when available, for the immediate improvements we contemplate. Still, without larger means than are now at our command, we must labor to great disadvantage, and perhaps retard and seriously injure our enterprise. Our farming, in a pecuniary view, has been successful. It has realized ten per cent. net gain on the value of the estate, which I believe is Mr. Phinney's mark; and our income is somewhat more than our current expenses. But we are called on for outlays, for absolutely necessary accommodations, [314] which, though conducted with a Spartan economy, exhaust our available funds, and leave us too restricted for successful operation.

Our resource, in this case, is to request some of those who have faith in us and in our enterprise, not to endow us, or to portion us, but to invest in our stock such sums as they can temporarily part with, and receive therefor a just equivalent. Our shares are $500 each; they are guaranteed five per cent. interest, and may be withdrawn at the pleasure of the subscribers, on giving three months' notice. I have no doubt that an investment would be equally safe, if not equally lucrative, as in any joint-stock company in the Commonwealth, besides essentially aiding the establishment of an institution, which is believed to contain the seeds of future good to men.

If my confessions should prompt you to seek the ownership of one or more of our shares, I need not say that we should be gratified and greatly forwarded in this the time of our infant struggle and hope; but if you have any cause to do otherwise, I am sure that you will be no less frank than I have been, and regard this request as if it had never been made.

Your young friend Frank Brown is very well and I hope will do well.

Ever yours sincerely,
GEORGE RIPLEY.

no. 29 ~

Elizabeth P. Peabody, "Plan of the West Roxbury Community," *The Dial*, II (January, 1842), 361-372. The text used here is that of a reprinting of *The Dial* for the Rowfant Club, Cleveland, Ohio, 1901-1902.

PLAN OF THE WEST ROXBURY COMMUNITY

In the last number of the Dial were some remarks, under the perhaps ambitious title, of "A Glimpse of Christ's Idea of Society;" in a note to which, it was intimated, that in this number, would be given an account of an attempt to realize in some degree this great Ideal, by a little company in the midst of us, as yet without name or visible existence. The attempt is made on a very small scale. A few individuals, who, unknown to each other, under different disciplines of life, reacting from different social evils, but aiming at the same object,— of being wholly true to their natures as men and women; have been made acquainted with one another, and have determined to become the Faculty of the Embryo University.

In order to live a religious and moral life worthy the name, they feel it is necessary to come out in some degree from the world, and to form themselves into a community of property, so far as to exclude competition and the ordinary rules of trade;—while they reserve sufficient private property, or the means of obtaining it, for all purposes of independence, and isolation at will. They have bought a farm, in order to make agriculture the basis of their life, it being the most direct and simple in relation to nature.

A true life, although it aims beyond the highest star, is redolent of the healthy earth. The perfume of clover lingers about it. The lowing of cattle is the natural bass to the melody of human voices.

On the other hand, what absurdity can be imagined greater than the institution of cities? They originated not in love, but in war. It was war that drove men together in multitudes, and compelled them to stand so close, and build walls around them. This crowded condition produces wants of an unnatural character, which resulted in occupations that regenerated the evil, by creating artificial wants. Even when that thought of grief,

> "I know, where'er I go
> That there hath passed away a glory from the Earth,"

came to our first parents, as they saw the angel, with the flaming sword of self-consciousness, standing between them [362] and the recovery of spontaneous Life and Joy, we cannot believe they could have anticipated a time would come, when the sensuous apprehension of Creation—the great symbol of God—would be taken away from their unfortunate children,—crowded together in such a manner as to shut out the free breath and the Universal Dome of Heaven, some opening their eyes in the dark cellars of the narrow, crowded streets of walled cities. How could they have believed in such a conspiracy against the soul, as to deprive it of the sun and sky, and glorious apparelled Earth!—The growth of cities, which were the embryo of nations hostile to each other, is a subject worthy the thoughts and pen of the philosophic historian. Perhaps nothing would stimulate courage to seek, and hope to attain social good, so much, as a profound history of the origin, in the mixed nature of man, and the exasperation by society, of the various organized Evils under which humanity groans. Is there anything, which exists in social or political life, contrary to the soul's Ideal? That thing is not eternal, but finite, saith the Pure Reason. It has a beginning, and so a history. What man has done, man may *undo*. "By man came death; by man also cometh the resurrection from the dead."

The plan of the Community, as an Economy, is in brief this: for all who have property to take stock, and receive a fixed interest thereon; then to keep house or board in commons, as they shall severally desire, at the cost of provisions purchased at wholesale, or raised on the farm; and for all to labor in community, and be paid at a certain rate an hour, choosing their own number of hours, and their own kind of work. With the results of this labor, and their interest, they are to pay their board, and also purchase whatever else they require at cost, at the warehouses of the Community, which are to be filled by the Community as such. To perfect this economy, in the course of time they must have all trades, and all modes of business carried on among themselves, from the lowest mechanical trade, which contributes to the health and comfort of life, to the finest art which adorns it with food or drapery for the mind.

All labor, whether bodily or intellectual, is to be paid at the same rate of wages; on the principle, that as the labor [363] becomes merely bodily, it is a greater sacrifice to the individual laborer, to give his time to it; because time is desirable for the cultivation of the intellect, in exact proportion to ignorance. Besides, intellectual labor involves in itself higher pleasures, and is more its own reward, than bodily labor.

Another reason, for setting the same pecuniary value on every kind of labor, is, to give outward expression to the great truth, that all labor is sacred, when done for a common interest. Saints and philosophers already know this, but the childish world does not; and very decided measures must be taken to equalize labors, in the eyes of the young of the community, who are not beyond the moral influences of the world without them. The community will have nothing done within its precincts, but what is done by its own members, who stand all in social equality;—that the children may not "learn to expect one kind of service from Love and Goodwill, and another from the obligation of others to render it,"—a grievance of the common society stated, by one of the associated mothers, as destructive of the soul's simplicity. Consequently, as the Universal Education will involve all kinds of operations, necessary to the comforts and elegances of life, every associate, even if he be the digger of a ditch as his highest accomplishment, will be an instructer in that to the young members. Nor will this elevation of bodily labor be liable to lower the tone of manners and refinement in the community. The "children of light" are not altogether unwise in their generation. They have an invisible but all-powerful guard of principles. Minds incapable of refinement will not be attracted into this association. It is an Ideal community, and only to the ideally inclined will it be attractive; but these are to be found in every rank of life, under every shadow of circumstance. Even among the diggers in the ditch are to be found some, who through religious cultivation, can look down, in meek superiority, upon the outwardly refined, and the book-learned.

Besides, after becoming members of this community, none will be engaged merely in bodily labor. The hours of labor for the Association will be limited by a general law, and can be curtailed at the will of the individual still more; and means will be given to all for intellectual im-[364]provement and for social intercourse, calculated to refine and expand. The hours redeemed from labor by community, will not be reapplied to the acquisition of wealth, but to the production of intellectual goods. This community aims to be rich, not in the metallic representative of wealth, but in the wealth itself, which money should represent; namely, LEISURE TO LIVE IN ALL THE FACULTIES OF THE SOUL. As a community, it will traffic with the world at large, in the products of Agricultural labor; and it will sell education to as many young persons as can be domesticated in the families, and enter into the common life with their own children. In the end, it hopes to be enabled to provide—not only all the necessaries, but all the elegances desirable for bodily and for spiritual health; books, apparatus, collections for science, works of art, means of beautiful amusement. These things are to be common to all; and thus that object, which alone gilds and refines the passion for individual accumulation, will no longer exist for desire, and whenever the Sordid passion appears, it will be seen in its naked selfishness. In its ultimate success, the community will realize all the ends which selfishness seeks, but involved in spiritual blessings, which only greatness of soul can aspire after.

And the requisitions on the individuals, it is believed, will make this the order forever. The spiritual good will always be the condition of the temporal. Every one must labor for the community in a reasonable degree, or not taste its benefits. The principles of the organization therefore, and not its probable results in future time, will determine its members. These principles are cooperation in social matters, instead of competition or balance of interests; and individual self-unfolding, in the faith that the whole soul of humanity is in each man and woman. The former is the application of the love of man; the latter of the love of God, to life. Whoever is satisfied with society, as it is; whose sense of justice is not wounded by its common action, institutions, spirit of commerce, has no business with this community; neither has any one who is willing to have other men (needing more time for intellectual cultivation than himself) give their best hours and strength to bodily labor, to secure himself immunity therefrom. And whoever does not measure what society owes to its members [365] of cherishing and instruction, by the needs of the individuals that compose it, has no lot in this new society. Whoever is willing to receive from his fellow men that, for which he gives no equivalent, will stay away from its precincts forever.

But whoever shall surrender himself to its principles, shall find that its yoke is easy and its burden light. Everything can be said of it, in a degree, which Christ said of his kingdom, and therefore it is believed that in some measure it does embody his Idea. For its Gate of entrance is strait and narrow. It is literally a pearl *hidden in a field.* Those only who are willing to lose their life for its sake shall find it. Its voice is that which sent the young man sorrowing away. "Go sell all thy goods and give to the poor, and then come and follow me." "Seek first the kingdom of Heaven, and its righteousness, and all other things shall be added to you."

This principle, with regard to labor, lies at the root of moral and religious life; for it is not more true that "money is the root of all evil," than that *labor is the germ of all good.*

All the work is to be offered for the free choice of the members of the community, at stated seasons, and such as is not chosen, will be hired. But it is not anticipated that any work will be set aside to be hired, for which there is actual ability in the community. It is so desirable that the hired labor should be avoided, that it is believed the work will all be done freely, even though at voluntary sacrifice. If there is some exception at first, it is because the material means are inadequate to the reception of all who desire to go. They cannot go, unless they have shelter; and in this climate, they cannot have shelter unless they can build houses; and they cannot build houses unless they have money. It is not here as in Robinson Crusoe's Island, or in the prairies and rocky mountains of the far west, where the land and the wood are not appropriated. A single farm, in the midst of Massachusetts, does not afford range enough for men to create out of the Earth a living, with no other means; as the wild Indians, or the United States Army in Florida may do.

This plan, of letting all persons choose their own departments of action, will immediately place the Genius of In-[366]struction on its throne. Communication is the life of spiritual life. Knowledge pours itself out upon ignorance by a native impulse. All the arts crave response. "WISDOM CRIES." If every man and woman taught only what they loved, and so many hours as they could naturally communicate, instruction would cease to be a drudgery, and we may add, learning would be no longer a task. The known accomplishments of many of the members of this association have already secured it an interest in the public mind, as a school of literary advantages quite superior. Most of the associates have had long practical experience in the details of teaching, and have groaned under the necessity of taking their method and law from custom and caprice, when they would rather have found it in the nature of the thing taught, and the condition of the pupil to be instructed. Each instructer appoints his hours of study or recitation, and the scholars, or the parents of the children, or the educational committee, choose the studies, for the time, and the pupils submit, as long as they pursue their studies with any teacher, to his regulations.

As agriculture is the basis of their external life, scientific agriculture, connected with practice, will be a prominent part of the instruction from the first. This obviously involves the natural sciences, mathematics, and accounts. But to classical learning justice is also to be done. Boys may be fitted for our colleges there, and even be carried through the college course. The particular studies of the individual pupils, whether old or young, male or female, are to be strictly regulated, according to their inward needs. As the children of the community can remain in the community after they become of age, as associates, if they will; there will not be an entire subserviency to the end of preparing the means of earning a material subsistence, as is frequently the case now. Nevertheless, as they will have had an opportunity, in the course of their minority, to earn three or four hundred dollars, they can leave the community at twenty years of age, if they will, with that sufficient capital, which, together with their extensive education, will gain a *subsistence* anywhere, in the best society of the world. It is this feature of the plan, which may preclude from parents any question as to their right to go into this community, and forego forever all hope of [367] great individual accumulation *for their children;* a customary plea for spending life in making money. Their children will be supported at free board, until they are ten years of age; educated gratuitously; taken care of in case of their parents' sickness and death; and they themselves will be supported, after seventy years of age, by the community, unless their accumulated capital supports them.

There are some persons who have entered the community without money. It is believed that these will be able to support themselves and dependents, by less work, more completely, and with more ease than elsewhere; while their labor will be of advantage to the community. It is in no sense an eleemosynary establishment, but it is hoped that in the end it will be able to receive all who have the spiritual qualifications.

It seems impossible that the little organization can be looked on with any unkindness by the world without it. Those, who have not the faith that the principles of Christ's kingdom are applicable to real life in the world, will smile at it, as a visionary attempt. But even they must acknowledge it can do no harm, in any event. If it realizes the hope of its founders, it will immediately become a manifold blessing. Its moral *aura* must be salutary. As long as it lasts, it will be an example of the beauty of brotherly love. If it succeeds in uniting successful labor with improvement in mind and manners, it will teach a noble lesson to the agricultural population, and do something to check that rush from the country to the city, which is now stimulated by ambition, and by something better, even a desire for learning. Many a young man leaves the farmer's life, because only by so doing can he have intellectual companionship and opportunity; and yet, did he but know it, professional life is ordinarily more unfavorable to the perfection of the mind, than the farmer's life; if the latter is lived with wisdom and moderation, and the labor mingled as it might be with study. This community will be a school for young agriculturalists, who may learn within its precincts, not only the skilful practice, but the scientific reasons of their work, and be enabled afterwards to improve their art continuously. It will also prove the best of normal schools, and as such, may claim the interest of those, who mourn over the inefficiency of our common school system, with its present ill-instructed teachers.

[368] It should be understood also, that after all the working and teaching, which individuals of the community may do, they will still have leisure, and in that leisure can employ themselves in connexion with the world around them. Some will not teach at all; and those especially can write books, pursue the Fine Arts, for private emolument if they will, and exercise various functions of· men.—From this community might go forth preachers of the gospel of Christ, who would not have upon them the odium, or the burthen, that now diminishes the power of the clergy. And even if *pastors* were to go from this community, to reside among congregations as now, for a salary given, the fact that they would have something to retreat upon, at any moment, would save them from that virtual dependence on their congregations, which now corrupts the relation. There are doubtless beautiful instances of the old true relation of pastor and people, even of teacher and taught, in the decaying churches around us, but it is in vain to attempt to conceal the ghastly fact, that many a taper is burning dimly in the candlestick, no longer silver or golden, because compassion forbids to put it quite out. But let the spirit again blow "where it listeth," and not circumscribe itself by salary and other commodity,—and the Preached word might reassume the awful Dignity which is its appropriate garment; and though it sit down with publicans and sinners, again speak "with authority and not as the scribes."

We write, as is evident perhaps, not as members, which we are not, but interested spectators of the growth of this little community. It is due to their modesty to apologize for bringing out so openly, what they have done simply and without pretension. We rest on the spirit of the day, which is that of communication. No sooner does the life of man become visible, but it is a part of the great phenomenon of na-

ture, which never seeks display, but suffers all to speculate thereon.
When this speculation is made in respect, and in love of truth, it is
most to be defended. We shall now proceed to make some observations that may sound like criticism, but this we do without apology,
for earnest seekers of a true life are not liable to be petulant.

The very liberality, and truth to nature of the plan, is a legitimate
reason for fearing it will not succeed as a special [369] community
in any given time. The vineyard does not always yield according to
the reasonable expectation of its Lord. When he looks for grapes, behold it brings forth wild grapes. For outward success there must always be compromise, and where it is so much the object to avoid the
dangers of compromise, as there very properly is here, there is perhaps danger of not taking advantage of such as nature offers.

One of these is the principle of antagonism. It is fair to take advantage of this in one respect. The members may be stimulated to
faithfulness and hope, by the spectacle of society around them, whose
unnecessary evils can be clearly seen to be folly, as well as sin, from
their retreat. The spirit of liberality must be discriminated from the
spirit of accommodation. Love is a stern principle, a severe winnower,
when it is one with the pure Reason; as it must be, to be holy, and
to be effective. It is a very different thing from indulgence. Some
persons have said that in order to [be] a true experiment, and to enact
a really generous faith in man, there should be any neighborhood
taken without discrimination, with the proportion that may happen
to be in it, of the good and bad, the strong and weak. But we differ as
to the application in this instance. They are so little fenced about with
rules and barriers, that they have no chance but by being strong in
the spirit. "Touch not, taste not, handle not," must be their watch-
word, with respect to the organized falsehoods they have protested
against; and with respect to means of successful manifestation, the
aphorism of St. Augustine, "God is patient because he is Eternal."

To be a little more explicit. The men and women of the world, as
they rise, are not at the present moment wise enough, in the Hebrew
sense of the word wisdom, even if they are good-intentioned enough,
to enter into a plan of so great mutual confidence. To all the evils
arising from constitutional infirmity and perversion they must, especially at first, be exposed. There will always be natures too cold to
satisfy the warm-hearted, too narrow for the enjoyment of the wide-
visioned, some will be deficient in reason, and some in sensibility, and
there will be many who, from defect of personal power, will let run
to waste beautiful hearts, and not turn to account great insight of natu-

ral wisdom. [370] Love, justice, patience, forbearance, every virtue under heaven, are always necessary in order to do the social duties. There is no knot that magnanimity cannot untie; but the Almighty Wisdom and Goodness will not allow any tower to be builded by the children of men, where they can understand one another *without* this solvent magnanimity. There must ever be sincerity of good design, and organic truth, for the evolution of Beauty.

Now there can be only one way of selecting and winnowing their company. The power to do this must be inherent in their constitution; they must keep sternly true to their principles.

In the first place, they must not compromise their principle of labor, in receiving members. Every one, who has any personal power, whether bodily or mental, must bring the contribution of personal service, no matter how much money he brings besides. This personal service is not to amount to drudgery in any instance, but in every able-bodied or sound-minded person, it should be at least equivalent to the care of their own persons. Exchange, or barter of labor, so as to distribute to each according to his genius, is to be the means of ease, indefinitely, but no absolute dispensation should be given, except for actual infirmity. "My Father worketh hitherto, and I work," is always the word of the divine humanity.

But granting that they keep the gate of entrance narrow, as the gate of life, which is being as liberal as the moral Law, a subtle temptation assails them from the side of their Organization. Woe be unto them if they lean upon it; if they ever forget that it is only what they have made it, and what they sustain it to be. It not only must be ever instinct with spirit, but it must never be thought, even then, to circumscribe the spirit. It can do nothing more, even if it work miracles, than make bread out of stones, and after all, man liveth not by bread alone, but by *every word that proceedeth out of the mouth of God.* Another temptation assails them, clothed as an angel of light. The lover of man finds in his benevolence a persuasive advocate, when the Devil proposes to him to begin by taking possession of the kingdoms of this world, according to his ability. In their ardor for means of success, they may touch the mammon of unrighteousness. They will be ex-[371]posed to endowment. Many persons, enlightened enough to be unwilling to let the wealth, they have gained by the accident of birth or of personal talent, go to exasperate the evil of present society, will be disposed to give it, or to leave it as a legacy to this community, and it would be asceticism to refuse it absolutely. But they should receive it greatly. "Thou shalt worship the Lord thy God, and Him *only* shalt thou *serve.*" No person who proposes to endow the com-

munity as a University, or as the true system of life, understands what
he does, unless he surrenders what he gives, unconditionally, in the
same spirit of faith, with which the members throw themselves in,
with their lives, their property, and sacred honor. At all events it
would violate their principle of progress to accept anything with conditions; unless it may be considered a condition, that they remain an
association, governed by the majority of members, according to its
present general constitution.

It were better even to forego the advantage of good buildings, apparatus, library, than to have these shackles.—Though space cannot
now be given to do more than state these points, it might be demonstrated that to keep to them is essential to independence, and can alone
justify the conscience of endower and endowed.

Another danger which should be largely treated is the spirit of
coterie. The breadth of their platform, which admits all sects; and the
generality of their plan, which demands all degrees of intellectual culture to begin with, is some security against this. But the ultimate
security must be in numbers. Some may say, "already this taint has
come upon them, for they are doubtless *transcendentalists*." But to
mass a few protestants together and call them transcendentalists, is a
popular cant. Transcendentalism belongs to no sect of religion, and no
social party. It is the common ground to which all sects may rise, and
be purified of their narrowness; for it consists in seeking the spiritual
ground of all manifestations. As already in the pages of this periodical,
Calvinist, and Unitarian, and Episcopalian, and Baptist, and Quaker,
and Swedenborgian, have met and spoken in love and freedom on
this common basis; so it would be seen, if the word were understood,
that transcendentalism, notwithstanding its [372] name is taken in vain
by many moonshiny youths and misses who assume it, would be the
best of all guards against the spirit of coterie. Much as we respect our
friends of the community, we dare not hope for them quite so much,
as to aver that they *transcend*, as yet, all the limitations that separate
men from love and mutual trust.

> Serene will be our days and bright,
> And happy will our nature be,
> When Love is an unerring light
> And Joy its own security.
> And blest are they who in the main
>   This faith, even now, do entertain;
>   Live in the spirit of this creed;
> Yet find the *strength of Law* according to their need!

We had intended to subjoin some further remarks, by way of inquiry, into the possibility of other portions of society, not able to emancipate themselves from the thralldom of city life, beginning also to act, in a degree, on the principles of cooperation. Ameliorations of present evils, initiations into truer life, may be made we believe everywhere. Wordly wisdom, for its own purposes, avails itself of what is outward in the community plan; at least of the labor-saving element. Why may not the children of light be equally wise?

There may be some persons, at a distance, who will ask, to what degree has this community gone into operation? We cannot answer this with precision, for we do not write as organs of this association, and have reason to feel, that if we applied to them for information, they would refuse it, out of their dislike to appear in public. We desire this to be distinctly understood. But we can see, and think we have a right to say, that it has purchased the Farm, which some of its members cultivated for a year with success, by way of trying their love and skill for agricultural labor;—that in the only house they are as yet rich enough to own, is collected a large family, including several boarding scholars, and that all work and study together. They seem to be glad to know of all, who desire to join them in the spirit, that at any moment, when they are able to enlarge their habitations, they may call together those that belong to them.

E. P. P.

no. 30 ～

Letter from R. W. Emerson, New York, March 3, 1842, to Lidian Emerson, here reprinted from *The Letters of Ralph Waldo Emerson*, edited by Ralph L. Rusk (New York: Columbia, 1939), III, 20-21.

. . . [21] And this P.M. Mr Brisbane indoctrinated me in the high mysteries of "Attractive Industry" in a conversation which I wish you all might have heard. He wishes me "with all my party," to come in directly & join him. What palaces! What concerts! What pictures lectures poetry & flowers. Constantinople it seems Fourier showed was the natural capital of the World, & when the Earth is planted & gardened & templed all over with "Groups" & "Communities" each of 2000 men & 6000 acres, Constantinople is to be the metropolis & we poets & Miscellaneous transcendental persons who are too great for your Concords & New Yorks will gravitate to that point for music

& architecture & society such as wit cannot paint nowadays. Well, tomorrow P.M. I am to hear the rest of the story, so you shall have no
more of it. . .

no. 31 ❧

Entry in the *Journals* of Ralph Waldo Emerson for a day early
in April, 1842. Here reprinted from *Journals of Ralph Waldo
Emerson*, edited by E. W. Emerson and W. E. Forbes (Boston:
Houghton Mifflin Company, 1911), VI, 193.

Mr. Clapp, of Dorchester, to whom I described the Fourier project,
thought it must not only succeed, but that agricultural association
must presently fix the price of bread, and drive single farmers into association in self-defence, as the great commercial and manufacturing
companies had done.

no. 32 ❧

Letter from R. W. Emerson, Concord, May 7 and 8, 1842, to
Charles King Newcomb, here reprinted from *The Letters of
Ralph Waldo Emerson*, edited by Ralph L. Rusk (New York:
Columbia, 1939), III, 51-52.

MY DEAR CHARLES,

I am glad you have been so happily employed, if I have lost the
benefit of seeing you when I had most leisure and when my jewels
were in my kingdom. Now my sister Elizabeth is in Boston, & Mr
Alcott sails for England today or tomorrow. But Thoreau is still here,
& E. H. will return again. Meantime I wish to secure the *first* Dolon
for the July *Dial*. I have set my heart on it & cannot be denied; so I
pray you to let no dreams, hallucinations 'delays of genius,' & the like,
interrupt the speedy ordering & transmission to me of that manuscript.
If you are at this instant of time enjoying the favor of heaven and receiving new communications, I shall not ask you to go back to the old,
for I am not impious. In that case, send me the papers & I will find
a Baruch who shall copy them. But on no other condition can I desist
from my claim.

The other claim I have to make is this. Caroline Sturgis has given
me leave to select anything that suits my purpose from her last sum-

mer's verses which, she says, you have. I desire that you will seal
them up & send them at your earliest opportunity to Miss Peabody in
West Street, addressed to me. So shall this muse again & other muses
hereafter if other such there be, be propitious to you.

I ask now only for the first Dolon, but I want the *second* to follow
this in October.

8 May

This letter was interrupted in the midst of the last page by Mr
Hawthorn's visit who came to Concord to look for a house. Cannot
you one day come hither to look for a house? Mr Bradford will also.
Those of us who do not believe in Communities, believe in neighbor-
hoods & that the kingdom of heaven may consist of such. Tell Mr
Ripley that Mr Edmund Hosmer, a farmer here of whom he has heard,
has a great [52] desire to see Brook Farm, and can only leave his
work conveniently on Sunday. Therefore if he do not forbid it, I shall
bring him on some Sunday soon. He should be your foreman at B. F.
We think him here an inestimable man. Farewell.

R. W. Emerson

no. 33 ～

Letter from Nathaniel Hawthorne, Boston, May 25, 1842, to
David Mack, here reprinted from Manning Hawthorne, "Hawthorne and Utopian Socialism," *The New England Quarterly*, XII
(1939), 729-730.

To David Mack, Esq.
My dear Sir:—

When I last met you I expressed my purpose of coming to Northampton in the course of the present month in order to gain information as to the situation and prospects of your community. Since our
interview, however, circumstances of various kinds have induced me
to give up the design of offering myself as a member. As a matter of
conscience, with my present impressions, I should hardly feel myself
justified in taking such a step; for, though I have much faith in the
general good tendency of insti-[730]tutions on this principle, yet I
am troubled with many doubts (after my experience of last year)
whether I, as an individual, am a proper subject for these beneficial
influences. In an economical point of view, undoubtedly, I would not

do so well anywhere else; but I feel that this ought not to be the primary consideration. A more important question is, how my intellectual and moral condition, and ability to be useful, would be affected by merging myself in a community. I confess to you, my dear Sir, it is my present belief that I can best attain the higher ends of my life by retaining the ordinary relation to society.

   With my best wishes for your prosperity and happiness,

I remain sincerely,
NATH. HAWTHORNE

no. 34 ～

> Letter from Georgianna Bruce to Sarah Edes Allen, Boston, which Lindsay Swift (p. 77) dates "certainly not before the summer of 1842." It is here reprinted from Lindsay Swift, *Brook Farm, Its Members, Scholars, and Visitors* (New York: The Macmillan Company, 1900), pp. 77-81. The relationship of Sarah Allen with Brook Farm is explained by the following paragraph from a letter to the editor of this volume from Miss Harriet Swift, Curator of Americana at the Public Library of the City of Boston, June 28, 1957: "My father, Lindsay Swift, was born in Boston on July 29, 1856. He was the son of John Lindsay Swift and Sarah Edes (Allen) Swift. Georgianna Bruce was a close friend of Sarah Allen and her brother, Daniel, when they were living in Boston. Sarah and Daniel both visited Georgianna in Brook Farm. I have a vague recollection that Daniel, who taught in a private school in Boston, was fond of Georgianna and it may be the reason she referred to herself in the quoted letter as 'Your loving sister.' Daniel died in Rio de Janeiro of yellow fever."

Eyrie, Brook Farm, *Saturday Night.*

I received yours, dearest, this afternoon by Dr. Dana, who, with I don't know how many others, was out here. We met Barbara Channing and others on the doorstep on our return from a boat ride. Three or four of the boys have clubbed together and bought a boat, painted it, fitted it up with sails, compass, etc., and especially a carpet (Paris they say) for the ladies' feet, in arranging which [78] they have taken, as you may suppose, clear comfort, as well as kept clear of mischief of some sort, I dare say. And this afternoon was the first time that it was honored with our presence. Four of us girls,—Mary G.[annett], Abby Morton, Caddy Stodder, and myself, with five boys, —our Spanish Manuel being Captain *for the day,*—set sail in Charles

River after having walked a mile through the fields and woods, not
to mention swamps. We sailed a good way up, passed under the Dedham bridge, then down, singing away, Abby and I. Oh! the woods
round Cow Island are so rich, the young pale green birch, down by the
bank, contrasted with the dark tall pines, the sky with just enough
of *life* in the clouds to satisfy me, and the deep water with just a
ripple on the surface, and so warm that you could hold your hand in,
formed a picture that seemed perfect. But then came in *man* to mar
and disfigure. Two men with hatchets cutting down those same beautiful trees and another with a line hooking the fish (for mere amusement, most likely). I really sympathize with Mr. Bradford who writes
me that "in cutting down the green young branches for pea-sticks
he is really afraid of the vengeance of the wood demon and looks
around to see if any Brownies are near." Well, we got home perfectly
safe as I informed you, and after tea a large party of all sorts came
up here to hear some music, so here I must stop to tell you that to my
inexpressible joy the piano and Mr. Dwight have at length come. The
piano is a handsome one of a sweet tone, and Mr. D. has some of the
best of music which I use, principally German. You will know that
every spare moment is devoted to music now. We are going to get up
a glee club forthwith. George and Burrill Curtis (of whom I will speak
or perhaps have spoken before) take the bass and tenor, I and Abby
the soprano and second. Then a large number who know very little
about music are going to commence with the rudiments. Poor Mr. D.
said to-night, when we [79] were washing up the tea things with two
or three of the gentlemen wiping, and groups here and there discussing, "How *fast* you *live* here; I *like* it, but really my head, my
head suffers," and then we had a talk about it, and Burrill said that he
had noticed how we seemed to drive with everything, but that we were
in debt and must not therefore be at leisure, and that we must be
willing to bear the consequences of the errors and sins of past time
for a season, and after all he could not think of living in the old way
again; it seemed like stagnation, vegetation. Burrill is not of age, and
his brother only eighteen. They both have large fortunes, I believe,
and have come out of the most fashionable society of New York, their
father entirely absorbed in *banks* and dollars. Burrill is a perfect
beauty, entirely unconscious, and then (as Sarah [Stearns] says) so
human. If you speak to him, he listens as if he thought there was *at*
least a chance that you were worth listening to. He stands alone and
acts for himself. His brother looks to him and is unconsciously influenced by him. George has a rich voice and they sing duets to-

gether—the Irish melodies which I love so much, etc. George plays beautifully and entirely by ear. Is it not grand to see them come out so independently and work away at the peas!!! We have had the Mortons from Plymouth to make a visit, leave two of their boys and Abby, and choose a building spot. You would like Mr. M. He looks just as you can fancy the most loving of the Puritans looked, and really *is* one, divested of all their superstition and bigotry. He read a letter to us before he left, that he had written to a nephew now in Germany, explaining the community principles, etc. I wish you could have heard it. It is so strange, as well as pleasant, to hear the ideas which different persons entertain of the same subject, expressed in their own peculiar way; and really if I should judge by the most beautiful letters I have read, written by one and another among us, I should [80] think that our *grandchildren* would not waste time were they to collect some of them if they wanted to trace the history of the *first community*.

We number over sixty and several more are coming. We have now a long table in the entry. Mrs. Barlow is going to New York for a week, and I have offered to take the *joys* and cares of a mother to her two boys during her absence, concerning which duties and pleasures we have had no little merriment. *"Orah dear"* [Gannett] has not returned, but her sister Mary has come—a smart, pleasant, trusting child. Of course I do not love her as well as Orah yet, but I have a sort of *motherly* feeling to her, and she turns to me as one does to a sister. Tomorrow I must write her. Only think of my writing all this after twelve o'clock with Sarah snoring away, and Sophia [Ripley] would not hear of my practising. And now I have not told you of the beautiful wild flowers I found in the woods and gave them to Mr. Dwight because he loves them, nor of how I took my scholars to walk this morning and we sang in the woods. But I must say good night, dearest, or shall lose my breakfast to-morrow. Now you will kiss dear little Kit for me, won't you? and give my love to all. I had an invitation to ride in and out last Sunday, but having sprained my ankle and not feeling very well, I did not think that even to *see you* I ought to risk making myself more sick. I got the medicine, etc. Be sure and come out if you can; I have much to tell you which I cannot write. I took a walk in the woods to-night. If I am ever so tired or excited, this always has a calming, quieting influence.

Your loving sister, GEORGY.

. . . .

no. 35 ~

From a letter from Margaret Fuller (Cambridge), October 16, 1842, here reprinted from *The Letters of Ralph Waldo Emerson*, edited by Ralph L. Rusk (New York: Columbia, 1939), III, 90, footnote 334.

. . . Alas! here I am at the end of my paper, and have told you nothing of my stay at Brook Farm, where I gave *conversations* on alternate evenings with the husking parties. But you will come to see me in my new home, & then I will tell you. My first visitor last Sunday was S. Ward. My second next day W. Channing. The following day I expected *you*, & since you were not so kind as to come, observe with pleasure that your letter dates from that day. Adieu, dear friend, be good to me, think of me, and write to me. The days of toil & care are coming, when I shall need your ray, mellow if distant. I owe to the protection of your roof, to the soothing influence of your neighborhood, and to the gentle beauty of the Concord wood, some weeks of health and peace which have revived my courage, so unusually dulled last summer. To Lidians unfailing and generous kindness also I owe much. But you must be the better to me for my thanks. . . .

no. 36 ~

Entry in the *Journals* of Ralph Waldo Emerson for November 26, 1842. Here reprinted from *Journals of Ralph Waldo Emerson*, edited by E. W. Emerson and W. E. Forbes (Boston: Houghton Mifflin Company, 1911), VI, 314.

London, New York, Boston, are phalanxes ready-made, where you shall find concerts, books, balls, medical lectures, prayers, or Punch and Judy, according to your fancy, on any night or day.

no. 37 ~

Entries in the *Journals* of Ralph Waldo Emerson for May 7, 1843. Here reprinted from *Journals of Ralph Waldo Emerson*, edited by E. W. Emerson and W. E. Forbes (Boston: Houghton Mifflin Company, 1911), VI, 391, 392, 392-393.

Yesterday George Bradford walked and talked of the Community and cleared up some of the mists which gossip had made: and expressed the conviction, shared by himself and his friends there, that plain dealing was the best defence of manners and morals between the sexes. I suppose that the danger arises whenever bodily familiarity grows up without a spiritual intimacy. The reason why there is purity in marriage is, that the parties are universally near and helpful, and not only near bodily. If their wisdoms come near and meet, there is no danger of passion. Therefore, the remedy of impurity is to come nearer.

[392] At Brook Farm this peculiarity, that there is no head. In every family, a paterfamilias; in every factory, a foreman; in a shop, a master; in a boat, a boatswain; but in Brook Farm, no authority, but each master and mistress of their own actions,—happy, hapless, *sansculottes*.

At Brook Farm again, I understand the authority of Mr. and Mrs. Ripley is felt unconsciously by all; and this is ground of regret to individuals, who see that this particular power is thrown into the conservative scale. But Mr. and Mrs. Ripley are the only ones who have identified themselves with the Community. They [393] have married it, and they are it. The others are experimenters who will stay by this if it thrives, being always ready to retire, but these have burned their ships, and are entitled to the moral consideration which this position gives. The young people agree that they have had more rapid experiences than elsewhere befel them; have lived faster.

no. 38 ⌖

An entry in the *Journals* of Ralph Waldo Emerson for June 22, 1843. Here reprinted from *Journals of Ralph Waldo Emerson*, edited by E. W. Emerson and W. E. Forbes (Boston: Houghton Mifflin Company, 1911), VI, 416-417.

I was at Brook Farm and had a cheerful time. Some confidences were granted me; and grief softened the somewhat hard nature of Mrs. George Ripley, so that I had never seen her to such advantage. Fine weather, cheerful uplands, and every person you meet is a character and in free costume. Charles Newcomb I saw, and was [417] relieved to meet again on something of the old footing, after hearing of so much illness and sensitiveness. But Charles is not a person to be seen on a holiday or in holiday places, but one should live in solitude and obscurity, with him for the only person in the county to speak to.

Also **George Bradford** let me a little into the spiritual history and relations that go forward, but one has this feeling in hearing of their
spiritualism,—ah! had they never heard of it first! and did not know
it was spiritualism.

no. 39 ～

> From a letter from Sophia Eastman to Mehitable Eastman, here
> reprinted from a true copy of the holograph in the Abernethy
> Library of American Literature, Middlebury College, Middlebury,
> Vermont. The true copy was supplied by the courtesy of Miss
> Mary Noel, Curator of the Abernethy Library.

West R July 25, 43

My dear Parents and Sisters

. . . .

I will describe to you the situation of the place. It is certainly a delightful place, although very different from what I imagined. There
are four separate buildings. The Pilgrim House, the Eyrie, Cottage
and Hive, where we eat our meals, and all that come stop. They are
situated about as far from each other as our house is from Mr Lum-
ley's (?) There is an aristocracy prevailing here, although many complain of being neglected. I think there should be a distinction made,
but you know it is against their principle, but they all treat me with
as much kindness and respect as though I paid five dollars a week for
board. You recollect the plan of this Community speaks of receiving
no individuals unless capable of refinement, a great taste for literature,
and possessed of superior abilities, but I assure you there are a great
many of the reverse. The fact is they are rather dull and backward in
there studies, and I am inclined to think some will always remain so,
though there are many pretty ladies and gentlemen and some mean
characters I should think (I judge only from looks and appearances).
There are three horns blown in the morning, the first is sounded a little
before five, the second half past five, and the third at six, to call them
to breakfast. Immediately after breakfast I proceed to the ironing
room, which is to the Pilgrim house (or to the washing room just as
they wish me to) and there remain until the horn sounds for dinner,
which is half past twelve. The work is very hard and wearing to the
constitution. It is now vacation many of the teachers are absent, and
we study at our rooms. Mr Ripleys sister is my teacher. She is a old

maid and is one of the most presise beings I ever saw. I can describe
her in no other way only to say she resembles old Mrs Clay very
much indeed (I think mother would like her on that account) though
she is called a very worthy person. We go to Miss Ripley's room at
four, and there remain three hours. The remainder of the time we
stay at our rooms. The advantages here are not as good as I imagined
neither do I think there can be so much improvement made here as at
some other institutions but I like [it] very well and I shall probably
stay here six months, or a year and prehaps I may finish my education.
But I find I have grown pale and poor already though I feel pretty
well most of the time. You will now wish to know what there religious principles are. I regret to say that many have no principles
at all. But very few attend church on the Sabbath, and it is a fact they
do knit and sew. On Sunday Mrs Ripley invites them to the Grove
where they spend a few hours in reading gipsy stories. I have seen
many things myself which I shall not mention here. A carriage is provided in the morning for those that wish to go to church. I have
walked one Sabbath, and rode two[.] The Unitarian [church] where
I attend is two miles from the community, the orthodox half mile. I
dislike the principles very much indeed and I know my parents and
sisters will not approve of this, but you know any one is not obliged
to imbibe these sentiments. There are four ministers here who have
renounced these sentiments and become Trancendentalists. They seldom attend Church on the Sabbath. A person that comes here is apt
to get into the habit of staying at home on the sabbath, but I mean
to attend constantly. The truth is that this institution is something like
the Shakers, after a person remains here a short time they become attached to the place, and are unwilling to leave and join the Association.
There are about sixteen or seventeen members, but I think I should
never be willing to join them, but I feel somewhat attached to the
place, although I have been here so short a time. I suppose you have
heard from me by way of Mr Ripley as he said he was going to write
to father. He enquired a great deal about Pa and said he hoped my
parents and sisters would visit the community. They have [word il-
legible under wax seal] from different cities and states, and always
treat them with great hospitality and politeness. I know you will enjoy a visit here and I want you to come in the fall it will be so
pleasant here Elizabeth Cone called on me in the morning, & in the
afternoon she sent for me to spend a few hours, had a pleasant time &
think her a very pleasant pretty young lady. They all thought me a
little girl about fourteen years of age, and seemed surprised when I
told them I was older. They seemed to think I possessed great courage

to come so far and among strangers but it is just what I like. I can see that they like me very much but it requires considerable policy to be in such a place, and to get the right side. They all appear uncommonly interested in my welfare. Why it is I cannot tell. The girls appear very fond of me because I appear so cheerful and happy. If they feel low spirited they come to my chamber. I have assisted many of the young ladies in there studies. Have written one letter for a lady to her mother who was 3 or 4 years my senior. My room mate is enjoying "Natures sweet repose" and I will describe her. She is a native of Ireland and is a orphan   She is a very good girl but rather ignorant not such a person as I should wish to have for a companion and friend. But I make a great deal of her and she appears to like me very much. She is a Catholic but I think she is a Christian. If father is sick be sure and let me know it immediately   I think a sight about this   You may send me a paper occasionally if you please. I would not send a paper to Mr Ripley very often he has so many he will not read for he has so much buisness to attend to   Answer this when you think propper and write all the news—you shall hear from me by way of Uncle Moses and the letter shall be written in a different style from this   There has been three or four in here all this evening and have kept up a continual talking   There is a dancing school tonight and it seems to be all confusion. They have balls   dancing schools   and all manner of amusements but I have attended none of them

It is nothing uncommon for people to get married and then part from there husbands. There are three who board here and there husbands have left them   Tell brother if he should get tired of Sarah he must come and live here   How I should like to have James and Sarah come here and see me. They would enjoy there visit so well.

Write when you shall be here   When you write tell me what Mr Ripley said [&] everything. But I feel excedingly tired and must bid you Good Night   It was six o'clock when I began this letter and it is now after ten   Tell mother not to be concerned about me for if I am sick I shall be taken care of   When you write tell me where Edward is that I may write him   Kiss Miss Betsy for me & should like to hear her sweet voice   If any of the family should be sick or suddenly taken away you had better write to the Rev. Mr. Ripley as I might get it sooner   The mail goes out and comes in every day.   Good Night.

SOPHIA

[Addressed to]
Miss Mehitable Eastman
  Franklin   N. H.

no. 40 ～

From a letter from Charles Lane, July 30, 1843, to the *New Age* (an English periodical), here reprinted from F. B. Sanborn, *A. Bronson Alcott, His Life and Philosophy*, 2 volumes (Boston: Roberts, 1893), II, 382-383.

Mr. Alcott and I returned last evening from a short visit to Boston, to purchase a few articles; and while [383] we were there, went out one evening to Roxbury, where there are eighty or ninety persons playing away their youth and daytime in a miserable, joyous, frivolous manner. There are not above four or five who could be selected as really and truly progressing beings. Most of the adults are there to pass "a good time;" the children are taught languages, etc. The animals occupy a prominent position; there being no less than sixteen cows, besides four oxen, a herd of swine, a horse or two, etc. The milk is sold in Boston, and they buy butter, to the extent of five hundred dollars a year. We had a pleasant summer evening conversation with many of them, but it is only in a few individuals that anything deeper than ordinary is found. The Northampton community is one of industry; the one at Hopedale aims at practical theology; this of Roxbury is one of taste; yet it is the best which exists here, and perhaps we shall have to say it is the best which *can* exist. . . . I could send you a description of works and crops,—our mowing, hoeing, reaping, ploughing in tall crops of clover and grass for next year's manure, and various other operations. But if we knew how to double the crops of the earth, it is scarcely to be hoped that any good would come by revealing the mode. We will therefore say little concerning the sources of external wealth.

no. 41 ～

Entries in the *Journals* of Ralph Waldo Emerson for late August, 1843. Here reprinted from *Journals of Ralph Waldo Emerson*, edited by E. W. Emerson and W. E. Forbes (Boston: Houghton Mifflin Company, 1911), VI, 441-442, 443.

We like the strong objectiveness of Homer and of the primitive poems of each country, ballads and the Chinese and Indian sentences, but that cannot be preserved in a large and civilized population. The scholar will inevitably be detached from the mechanic, and will not dwell in the same house, nor see his handiworks so near by, and must adopt new classification and a more metaphysical vocabulary. Hawthorne boasts that he lived at Brook Farm during its heroic [442] age: then all were intimate and each knew the other's work: priest and cook conversed at night of the day's work. Now they complain that they are separated and such intimacy cannot be; there are a hundred souls.

[443] The founders of Brook Farm ought to have this praise, that they have made what all people try to make, an agreeable place to live in. All comers, and the most fastidious, find it the pleasantest of residences.

no. 42 ⌇

An entry in the *Journals* of Ralph Waldo Emerson for about September 23, 1843. Here reprinted from *Journals of Ralph Waldo Emerson*, edited by E. W. Emerson and W. E. Forbes (Boston: Houghton Mifflin Company, 1911), VI, 449.

Ellery [Channing] says that at Brook Farm they keep Curtis and Charles Newcomb and a few others as decoy-ducks.

no. 43 ⌇

From the *Phalanx or Journal of Social Science, Devoted to the Cause of Association or Social Reform*, published at New York, Volume I, Number 1 (Thursday, October 5, 1843), pp. 15-16.

THE ROXBURY COMMUNITY

This is almost exclusively an Educational establishment, relying mainly upon the income of its excellent school, which, from the peculiar nature of its organization and management is, in our opinion, the best [16] in the country, and depends but slightly upon its industrial income. It is situated about 8 miles from Boston, and possesses at present about 250 acres of fine land; the cultivation of which constitutes its only branch of industry. It is, however, wished to establish some branches of mechanics, and good mechanics who have some capital would find an advantageous location there. Letters may be addressed, *post paid*, to the Rev. GEO. RIPLEY, Roxbury, Mass.

no. 44 ❧

Letter from George Ripley to Phinehas Eastman, here reprinted
from a true copy of the holograph in the Abernethy Library of
American Literature, Middlebury College, Middlebury, Vermont.
The true copy was supplied by the courtesy of Miss Mary Noel,
Curator of the Abernethy Library.

Brook Farm, Nov 24, 1843

DEAR SIR

I was about writing you in reference to your daughter when I received your favor of the 20th inst.

We have thought for a long time that she was not adequate to the
work of the place, which for the present is quite severe, & should have
proposed her return, if we had not understood that she was making
arrangements to that effect, & were unwilling to seem to hurry her
departure. Neither is she sufficiently advanced in the common branches
of education to enable her to pursue our course to advantage, without
devoting the whole or nearly the whole of her time to her studies.

In truth, although a very deserving girl, she is not the kind of person contemplated in our plan of admitting a few pupils to defray their
expenses by their services. We are obliged to restrict this arrangement
to a very few: to those who are capable of going forward in all sorts
of labor; & who are old enough to make a good use of the portion of
the time which is left at their disposal.

When Mr Wellington requested admission for your daughter, we
had several applications on hand of the same kind; we told him what
we wanted; that the duties were very laborious, the work of the heaviest kind; & that none but a very efficient & experienced person could
answer the purpose; but from his description, we decided upon her in
preference to four others. We supposed her to be a strong, hearty
Granite-State girl, skilled in all sorts of domestic labor, & capable of
taking the lead in the most fatiguing duties. We soon found that this
was not the case; & that her labors were more burdensome to her than
advantageous to us. She has not performed any labors, however, which
are not shared by the most delicate ladies of the Association with
cheerfulness & alacrity.

We do not find any fault with your daughter when we say that she
is better adapted for some other situation than any which we can offer
at present; & when she leaves us, it will be with our cordial good wishes.

I shall be happy to do any thing in my power to aid her in procuring a situation. I know nothing of the school in Charlestown, to which you allude, & should probably have little influence in that quarter. It seems to me her wisest course would be to return to her friends at home, who could arrange a plan for her better than she can for herself; & I shall advise her to that effect.

                                        Yours, with esteem
[Addressed to]   GEO. RIPLEY
Phinehas Eastman
   Franklin

no. 45 ⮞

From Albert Brisbane, "Spread of the Doctrine of Association," *Phalanx*, Volume I, Number 3 (Tuesday, December 5, 1843), p. 34.

. . . It must be deeply gratifying to the friends of Association to see the unexampled rapidity with which our Principles are spreading throughout this vast country. Would it not seem that this very general response to, and acceptance of, *an entirely new and radically reforming doctrine* by intelligent and practical men, prove that there is something in it harmonizing perfectly with the ideas of truth, justice, economy, and order, and those higher sentiments implanted in the soul of man—which, although so smothered at present, are awakened when the correspondences in doctrine or practice are presented to them clearly and understandingly.

The name of FOURIER is now heard from the Atlantic to the Mississippi; from the remotest parts of Wisconsin and Louisiana responsive echoes reach us, heralding the spread of the great principles of Universal Association; and this important work has been accomplished in a few years, and mainly within two years, since Horace Greeley, Esq., the Editor of the Tribune, with unprecedented courage and liberality, opened the columns of his widely circulated Journal to a fair exposition of this subject. What will the next ten years bring forth?

We are well aware that the conviction of the majority is not scientific, and is not so profound as it should be, for they have not had the works and means of instruction necessary to gain it; the practical part of the system only has been taught; but now the works of the Master will be translated, and through THE PHALANX, the Organ of the Doctrine, the discoveries which they contain will be laid before the Country in all their depth and grandeur.

The conviction of the majority of adherents is mainly of the Truth of the great (Christian and Uniting) principle of Association, of that of unity of interests, of concert of action, of the noble idea of AT-TRACTIVE INDUSTRY, and the possibility of combining full and unrestricted individual liberty with associated efforts and the maintenance of all individual rights.

A strong interest is aroused in thousands of minds, which will lead them on to obtain a more complete and scientific knowledge of the System, and this knowledge will excite a correspondingly increased energy and enthusiasm on their part. The seeds are sown of a mighty harvest, such as the world has not yet looked upon.

A. B.

no. 46 ～

Charles Lane, "Brook Farm," *The Dial,* IV (January, 1844), 351-357. The text used here is that of a reprinting of *The Dial* for the Rowfant Club, Cleveland, Ohio, 1901-1902.

BROOK FARM

Wherever we recognize the principle of progress, our sympathies and affections are engaged. However small may be the innovation, however limited the effort towards the attainment of pure good, that effort is worthy of our best encouragement and succor. The Institution at Brook Farm, West Roxbury, though sufficiently extensive in respect to number of persons, perhaps is not to be considered an experiment of large intent. Its aims are moderate; too humble indeed to satisfy the extreme demands of the age; yet, for that reason probably, the effort is more valuable, as likely to exhibit a larger share of actual success.

Though familiarly designated a "Community," it is only so in the process of eating in commons; a practice at least, as antiquated, as the collegiate halls of old England, where it still continues without producing, as far as we can learn, any of the Spartan virtues. A residence at Brook Farm does not involve either a community of money, of opinions, or of sympathy. The motives which bring individuals there, may be as various as their numbers. In fact, the present residents are divisible into three distinct classes; and if the majority in numbers were considered, it is possible that a vote in favor of self-sacrifice for the common good would not be very strongly carried. The leading portion of the adult inmates, they whose presence imparts the greatest peculiarity and the fraternal tone to the household, believe that an improved state of existence would be developed in association, and are therefore anxious to promote it. Another class consists of those who join with the view of bettering their condition, by being exempted from some portion of worldly strife. The third portion, comprises those who have their own development or education, for their principal object. Practically, too, the institution manifests a threefold improvement over the world at large, corresponding to these three motives. In consequence of the first, the companionship, the personal intercourse, the social bearing are of a marked, and very superior character. [352] There may possibly, to some minds, long accustomed to other modes, appear a want of homeness, and of the private fireside; but all observers must acknowledge a brotherly and softening condition, highly conducive to the permanent, and pleasant growth of all the better human qualities. If the life is not of a deeply religious cast, it is at least not inferior to that which is exemplified elsewhere; and there is the advantage of an entire absence of assumption and pretence. The moral atmosphere so far is pure; and there is found a strong desire to walk ever on the mountain tops of life; though taste, rather than piety, is the aspect presented to the eye.

In the second class of motives, we have enumerated, there is a strong tendency to an important improvement in meeting the terrestrial necessities of humanity. The banishment of servitude, the renouncement of hireling labor, and the elevation of all unavoidable work to its true station, are problems whose solution seems to be charged upon association; for the dissociate systems have in vain sought remedies for this unfavorable portion of human condition. It is impossible to introduce into separate families even one half of the economies, which the present state of science furnishes to man. In that particular, it is probable that even the feudal system is superior to the civic: for its combinations permit many domestic arrangements of an economic character, which are impracticable in small households. In order to economize labor, and dignify the laborer, it is absolutely necessary that men should cease to work in the present isolate competitive mode, and adopt that of cooperative union or association. It is as false and as ruinous to call any man "master" in secular business, as it is in theological opinions. Those persons, therefore, who congregate for the purpose, as it is called, of bettering their outward relations, on principles so high and universal as we have endeavored to describe, are not engaged in a petty design, bounded by their own selfish or temporary improvement. Every one who is here found giving up the usual chances of individual aggrandize-

ment, may not be thus influenced; but whether it be so or not, the outward demonstration will probably be equally certain.

In education, Brook Farm appears to present greater mental freedom
than most other institutions. The tuition [353] being more heart-
rendered, is in its effects more heart-stirring. The younger pupils as well
as the more advanced students are held, mostly if not wholly, by the
power of love. In this particular, Brook farm is a much improved
model for the oft-praised schools of New England. It is time that the
imitative and book-learned systems of the latter should be superseded
or liberalized by some plan, better calculated to excite originality of
thought, and the native energies of the mind. The deeper, kindly sympathies of the heart, too, should not be forgotten; but the germination
of these must be despaired of under a rigid hireling system. Hence,
Brook farm, with its spontaneous teachers, presents the unusual and
cheering condition of a really "free school."

By watchful and diligent economy, there can be no doubt that a
community would attain greater pecuniary success, than is within the
hope of honest individuals working separately. But Brook Farm is not
a Community, and in the variety of motives with which persons associate there, a double diligence, and a watchfulness perhaps too costly,
will be needful to preserve financial prosperity. While, however, this
security is an essential element in success, riches would, on the other
hand, be as fatal as poverty, to the true progress of such an institution.
Even in the case of those foundations which have assumed a religious
character, all history proves the fatality of wealth. The just and happy
mean between riches and poverty is, indeed, more likely to be attained
when, as in this instance, all thought of acquiring great wealth in a
brief time, is necessarily abandoned, as a condition of membership. On
the other hand, the presence of many persons, who congregate merely
for the attainment of some individual end, must weigh heavily and un-
fairly upon those whose hearts are really expanded to universal results.
As a whole, even the initiative powers of Brook Farm have, as is found
almost everywhere, the design of a life much too objective, too much
derived from objects in the exterior world. The subjective life, that in
which the soul finds the living source and the true communion within
itself, is not sufficiently prevalent to impart to the establishment the
permanent and sedate character it should enjoy. Undeniably, many
devoted individuals are there; several who have as generously [354] as
wisely relinquished what are considered great social and pecuniary advantages; and by throwing their skill and energies into a course of the
most ordinary labors, at once prove their disinterestedness, and lay the
foundation of industrial nobility.

An assemblage of persons, not brought together by the principles of community, will necessarily be subject to many of the inconveniences of ordinary life, as well as to burdens peculiar to such a condition. Now Brook Farm is at present such an institution. It is not a community: it is not truly an association: it is merely an aggregation of persons, and lacks that oneness of spirit, which is probably needful to make it of deep and lasting value to mankind. It seems, even after three years' continuance, uncertain, whether it is to be resolved more into an educational, or an industrial institution, or into one combined of both. Placed so near a large city, and in a populous neighborhood, the original liability for land, &c., was so large, as still to leave a considerable burden of debt. This state of things seems fairly to entitle the establishment to re-draw from the old world in fees for education, or in the sale of produce, sufficient to pay the annual interest of such liabilities. Hence the necessity for a more intimate intercourse with the trading world, and a deeper involvement in money affairs than would have attended a more retired effort of the like kind. To enter into the corrupting modes of the world, with the view of diminishing or destroying them, is a delusive hope. It will, notwithstanding, be a labor of no little worth, to induce improvements in the two grand departments of industry and education. We say *improvement,* as distinct from *progress;* for with any association short of community, we do not see how it is possible for an institution to stand so high above the present world, as to conduct its affairs on principles entirely different from those which now influence men in general.

There are other considerations also suggested by a glance at Brook Farm, which are worthy the attention of the many minds now attracted by the deeply interesting subject of human association. We are gratified by observing several external improvements during the past year; such as a larger and a more convenient dining room, a labor-saving cooking apparatus, a purer diet, a more orderly [355] and quiet attendance at the refections, superior arrangements for industry, and generally an increased seriousness in respect to the value of the example, which those who are there assembled may constitute to their fellow beings.

Of about seventy persons now assembled there, about thirty are children sent thither for education; some adult persons also place themselves there chiefly for mental assistance; and in the society there are only four married couples. With such materials it is almost certain that the sensitive and vital points of communication cannot well be tested. A joint-stock company, working with some of its own members and with others as agents, cannot bring to issue the great question, whether

the existence of the marital family is compatible with that of the universal family, which the term "Community" signifies. This is now the
grand problem. By mothers it has ever been felt to be so. The maternal
instinct, as hitherto educated, has declared itself so strongly in favor of
the separate fire-side, that association, which appears so beautiful to the
young and unattached soul, has yet accomplished little progress in the
affections of that important section of the human race—the mothers.
With fathers, the feeling in favor of the separate family is certainly
less strong; but there is an undefinable tie, a sort of magnetic *rapport*,
an invisible, inseverable, umbilical chord [*sic*] between the mother and
child, which in most cases circumscribes her desires and ambition to her
own immediate family. All the accepted adages and wise saws of society,
all the precepts of morality, all the sanctions of theology, have for ages
been employed to confirm this feeling. This is the chief corner stone
of present society; and to this maternal instinct have, till very lately,
our most heartfelt appeals been made for the progress of the human
race, by means of a deeper and more vital education. Pestalozzi and
his most enlightened disciples are distinguished by this sentiment. And
are we all at once to abandon, to deny, to destroy this supposed strong-
hold of virtue? Is it questioned whether the family arrangement of mankind is to be preserved? Is it discovered that the sanctuary, till now
deemed the holiest on earth, is to be invaded by intermeddling skepticism, and its altars sacrilegiously destroyed by the rude hands of in-
novating progress? Here "social science" must be brought to issue.
[356] The question of association and of marriage are one. If, as we
have been popularly led to believe, the individual or separate family is
in the true order of Providence, then the associative life is a false effort.
If the associative life is true, then is the separate family a false arrangement. By the maternal feeling, it appears to be decided that the co-
existence of both is incompatible, is impossible. So also say some religious sects. Social science ventures to assert their harmony. This is
the grand problem now remaining to be solved, for at least, the en-
lightening, if not for the vital elevation of humanity. That the affections can be divided or bent with equal ardor on two objects, so opposed as universal and individual love, may at least be rationally
doubted. History has not yet exhibited such phenomena in an associate body, and scarcely perhaps in any individual. The monasteries and
convents, which have existed in all ages, have been maintained solely by
the annihilation of that peculiar affection on which the separate family
is based. The Shaker families, in which the two sexes are not entirely
dissociated, can yet only maintain their union by forbidding and pre-

venting the growth of personal affection other than that of a spiritual character. And this in fact is not personal in the sense of individual, but ever a manifestation of universal affection. Spite of the speculations of hopeful bachelors and aesthetic spinsters, there is somewhat in the marriage bond which is found to counteract the universal nature of the affections, to a degree tending at least to make the considerate pause, before they assert that, by any social arrangements whatever, the two can be blended into one harmony. The general condition of married persons at this time is some evidence of the existence of such a doubt in their minds. Were they as convinced as the unmarried of the beauty and truth of associate life, the demonstration would be now presented. But might it not be enforced that the two family ideas really neutralize each other? Is it not quite certain that the human heart cannot be set in two places; that man cannot worship at two altars? It is only the determination to do what parents consider the best for themselves and their families, which renders the o'er populous world such a wilderness of selfhood as it is. Destroy this feeling, they say, and you prohibit every motive to exertion. Much [357] truth is there in this affirmation. For to them, no other motive remains, nor indeed to any one else, save that of the universal good, which does not permit the building up of supposed self-good, and therefore, forecloses all possibility of an individual family.

These observations, of course, equally apply to all the associative attempts, now attracting so much public attention; and perhaps most especially to such as have more of Fourier's designs than are observable at Brook Farm. The slight allusion in all the writers of the "Phalansterian" class, to the subject of marriage, is rather remarkable. They are acute and eloquent in deploring Woman's oppressed and degraded position in past and present times, but are almost silent as to the future. In the meanwhile, it is gratifying to observe the successes which in some departments attend every effort, and that Brook Farm is likely to become comparatively eminent in the highly important and praiseworthy attempts, to render labor of the hands more dignified and noble, and mental education more free and loveful.

C. L.

no. 47 ～

From Albert Brisbane and Osborne Macdaniel, "What Is Association?" *Phalanx*, Volume I, Number 4 (Friday, January 5, 1844), pp. 56-57.

WHAT IS ASSOCIATION?

. . . An Association is a body of persons (1800 individuals, men, women and children, or about 300 families, are the proper number for a complete Association) united voluntarily for the purpose of prosecuting with method and order, Industry, Education, Commerce, and the Arts and Sciences—of establishing concert of action and unity of interests (not community of property)—of applying their efforts in the best and most judicious manner—of dignifying Labor and rendering it honorable and ATTRACTIVE—of dividing equitably the product of their labor, every individual receiving a share according to the part taken in producing it, and giving to Labor, Skill and Capital, each, a just proportion or dividend—of realizing great collective economies—of introducing every facility [57] and the most efficient means of education, moral, mental and physical, which will be extended to all children without exception—of living together in friendly union and concord, and enjoying the varied pleasures of extended and congenial social relations, and the pursuits of useful industry and exalting art and science, and of directing their energies and talents so as to conduce to the greatest happiness of the Whole.

no. 48 ∾

Constitution of the Brook Farm Association, for Industry and Education, West Roxbury, Mass. With An Introductory Statement (Boston: I. R. Butts, Printer, No. 2 School Street, 1844), pp. 3-12.

BROOK FARM ASSOCIATION.

The Association at Brook Farm, has now been in existence upwards of two years. Originating in the thought and experience of a few individuals, it has hitherto worn, for the most part, the character of a private experiment, and has avoided rather than sought, the notice of the public. It has, until the present time, seemed fittest to those engaged in this enterprise to publish no statements of their purposes or methods, to make no promises or declarations, but quietly and sincerely to realise, as far as might be possible, the great ideas which gave the central impulse to their movement. It has been thought that a steady endeavor to embody these ideas more and more perfectly in life, would give the best answer, both to the hopes of the friendly and the cavils of the sceptical, and furnish in its results the surest grounds for any larger efforts.

Meanwhile every step has strengthened the faith with which we set out; our belief in a divine order of human society, has in our own minds become an absolute certainty; and considering the present state of humanity and of social science, we do not hesitate to affirm, that the world is much nearer the attainment of such a condition than is generally supposed.

The deep interest in the doctrine of Association, which [4] now fills the minds of intelligent persons every where, indicates plainly that the time has passed when even initiative movements ought to be prosecuted in silence, and makes it imperative on all who have either a theoretical or practical knowledge of the subject to give their share to the stock of public information.

Accordingly, we have taken occasion at several public meetings recently held in Boston, to state some of the results of our studies and experience, and we desire here to say emphatically, that while on the one hand we yield an unqualified assent to that doctrine of universal unity which Fourier teaches, so on the other, our whole observation has shown us the truth of the practical arrangements which he deduces therefrom. The law of groups and series is, as we are convinced, the law of human nature, and when men are in true social relations their industrial organization will necessarily assume those forms.

But beside the demand for information respecting the principles of association, there is a deeper call for action in the matter. We wish, therefore, to bring Brook Farm before the public, as a location offering at least as great advantages for a thorough experiment as can be found in the vicinity of Boston. It is situated in West Roxbury, three miles from the depot of the Dedham Branch Rail Road, and about eight miles from Boston, and combines a convenient nearness to the city with a degree of retirement and freedom from unfavorable influences, unusual even in the country. The place is one of great natural beauty, and indeed the whole landscape is so rich and various as to attract the notice even of casual visitors. The farm now owned by the Association contains two hundred and eight acres, of as good quality as any land in the neighborhood of Boston, and can be enlarged by the purchase of land adjoining to any necessary extent. The property now in the hands of the Association is worth nearly or quite thirty thousand dollars, of which about twenty-two thousand dollars is invested either in the stock of the company, or in permanent loans at six per cent, which can remain as long as the Association may wish.

The fact that so large an amount of capital is already invested and at our service as the basis of more extensive operations, furnishes a reason why Brook Farm should be chosen as the scene of that practical trial of association which the public feeling calls for in this immediate vicinity, instead of forming an entirely new organization for that purpose. [5] The completeness of our educational department is also not to be overlooked. This has hitherto received our greatest care, and in forming it we have been particularly successful. In any new Association it must be many years before so many accomplished and skillful teachers in the various branches of intellectual culture could be enlisted. Another strong reason is to be found in the degree of order our organization has already attained, by the help of which a large Association might be formed without the losses and inconveniences which would otherwise necessarily occur. The experience of nearly three years in all the misfortunes and mistakes incident to an undertaking so new and so little understood, carried on throughout by persons not entirely fitted for the duties they have been compelled to perform, has, as we think, prepared us to assist in the safe conduct of an extensive and complete Association.

Such an institution, as will be plain to all, cannot by any sure means, be brought at once and full grown into existence. It must at least in the present state of society, begin with a comparatively small number of select and devoted persons, and increase by natural and gradual aggregations. With a view to an ultimate expansion into a perfect Phalanx, we desire without any delay to organize the three primary departments of labor, namely, Agriculture, Domestic Industry, and the Mechanic Arts.

For this purpose additional capital will be needed, which it is most desirable should be invested by those who propose to connect themselves personally with the institution. These should be men and women accustomed to labor, skilful, careful, in good health, and more than all imbued with the idea of Association, and ready to consecrate themselves without reserve to its realization. For it ought to be known that the work we propose is a difficult one, and except to the most entire faith and resolution will offer insurmountable obstacles and discouragements. Neither will it be possible to find in Association at the outset the great outward advantages it ultimately promises. The first few years must be passed in constant and unwearied labor, heightened chiefly by the consciousness of high aims and the inward content that devotion to a universal object cannot fail to bring. Still there are certain tangible compensations which Association guaranties immediately.

These are freedom from pecuniary anxiety, and the evils of competitive industry, free and friendly society, and the education of children. How great these are, those [6] who have felt the terrible burdens which the present civilized society imposes in these respects will not need to be informed.

Those who may wish to further this course by investments of money only will readily perceive that their end is not likely to be lost in an Association whose means are devoted mainly to productive industry, and where nothing will ever be risked in uncertain speculations.

The following Constitution is the same as that under which we have hitherto acted, with such alterations as on a careful revision seemed needful. All persons who are not familiar with the purposes of Association, will understand from this document that we propose a radical and universal reform, rather than to redress any particular wrong or to remove the sufferings of any single class of human beings. We do this in the light of universal principles, in which all differences, whether of religion, or politics, or philosophy, are reconciled, and the dearest and most private hope of every man has the promise of fulfilment. Herein, let it be understood, we would remove nothing that is truly beautiful or venerable; we reverence the religious sentiment in all its forms, the family, and whatever else has its foundation either in human nature or the Divine Providence. The work we are engaged in is not destruction, but true conservation: it is not a mere revolution, but, as we are assured, a necessary step in the course of social progress which no one can be blind enough to think has yet reached its limit. We believe that humanity, trained by these long centuries of suffering and struggle, led onward by so many saints and heroes and sages, is at length prepared to enter into that universal order, toward which it has perpetually moved. Thus we recognize the worth of the whole Past and of every doctrine and institution it has bequeathed us; thus also we perceive that the Present has its own high mission, and we shall only say what is beginning to be seen by all sincere thinkers, when we declare that the imperative duty of this time and this country, nay more, that its only salvation, and the salvation of all civilized countries, lies in the Reorganization of Society, according to the unchanging laws of human nature and of universal harmony.

We look, then, to the generous and hopeful of all classes for sympathy, for encouragement and for actual aid, not to ourselves only, but to all those who are engaged in this great work. And whatever may be the result of any special efforts, we can never doubt that the object we have in view [7] will finally be attained; that human life shall yet be developed, not in discord and misery, but in harmony and joy, and that the perfected earth shall at last bear on her bosom a race of men worthy of the name.

GEORGE RIPLEY,
MINOT PRATT,   } Directors.
CHARLES A. DANA,

Brook Farm, West Roxbury, Mass., }
     January 18, 1844

[8]   CONSTITUTION

In order more effectually to promote the great purposes of human culture; to establish the external relations of life on a basis of wisdom and purity; to apply the principles of justice and love to our social organization in accordance with the laws of Divine Providence; to substitute a system of brotherly cooperation for one of selfish competition; to secure to our children and those who may be entrusted to our care the benefits of the highest physical, intellectual and moral education, which in the progress of knowledge the resources at our command will permit; to institute an attractive, efficient, and productive system of industry; to prevent the exercise of worldly anxiety, by the competent supply of our necessary wants; to diminish the desire of excessive accumulation, by making the acquisition of individual property subservient to upright and disinterested uses; to guarantee to each other forever the means of physical support, and of spiritual progress; and thus to impart a greater freedom, simplicity, truthfulness, refinement, and moral dignity, to our mode of life;—we the undersigned do unite in a voluntary Association, and adopt and ordain the following articles of agreement, to wit:

[9]   ARTICLE I.

NAME AND MEMBERSHIP

Sec. 1. The name of this Association shall be "THE BROOK-FARM ASSOCIATION FOR INDUSTRY AND EDUCATION." All persons who shall hold one or more shares in its stock, or whose labor and skill shall be considered an equivalent for capital, may be admitted by the vote of two-thirds of the Association, as members thereof.

Sec. 2. No member of the Association shall ever be subjected to any religious test; nor shall any authority be assumed over individual freedom of opinion by the Association, nor by one member over another; nor shall any one be held accountable to the Association, except for such overt acts, or omissions of duty, as violate the principles of justice, purity, and love, on which it is founded; and in such cases the relation of any member may be suspended or discontinued, at the pleasure of the Association.

ARTICLE II.

Capital Stock.

Sec. 1. The members of this Association shall own and manage such real and personal estate in joint stock proprietorship, divided into shares of one hundred dollars each, as may from time to time be agreed on.

Sec. 2. No share-holder shall be liable to any assessment whatever on the shares held by him; nor shall he be held responsible individually in his private property on account of the Association; nor shall the Trustees or any officer or agent of the Association have any authority to do any thing which shall impose personal responsibility on any share-holder, by making any contracts or incurring any debts for which the share-holders shall be individually or personally responsible.

Sec. 3. The Association guaranties to each share-holder the interest of five per cent. annually on the amount of stock held by him in the Association, and this interest may be paid [10] in certificates of stock and credited on the books of the Association; provided that each share-holder may draw on the funds of the Association for the amount of interest due at the third annual settlement from the time of investment.

Sec. 4. The share-holders on their part for themselves, their heirs and assigns, do renounce all claim on any profits accruing to the Association for the use of their capital invested in the stock of the Association, except five per cent. interest on the amount of stock held by them, payable in the manner described in the preceding section.

ARTICLE III.

Guaranties.

Sec. 1. The Association shall provide such employment for all its members as shall be adapted to their capacities, habits, and tastes; and each member shall select and perform such operations of labor, whether corporal or mental, as shall be deemed best suited to his own endowments and the benefit of the Association.

Sec. 2. The Association guaranties to all its members, their children and family dependents, house-rent, fuel, food, and clothing, and the other necessaries of life, without charge, not exceeding a certain fixed amount to be decided annually by the Association; no charge shall ever be made for support during inability to labor from sickness or old age, or for medical or nursing attendance, except in case of share-holders, who shall be charged therefor, and also for the food and clothing of children, to an amount not exceeding the interest due to them on settlement; but no charge shall be made to any member for education or the use of the library and public rooms.

Sec. 3. Members may withdraw from labor, under the direction of the Association, and in that case, they shall not be entitled to the benefit of the above guaranties.

Sec. 4. Children over ten years of age shall be provided with employment in suitable branches of industry; they shall [11] be credited for such portions of each annual dividend, as shall be decided by the Association, and on the completion of their education in the Association at the age of twenty, shall be entitled to a certificate of stock to the amount of credits in their favor, and may be admitted as members of the Association.

ARTICLE IV

DISTRIBUTION OF PROFITS.

Sec. 1. The nett [*sic*] profits of the Association, after the payment of all expenses, shall be divided into a number of shares corresponding to the number of day's labor; and every member shall be entitled to one share for every day's labor performed by him.

Sec. 2. A full settlement shall be made with every member once a year, and certificates of stock given for all balances due; but in case of need to be decided by himself, every member may be permitted to draw on the funds in the Treasury to an amount not exceeding the credits in his favor for labor performed.

ARTICLE V.

GOVERNMENT.

Sec. 1. The government of the Association shall be vested in a board of Directors, divided into four departments, as follows: 1st, General Direction; 2d, Direction of Education; 3d, Direction of Industry; 4th, Direction of Finance; consisting of three persons each, provided that the same person may be elected member of each Direction.

Sec. 2. The General Direction and Direction of Education shall be chosen annually, by the vote of a majority of the members of the Association. The Direction of Finance shall be chosen annually, by the vote of a majority of the share-holders and members of the Association.

The Direction of Industry shall consist of the chiefs of the three primary series. [12]

Sec. 3. The chairman of the General Direction shall be the President of the Association, and together with the Direction of Finance, shall constitute a board of Trustees, by whom the property of the Association shall be held and managed.

Sec. 4. The General Direction shall oversee and manage the affairs of the Association, so that every department shall be carried on in an orderly and efficient manner.

Sec. 5. The departments of Education and Finance shall be under the control each of its own Direction, which shall select, and in concurrence with the General Direction, shall appoint such teachers, officers, and agents, as shall be necessary to the complete and systematic organization of the department. No Directors or other officers shall be deemed to possess any rank superior to the other members of the Association, nor shall they receive any extra remuneration for their official services.

Sec. 6. The department of Industry shall be arranged in groups and series, as far as practicable, and shall consist of three primary series; to wit, Agricultural, Mechanical, and Domestic Industry. The chief of each series shall be elected every two months by the members thereof, subject to the approval of the General Direction. The chief of each group shall be chosen weekly by its members.

ARTICLE VI.

Miscellaneous.

Sec. 1. The Association may from time to time adopt such bye-laws, not inconsistent with the spirit and purpose of these articles, as shall be found expedient or necessary.

Sec. 2. In order to secure to the Association the benefits of the highest discoveries in social science, and to preserve its fidelity to the principles of progress and reform, on which it is founded, any amendment may be proposed to this Constitution at a meeting called for the purpose; and if approved by two-thirds of the members at a subsequent meeting, at least one month after the date of the first, shall be adopted.

PART THREE ~~~

From Phalanx

to the Fire

~~~ *1844–1846*

Editor's Preface

"The *correspondence* of that place would be a historiette of the Spirit of this Age," wrote Emerson in his *Journal*. And it is interesting to reflect on what manner of Age this correspondence records.

Of all the letters written at Brook Farm, Marianne Dwight's are the best preserved and most easily accessible. She poured out letters by the score to Anna Parsons, her friend, and to her brother Frank, who was employed in an architect's office in Boston. If a good letter writer is one whose letters convey precisely the moods, impressions, and involvements of their author, then Marianne was a very fine letter writer indeed. She and Hawthorne are the two Farmers of whose characters we have most detailed knowledge. It is worth while to contrast their personalities and their attitudes toward life at the Farm.

But if Marianne records her own character, she tells us of the Farm as well. She was an observer of persons. She wrote about the people, about what they said and did. When a question arises concerning the precise day on which an individual arrived, departed, lectured, or lost his temper, the answer is more likely to occur in her letters than in any other place. Even a casual, discursive reading of them makes Brook Farm firm and lively in the imagination.

Furthermore, it is Marianne who tells us most of what we know about the "industry" to which, with education, Brook Farm was nominally devoted. Her lamp shades were "industrial" products. From her we learn what the word "industrial" meant at Brook Farm in 1844.

Another correspondent of especial interest is George William Curtis. The letters of his which are accessible to us are addressed to John Sullivan Dwight, who remained at Brook Farm, and therefore they were written when Curtis was away. He does not report the details of life at the Farm, but his letters develop the topics which he knew to be of interest there. Both Curtis and Dwight were artists of a sort. Curtis later won considerable reputation as a man of letters. John S. Dwight, one of the most unselfish and appealing of all Brook Farmers, was a musician who worked quietly throughout his life to teach America the true value of the great composers, especially the "strange" and "modern" Beethoven.

Curtis lived at Brook Farm only briefly. Dwight remained to the end. In Curtis' letters and in Dwight's lectures and articles the reasons why they parted are clearly argued out.

Another vein of ideas recurring in many of the letters is that of religion. To Elizabeth Peabody, Ripley's original plan had appeared essentially religious in effect. Charles Dana lectured on the subject, and it seems strange that he should have been the one assigned this particular topic. William H. Channing was a central figure in the religious activities of the Farm itself. But most important in subsequent years was Isaac Hecker, a quiet young baker from New York, who left the Farm to begin a long period of training in Europe, and who returned at last to found the order of the Paulist Fathers. While he was at the Farm he met and was strongly drawn to a neighbor and occasional visitor, Henry David Thoreau. The attraction was in one sense an attraction of opposites, for Thoreau, no associationist, was planning a different way. He made his own one-man community at Walden Pond, and set up housekeeping there on July 4, 1845. In another sense they were kindred spirits, for in both of them quiet and intense vocations glowed.

Finally, there was *The Harbinger*. The selections drawn from it are representative, but only a vague sense of general tone and policy may be imagined on this slight evidence. There is too little room in this volume for the translations of George Sand and Fourier that filled many of its clearly printed pages. If on the basis of this sparse selection readers decide that *The Harbinger* was a journal composed chiefly of editorials, it will be a pity, but it will be not altogether untrue.

The Phalanstery and its spectacular end provide a theme and a crisis of the Brook Farm story. Critics differ on the question of whether it determined the fate of Ripley's plan. What if the Phalanstery had never been begun? What if it had been finished and put into use?—Take either side.

Additional Books

John Sullivan Dwight and Charles A. Dana. *Association in its Connection with Education and Religion*. Boston: Benjamin H. Greene, 1844.

The Journals of Bronson Alcott. Edited by Odell Shepard. Boston: Little, Brown & Company, 1938.

Early Letters of George William Curtis to John S. Dwight. Edited by G. W. Cooke. New York: Harper & Brothers, 1898.

Marianne Dwight. *Letters from Brook Farm 1844-1847*. Edited by Amy L. Reed. Poughkeepsie, N. Y.: Vassar College, 1928.

E. H. Russell. "A Bit of Unpublished Correspondence between Henry Thoreau and Isaac Hecker," *Atlantic Monthly*, XC (July-December 1902), 370-376.

The Elijah P. Grant Papers, holograph, Manuscript Room, University of Chicago Libraries.

John Thomas Codman. *Brook Farm, Historic and Personal Memoirs*. Boston: Arena, 1894.

G. W. Cooke. *John Sullivan Dwight . . . A Biography*. Boston: Small, Maynard and Company, 1898.

The Harbinger, 4 volumes, 26 numbers in each volume, published weekly by the Brook Farm Phalanx, Number 1 of Volume I on Saturday, June 14, 1845, and the final number (Volume IV, No. 26) on Saturday, June 5, 1847.

no. 49 ✺

An entry in the *Journal* of Ralph Waldo Emerson, probably for January 30, 1844. Here reprinted from *Journals of Ralph Waldo Emerson*, edited by E. W. Emerson and W. E. Forbes (Boston: Houghton Mifflin Company, 1911), VI, 491-492.

"And fools rush in where angels fear to tread." So say I of Brook Farm. Let it live. Its merit is that it is a new life. Why should we have only two or three ways of life, and not thousands and millions? This a new one so fresh and expensive [*sic*] that they are all homesick when they go away. The shy sentiments are there expressed. The *correspondence* of that place would be a historiette of the Spirit of this Age. They [492] might see that in the arrangements of Brook Farm, as out of them, it is the person, not the communist, that avails.

no. 50 ⌒

Entry in the journal of Abigail May (Mrs. Bronson) Alcott, February 3, 1844, here reprinted from *The Journals of Bronson Alcott*, selected and edited by Odell Shepard (Boston: Little, Brown & Company, 1938), p. 157.

February 3

Returned from visiting Communities, quite convinced that there is nothing there for us, no sphere in which we could act without an unwarrantable alienation from our children. At Northampton the life is quite elementary and aimless, except to pay off the debt. At Hopedale I could find nothing higher than living quite inoffensive lives and aiding in all the moral reforms by going into the world and lecturing. —There was some "sackcloth and ashes" there. Brook Farm—there was more neatness, order, beauty, and life than in either of the other places. Still I could find no advance on the old world. Education at Brook Farm is of a higher and more elaborate kind, but no better than our schools afford, and I see but little gained in the assocation in labour.

no. 51 ⌒

Opening paragraph of a lecture on "Association in its Connection with Education," by John Sullivan Dwight, delivered before the New England Fourier Society, in Boston, February 29, 1844. Here reprinted from *Association in its Connection with Education and Religion* (Boston: Benjamin H. Greene, 1844), pp. 3-4.

The system of FOURIER, though it proposes no less than a complete reorganization of society, rightly calls itself the system of '*Attractive Industry*.' Its claims to the rank of a social *science* rest upon the success of its attempt to reconcile the productive industry of man with man's natural tendencies, or 'passional attractions.' Could this be done, the word 'necessity' would acquire an altogether new and pleasanter meaning; the outward necessity and the inward prompting for every human being would be one and identical, and his life a living harmony. The tendency of our whole nature is to Unity. Every man is a lover of harmony; the very discord of his life is a crying out for harmony. The mind tends to Truth, Science; which is the perception of Unity.

The heart tends to Love; which is the enjoyment of Unity. Ignorance is only another name for the mental confusion of losing one's place in the Universal Order. Selfishness and Sin, in the same manner, are only involuntary discord, unwelcome isolation; every one tries to love, tries to work his way somehow, even by his selfishness, to the central heart of things, that he may feel and return its warmth. Yet the blind earnestness of this very effort brings him into conflict with his neighbor. Striving to love him and draw near to him, he finds himself in competition with him; one succeeds by the other's failing. All these individual wills, or natures, born for harmony, and seeking it, but seeking it by private paths that lead to private ends, have only multiplied strife by all their earnestness, and failing of the Combined Order, failing of anything which can be called Society, have thus far only realized certain successive stages of a chaotic striving after society, which we call Savageism, Patriarchalism, Barbarism, Feudalism, and, finally, Civilization, with its admirable outward order cemented by individual selfishness and held together by most curious checks and balances, curious as are all its 'improvements' for the multiplication of [4] wealth and misery at once, its machinery for producing more, that more may starve. The history of all these periods is but the record of strife. And still it goes on whirling and widening, none the less under the decent, peaceful smile of what we call our Civilization. Whence came the strife? Not from man's natural passions: have we not said that their final cause is harmony, and that no heart loves discord, no mind thinks in order to get lost? Not from any mal-adaptation between our nature and our sphere:—was not the law of my individual being appointed with perfect knowledge of all the laws of the whole universe of things, and with full regard to the laws of all other individual natures like myself, so that I in my true self-development must harmonize with others, and not clash? Whence *did* it come? We are harmonies, born each into our preëstablished place in an infinite system of harmonies; every man is a microcosm, or world in miniature, reflecting all the laws of all things; and each mortal child is as indispensable to the balance and completeness of the world into which he comes so small an atom, as is each planet in the system of our sun, or each sun in the celestial sphere, or each note in the great music of God. How comes it, then, that we clash? that our noblest aspirations prove our keenest misery? that we cannot put forth our hands to accept the promises of life without stealing food and joy from our neighbor? that we cannot seek our neighbor's good without being trampled under foot ourselves?

no. 52 ✍

A letter from George William Curtis to John S. Dwight. Here re-
printed (in part) from *Early Letters of George William Curtis to
John S. Dwight*, edited by G. W. Cooke (New York: Harper &
Brothers, 1898), pp. 152-160.

New York, March 3, 1844

Your letter was very grateful to me. I had supposed the silence would
be broken by some music burst of devotion, and that all friends would
be dearer to you the more imperative [153] the call upon your
strength to battle for the Ideal. It half reproved me for the meagre
sheet the same day brought to your hand. And yet could we see how
all the forces of heaven and earth unite to shape the particle that floats
idly by us, we should never see meagreness more.

    I do not think (and what a heresy!) that your life has found more
than an object, not yet a centre.[1] The new order will systematize your
course; but I do not see that it aids your journey. Is it not the deeper
insight you constantly gain into music which explains the social economy you adopt, and not the economy the music? One fine symphony
or song leads all reforms captive, as the grand old paintings in St. Peter's
completely ignore all sects. Association will only interpret music so
far as it is a pure art, as poetry and sculpture and painting explain
each other. But necessarily Brook Farm, association and all, do not
regard it artistically, but charitably. It regenerates the world with them
because it does tangible good, not because it refines. We must view
all pursuits as arts before we can accomplish.

    With respect to association as a means of reform, I have seen no
reason to change my view. Though, like the monastic, a life of devotion, to severe criticism it offers a selfish and an unheroic aspect. When
your letter first spoke [154] of your personal interest in the movement, I had written you a long statement of my thought, which I did
not send, and then partly spun into an article for *The Present*, which
I did not entirely finish. It was only a strong statement of Individualism, which would not be new to you, perhaps, and the essential reason
of which could not be readily treated. What we call union seems to
me only a name for a phase of individual action. I live only for myself;
and in proportion to my own growth, so I benefit others. As Fourier
seems to me to have postponed his life, in finding out how to live, so
I often felt it was with Mr. Ripley. Besides, I feel that our evils are

---

[1] Dwight had recently become a full member of the Brook Farm Association.

entirely individual, not social. What is society but the shadow of the single men behind it. That there is a slave on my plantation or a servant in my kitchen is no evil; but that the slave and servant should be unwilling to be so, that is the difficulty. The weary and the worn do not ask of me an asylum, but aid. The need of the most oppressed man is strength to endure, not means of escape. The slave toiling in the Southern heats is a nobler aspect of thought than the freed black upon the shore of England. That is just now the point which pains me in association, its lack of heroism. Reform is purification, forming anew, not forming again. Love, like genius, uses the means that are, and the opportunities of today. If paints are want-[155]ing, it draws charcoal heads with Michael Angelo. These crooked features of society we cannot rend and twist into a Roman outline and grace; but they may be animated with a soul that will utterly shame our carved and painted faces. A noble man purges these present relations, and does not ask beautiful houses and landscapes and appliances to make life beautiful. In Wall Street he gives another significance to trade; in the City Hall he justifies its erection; in the churches he interprets to themselves the weekly assembly of citizens. He uses the pen with which, just now, the coal-man scrawled his bill, and turns off an epic with the fife that in the band so sadly pierced our ears. He moves our trudging lives to the beauties of golden measures. He laughs heartily at our absorbing charities and meetings, upon which we waste our health and grow thin. He answers our distressing plea for the rights of the oppressed, and the "all-men-born-to-be-free-and-equal" with a smiling strength, which assures us therein lies the wealth and the equality which we are trying to manufacture out of such materials as association, organization of society, copartnership, no wages, and the like. While this may be done, why should we retire from the field behind the walls which you offer? Let us die battling or victorious. And this, true for me and you, is true to the uttermost. The love which alone can make [156] your Phalanx beautiful, also renders it unnecessary. You may insure food and lodgings to the starving beggar, I do not see that strength is afforded to the man. Moreover, a stern divine justice ordains that each man stand where he stands, and do his utmost. Retreat, if you will, behind this prospect of comfortable living, but you do so at a sacrifice of strength. Your food must be eternal, for your life is so. I do not feel that the weary man outworn by toil needs a fine house and books and culture and free air; he needs to feel that his position, also, is as good as these. When he has, by a full recognition of that, earned the right to come to you, then his faith is deeper than the walls of association, and the desolate cellar is a cheerful room for his shining lore. Men do not want opportunities, they do not want to start fair, they do not want to reach the same goal; they want only perfect submission. The gospel now to be preached is not, "Away with me to the land where the fields are fair and the waters flow," but, "Here in your penury, while the rich go idly by and scoff, and the chariot wheels choke you with dust, make here your golden age."

> "Who cannot on his own bed sweetly sleep,
>   Can on another's hardly rest."

So sings the saintly George Herbert, no new thought in these days of ours. [157]

The effect of a residence at the Farm, I imagine, was not greater willingess to serve in the kitchen, and so particularly assert that labor was divine; but discontent that there was such a place as a kitchen. And, however aimless life there seemed to be, it was an aimlessness of the general, not of the individual life. Its beauty faded suddenly if I remembered that it was a society for special ends, though those ends were very noble. In the midst of busy trades and bustling commerce, it was a congregation of calm scholars and poets, cherishing the ideal and the true in each other's hearts, dedicate to a healthy and vigorous life. As an association it needed a stricter system to insure success; and since it had not the means to justify its mild life, it necessarily grew to this. As reformers, you are now certainly more active, and may promise yourselves heaven's reward for that. That impossibility of severance from the world, of which you speak, I liked, though I did not like that there should be such a protest against the world by those who were somewhat subject to it. This was not my first feeling. When I went, it seemed as if all hope had died from the race, as if the return to simplicity and beauty lay through the woods and fields, and was to be a march of men whose very habits and personal appearance should wear a sign of the coming grace. The longer I stayed, the more surely that thought [158] vanished. I had unconsciously been devoted to the circumstance, while I had earnestly denied its value. Gradually I perceived that only as a man grew deeper and broader could he wear the coat and submit to the etiquette and obey the laws which society demands. Now I feel that no new order is demanded, but that the universe is plastic to the pious hand. . . . [160]

I wish this was me instead of my letter, for a warm grasp of the hand might say more than all these words.

Yr friend,
G. W. C.

no. 53 ⤨

Opening paragraphs of a lecture on "Association, in its Connection with Religion," by Charles A. Dana, delivered before the New England Fourier Society in Boston, March 7, 1844. Here reprinted from *Association in its Connection with Education and Religion* (Boston: Benjamin H. Greene, 1844), pp. 25-27.

Association, in its simplest aspect, belongs to the natural or outward world. It asserts the immense advantages of union in material interests, and demonstrates the entire practicability of such a union. To this end it proves, beyond the possibility of doubt, that combination in industry and in domestic economy, will, without any diminution of individual freedom or happiness, bring about a large increase in the means of worldly comfort and independence. And here, as advocates of Association, we might rest our cause, with the best assurance that we had pointed out a sure road to the most desirable results, even if no universal end lay beyond.

For no one could consider *that* a discovery of trifling importance, which gave a hope of ending the material poverty by which so many millions of human beings are afflicted. No one who has had any experience in our cities, where, within the sound of music and gay company, with half frantic eyes lighted only by gleams from luxurious halls, hunger and pain lie gasping; no one, we might suppose, who has seen any of the thousand sadder spectacles that on all sides meet the most superficial observation, could fail of regarding with peculiar gratitude a method of escape from such fearful evils, which, in offering abundance to all, invades the established rights of none, and in conducting us to general prosperity, lays violent hands on nothing that is justly dear to any one of us. It is an essential characteristic of the new Social Science, that it is pacific and not destructive. It does not so much seek to overturn the old order of things, as to supplant it; it does not tear down our rotten and creaking shelter, until its own beautiful mansion invites us to a more secure abode. It aims first of all at a reconciliation of interests: it appears in the world with only words of peace in its mouth, and only implements of peace in its hands. It calls on individuals, on parties, and on nations, to lay aside their [26] differences, and to find, in a just union of material forces, the only sure means of private success, and of public well-being.

The immediate object, then, of all our labors, is the establishment of Industrial Association, which is possible under any form of civilized government, and without any uncommon developments of intellect or character. Without seeking any Utopia, without traveling to any unknown region of peace or freedom, we take our stand wherever we are, whether here in Boston, or in Vienna, or London, or St. Petersburg, and today, from the existing condition of men and things, we announce the realization of the visions and promises of the past, and of the hopes of the present.

Our ulterior aim is nothing less than Heaven on Earth,—the conversion of this globe, now exhaling pestilential vapors and possessed by unnatural climates, into the abode of beauty and health, and the restitution to Humanity of the Divine Image, now so long lost and forgotten. As the first step to this end, we advocate Industrial Association, which, considered alone, without any reference to its consequences and final purposes, is fortified by the most conclusive arguments, and commends itself to the common sense of every unprejudiced man. And, indeed, one great evidence that the general system is true, that is, founded in the nature of things, and not in human wisdom or imagination, is the fact that separate parts of it can be proven by reasonings drawn from the peculiar sphere of each, without regard to the fundamental principles of the whole.

Here let me say distinctly, that the practical result we first aim at is Wealth. We declare, without hesitation, that universal wealth is a necessary condition of the universal development of Humanity; without the one the other is impossible.

We do not make war upon any part of human nature, but only upon its false circumstances and subversive conditions. God has formed no creature with innate desires and necessities, for which there is no means of supply. Nor is man an exception to this universal law, and only in false and unnatural circumstances and relations, can he fail to be a partaker of the universal satisfactions. The first result, then, of a true order of society, will be the means of complete and just satisfaction for the fundamental or sensuous wants of man; and as this is attained, we shall see a development of his social and spiritual nature which we do not now imagine.

And not only does the new philosophy announce itself as a peacemaker in the world of material discord, but, in the fiercer strife of opinions and prejudices, in the chaos of skepticism and intellectual despair, [27] she appears with the same beneficent promise. Thus only, can she vindicate her claim to the title of a universal philosophy. For it is plainly the office of such a philosophy, in perceiving the worth of each phenomenon, to show the essential oneness of all, and in bringing down to us the pure light of truth, to do justice to the glimpses of the

same which have been had in all ages and among all men. And if the
disciples of what ought to be delivered only with the calmness of entire faith, appear upon the field rather as armed combatants than as
peaceful heralds; if, instead of positive teaching and affirmation, they
are led into criticism and controversy, let the fault rest with those who
make such a procedure necessary.

no. 54 ~

Letter from Marianne Dwight to Anna Parsons, here reprinted
from Marianne Dwight, *Letters from Brook Farm 1844-1847*,
edited by Amy L. Reed (Poughkeepsie, N. Y.: Vassar College,
1928), pp. 1-4.

Brook Farm, West Roxbury, Mass.
Thursday a.m., [Spring, 1844].

DEAREST ANNA,

Thanks, thanks for your note and all the interesting things you told
me. . . . And now where do you think I am and what do you think
I am about? In the *barn* taking care of *three babies* about eighteen
months old! The sun shines warm, the breeze is gentle and spring
like, and fragrant with hay. It is one of the loveliest of spring days,—
a day to be out of doors, and therefore I have chosen to fix the
nursery for today in the open barn. This is my first entrance upon
duty. For company, besides the babies, I have a goodly row of cows
and oxen—a great, good natured dog,—occasionally a call from one and
another,—and a parcel of little romping girls and boys who are keeping
fast day as a holiday. I have had calls from Horace,[1] Fred Cabot,[2]
Mr. Pratt,[3] Lucas,[4] Mr. [2] Bradford,[5] who has just arrived, father,[6]

---

[1] Horace Sumner, brother of Charles Sumner.

[2] The manuscript records of Brook Farm in the library of the Massachusetts
Historical Society show that seventy-three members of the Brook Farm Associa-
tion for Industry and Education signed the revised constitution of 1844. There
Mary Ann Dwight of Boston, born 1816, gives her occupation as that of a teacher.
Frederick S. Cabot, of Boston, "clerk," was some six years younger. Anna Parsons
was about three years older than Mary Ann (or Marianne) Dwight.

[3] Minot Pratt, the head farmer.

[4] The brothers, Lucas and José Corrales, young Spaniards from Manila, were
pupils in the school.

[5] George P. Bradford, formerly a Unitarian clergyman.

[6] Dr. John Dwight's medical skill served the community well in more than one
serious situation.

John,[7] etc., etc., and many of the ladies. Fanny[8] has been doing the dormitory. But I must go back to the beginning and tell you all from our arrival. Our ride out was very pleasant, all the *bees*[9] were in the Hive at supper when the stage stopped, and our arrival created quite a sensation. John, Dana[10] and Horace waited on us in, Dora[11] and others welcomed us in the entry. We were ushered to the table where everything wore the same appearance of neatness and refinement I have always observed when I have been here. After supper we went, Mother to the Eyrie,[12] and Fanny and I to the Morton House[13] to inspect our apartment and put *to rights*. Thanks to the kind foresight of friends, we found our carpet spread out and our beds up. In my little room everything fits nicely. It is more roomy and convenient than I had an idea. They had placed the bed, bureaus, and washstand just where I wished, and soon we shall be in prime order,—didn't do much to the room on that [3] first visit, but went over to the Eyrie to spend the evening, where we had flute and piano music. And oh! what a magnificent evening! Full moonlight from the Eyrie parlor was splendid; everything glittered like pure white snow. Again and again I wished you and Helen[14] were here. Before nine o'clock Mr. and Mrs. Ripley[15] came home and gave us a cordial welcome. Dora came in and we had quite a nice talk together. Mrs. Ripley ran across the room to us and said to me, "I really envy you, you are having such a good talk;—Dora never finds time to talk to me,—has never had-any talk with me since she came." I asked her to take my seat for a talk with Dora—"No, I won't, I'm so *offended*." Mrs. Ripley said we were tired and must rest several days, for if we once began to work, we should never think we could stop. She charged Fanny and me not to

---

[7] John Sullivan Dwight, editor, teacher, and musical critic. His biography is by George Willis Cooke, Boston, 1898.

[8] Marianne's sister, Frances Ellen Dwight, was at this time twenty-five years old. She assisted her brother John in teaching music at Brook Farm.

[9] The Brook Farmers. The largest building was called the Hive.

[10] Charles A. Dana, later famous as editor of the New York *Sun*, was one of the original shareholders and always an influential member of the community. He taught Greek and German in the school. He was at this time twenty-five years old.

[11] Dora Wilder.

[12] The Eyrie, built on the highest point in the Farm, contained the school, the library, and pianos, as well as rooms for residence.

[13] The Morton House, named after its first owner, was presently rechristened the Pilgrim House.

[14] Helen Parsons, sister of Anna.

[15] George Ripley and Sophia Willard (Dana) Ripley, the founders of Brook Farm.

get up to breakfast the next morning saying we should have our breakfast sent up to the house.

But the next—(I've forgotten something and must go back. Fanny and Horace walked into the Pine Woods in the evening moonlight, and described the scene as surpassingly beautiful. I was too tired to go with them.) The next morning we rose soon after six—Horace knocked at our chamber door, and waited upon us down to the Hive for breakfast. After this we went back and went to work putting our rooms in order. We were busied so nearly all day, when we were not sitting still to rest. My box of books is not yet opened—when I get it unpacked and all its contents arranged, our room will look very pleasant and homelike. Directly after dinner, Messrs. Ripley, Dana, [4] Ryckman[16] and List[17] started for New York. Dana carried our regards to Cranch.[18] Before leaving . . . Mr. Ripley told Fanny and me in a very amusing way, how "pleasant it was to him to see *Christian people* about (alluding to us) and *proper, grown up,* well *behaved* young women, free from all the vices of the *world,* and *filled with all the virtues of association.*" In the afternoon came the rest of our furniture (except what didn't) and the piano-forte, and about tea time came father. He said the supper reminded him of college commons, except that there were ladies present. Father is pleased with the place, and we are all thus far pleased and happy. I must own to one little *twinge of heart.*

MARIANNE

Thursday eve.

Have been in the refectory—had a grand time setting table. Mary Ann R.[19] said it was set uncommonly well. After tea washed *all* the cups and saucers, Fred C. wiped them—Had a *grand* time—To night will be a meeting in our parlor for rustic amusements—and tomorrow morning, what think you, I am *to wait on the table.*

MARY ANN

---

16 Lewis K. Ryckman, a cordwainer.

17 Christopher List.

18 The poet and artist, Christopher Pearse Cranch, a close friend of John S. Dwight, was a frequent visitor at the Farm, where his singing and playing gave much pleasure.

19 Marianne, or Mary Ann, Ripley, sister of George Ripley, headed the primary department of the school and was in charge of the Nest, a small building across the road from the entrance to Brook Farm. Her advice was always influential with her brother.

no. 55 ～

Letter from Marianne Dwight to Franklin Dwight, here reprinted from Marianne Dwight, *Letters from Brook Farm 1844-1847*, edited by Amy L. Reed (Poughkeepsie, N. Y.: Vassar College, 1928), pp. 7-10.

Brook Farm, Sunday, April 14, '44.

DEAR BROTHER FRANK,[1]

I did not mean it should be so long before you had a letter from me, but so many different things have taken up my time that I hardly know when I could have written. . . . I have taken a joyful leave of the nursery and the babies,—with one exception, the sweet little innocents were not to my taste, and not *such* angels as I love to minister to. Now my business is as follows (but perhaps liable to frequent change): I wait on the breakfast table (½ hour), help M. A. Ripley[2] clear away breakfast things, etc. (1½ hours), go into the dormitory group till eleven o'clock,—dress for dinner [8] —then over to the Eyrie and sew till dinner time,—half past twelve. Then from half past one or two o'clock until ½ past five, I teach drawing in Pilgrim Hall and sew in the Eyrie. At ½ past five go down to the Hive, to help set the tea table, and afterwards I wash tea cups, etc., till about ½ past seven. Thus I make out a long day of it, but alternation of work and pleasant company and chats make it pleasant. I am about entering a flower garden group[3] and assisting Miss Russell in doing up muslins. I have one very

[1] Benjamin Franklin Dwight, Marianne's brother, was in an architect's office in Boston.

[2] Mary Ann Ripley.

[3] When the Dwight family joined the Brook Farm Association, the community was well on its way to becoming a Fourier phalanx on a much smaller scale. Fourier's organization of workers into "groups and series" according to their preference ("passional attraction") for certain kinds of work is elaborately explained in *The Harbinger* for Saturday, October 10, 1846, in an article on "Objections to Association"; more simply in Lindsay Swift's *Brook Farm*, pp. 44-45.

Francois Charles Marie Fourier (1772-1837), son of a French linen draper, wrote a number of socialistic books of which *Le nouveau Monde industriel*, 1829-30, contains the fullest exposition of his ideas. His system was based on the belief that the free play of strong individual desire was likely to bring about the most harmonious social living. Without advocating community of property or the abolition of the family, he planned the regrouping of society in "phalanxes" of about 1600 persons, living in large communal houses and subdivided into series and groups, working cooperatively under elective heads. The small numbers at Brook Farm prevented anything like the complete carrying out of Fourier's idea. But they did their best.

pleasant drawing class, consisting of the young ladies and the young men, José, Martin Cushing, etc. The other class is composed of the children in the regular school. We enjoy ourselves here very well, and I can't but think that after some weeks I shall become deeply attached to the place—I have felt perfectly at home from the first. We need more leisure, or rather, we should like it. There are so many, and so few women to do the work, that we have to be nearly all the time about it. I can't find time to write till it comes [9] evening, and then we generally assemble in little bands somewhere for a little talk or amusement. Fred Cabot and Martin Cushing have moved into Horace's room, and I wish for the fun of it, you could look in and see how they have placed their beds,—across the door, so they are obliged to vault over them to get at what they call their parlor, which is by the window. They are full of fun and roguery. A day or two since, we looked in there and behold they had got our *images,*—cologne bottle, ink stand, etc., paraded out on their table. Martin is a good fellow, and makes a great deal of amusement for the whole house. He says he means to carry Fanny and me into Boston some Sunday. Oh! I love the Sundays here. This whole afternoon I have spent in the Pine Woods, and have wanted you here more than I can tell. We have much sickness here now, cases of scarlatina. Carry Pratt's[4] and Alfred Kay's are pretty severe cases, but all are now mending. Father came at the right time.

I really think you would enjoy living here, Frank, and hope that, if we stay, you will come. Come out that evening you have talked about when next we have full moon. . . . The Codmans[5] have come. The Campbells won't do, and are going away. I believe eight or ten more men are to come this next week. You can't think how we want to see you. . . . This evening in a few minutes will be a general gathering at the Hive to hear an account of the New York convention,[6] which I wish to attend. So must bid you good [10] bye now—will add a few words afterwards, if not too late. . . .

Your affectionate sister
MARY ANN

---

[4] One of Minot Pratt's three children.

[5] The Codman family consisted of the parents, one daughter, Rebecca, and two sons, Charles H. and John T., the author of *Brook Farm: Historical and Personal Memoirs*, Boston, 1894.

[6] A socialist convention held at Clinton Hall, New York, George Ripley presiding. The meeting laid emphasis on the religious aspect of the socialist movement and indorsed Fourier's principles of industrial organization. Frothingham, O. B., *Memoir of William Henry Channing*, p. 207.

P. S. Mr. Ripley brought letters yesterday from you, Anna, and Helen.[7] We had quite a party in the evening in our little room.

no. 56 ～

Letter from Marianne Dwight to Anna Parsons, here reprinted from Marianne Dwight, *Letters from Brook Farm 1844-1847*, edited by Amy L. Reed (Poughkeepsie, N. Y.: Vassar College, 1928), pp. 12-15.

Brook Farm, Sat. a. m., April 27, 1844.

DEAREST ANNA,

I intended to have written you a full letter last evening, but we had company come in (up in our room), Fred C. and William Coleman, and were drawn into playing whist and talking til! *eleven o'clock*, which in these working days, is as late an hour as I like to keep. Evening before last went into the Pine Woods about sunset, with Dora, Miss Codman, Fanny, Fred C. and one or two more. Oh! how sacred and solemn were those deep shades, and the sombre light! We threw ourselves upon our backs, Dora, Frederick and I, and whilst the rest walked on, and finally walked home, we staid (imprudent children) and talked till about nine [13] o'clock when the dampness warned us home. How beautiful the moonbeams flickering through the leaves, as we gazed up into the sky, and here and there a star spangled the magically figured firmament above us! . . . Our earnest talk strengthened by faith in Association and in Brook Farm.—In which latter, strange to say, Dora's heart fails her.—But she will and must, I think, alter her mind. Oh! it is so pleasant here, even with all the work! I am sorry if Frank[1] carried you my last note, for I did not finish what I had begun to say and now forget about it. I believe I was going to tell you that, owing to Mary Ann Ripley's being ill two or three days, I had had more work to do than usual, as I endeavored in part, to supply her place.—Have you recovered your impressibility? We had a gentleman here a few days ago, by name John Orvis,[2] who has

---

[7] One of Minot Pratt's three children.

---

[1] Frank Dwight.

[2] John Orvis, "farmer," Ferrisburgh, Vermont, about the same age as Mary Ann Dwight and destined to be of considerable importance in her life. He was already interested in Fourierism. Swift, *Brook Farm*, p. 278.

lived at Skaneateles with Collins.³ He is a very interesting and delightful young man—is *very* impressible, reads characters thro' letters, or
by coming in contact with a person.—Fred put him to sleep in a few
moments, and also cured him of sore throat and head-ache, which
complaints he had taken from Frances by relieving her of them. Frances
proves to be rather impressible. Mr. Orvis did not undertake to examine any letters, in consequence of his head-ache, but read Abby
Foord's character finely by putting his hand on [14] her head.—Well,
the best of it is that he is coming here to live in two or three weeks, in
consequence of being so much pleased with his visit, and he wants to
be in *our entry* in Pilgrim Hall, and perhaps Fred will take him in with
him if Martin leaves soon. Oh! how Mr. Kay⁴ has teazed us about
inveigling Mr. Orvis into our house! Then the Macdaniels⁵ are to
come this week and have one of our parlors. He insists upon it that
the character of our house is to be changed, that the elegance and refinement of the place are tending this way. I tell him no—the Eyrie—
the Eyrie! So has it been and will ever be till we get our Phalanstery.⁶

The boys have brought us some anemones and cowslips,—wish I had
some now to send.—But I write particularly to ask that when the rest
of you come out here (I refer to the party by moonlight) you will
by some means, bring little Fanny.⁷ She can be tucked in anywhere
and will not [15] take up any room. A great deal of love to her, and
tell her we shall be very much disappointed, if when your vehicles
unpack at the Hive, she should not come to light. Love to all,—I am
desirous of knowing what evening you will come;—will you send us

---

³ John A. Collins, founder of the Skaneateles Community, which adopted Fourier's principles. Orvis was one of the signers of the call for the Association meeting at Skaneateles, March 22, 1843.

⁴ Mr. Kay, a New York businessman, father of "Allie" Kay, was much interested in the success of Brook Farm. He was often called on for financial advice.

⁵ The Macdaniels, mother, two daughters, Fanny and Eunice, and a son, Osborne, were a southern family. The son lived in New York, where he assisted
Brisbane in editing the *Phalanx*. However, he visited the Farm frequently and for
long periods.

⁶ The Phalanstery, the central community house ("unitary building"), was begun in the summer of 1844. Hence the influx of carpenters. "All the public rooms
were to be in this building, which was almost in the middle of the estate (of 200
acres). The parlors, reading room, reception rooms, general assembly hall, dining
room capable of seating over three hundred people, kitchen, and bakery were
carefully planned for a common use." (There were also single rooms and suites
for families.) "The building was of wood and 175 feet long. Thus the larger
families, whose members had been scattered by reason of the crowded condition
of the other houses, could be insured a secluded family life, and such rooms in the
older buildings as were in use for other than living purposes might be available for
this legitimate need." Swift, *Brook Farm*, pp. 35-36.

⁷ Anna Parsons' younger sister.

word? perhaps Monday or Tuesday.—I don't know when the moon fulls,—but we are to have glorious evenings—Farewell.

Yours ever
MARY ANN

no. 57 ~

> From a letter from Convers Frances, Cambridge, Mass., to Theo-
> dore Parker, in London, dated June 22, 1844, here printed from a
> photostatic copy of the holograph in the Abernethy Library of
> American Literature, Middlebury College, Middlebury, Vermont.
> Photostats were secured through the courtesy of Miss Mary Noel,
> Curator of the Abernethy Library.

. . . Geo. Ripley is doing better than ever,—at least, so they report of him. The Community is much enlarged by the addition of
many families . . mechanics & . . & [sic] a greater variety of occupations introduced. I understand they are trying to come, as much as possible, into the Fourier system. I have great regard for these people; at
any rate they are willing to make some attempt towards the true doctrines of labor & life; & are trying to live out what they believe to be
the truth. Yet I always feel a distrust (arising I presume from old
prejudices) of all plans like Fourier's, which would seem to say, "go
to now, by means of mechanical arrangements & progressive series we
will construct a perfect form of society." It seems too much like applying mathematics & mechanism to a free soul, too much like attempting so to arrange mankind, that the square of the oblique diagonal
of conduct shall be equal to the two squares of the base of nature, &
the perpendicular of education. But I find the Swedenborgians are
much struck with Fourier's systems; it is, they think, a correspondence
of outward organization to what Swedenborg has revealed of spirit
life,—the form which represents the social theory of souls in the spirit-
world. So at least it is spoken of. God speed any attempt to emancipate us from the perverse and artificial ways of living which so often
oppress us we know not why. . . .

no. 58 ~

> A letter from Isaac Hecker to Henry David Thoreau, here re-
> printed from E. H. Russell, "A Bit of Unpublished Correspond-

ence between Henry Thoreau and Isaac Hecker," *Atlantic Monthly*, XC (July-December, 1902), 370-376.

HENRY THOREAU,—It was not altogether the circumstance of our imme-
[372]diate physical nearness, though this may have [been] the consequence of a higher affinity, that inclined us to commune with each
other. This I am fully sensible [of] since our separation. Oftentimes
we observe ourselves to be passive or cooperative agents of profounder
principles than we at the time even dream of.

I have been stimulated to write to you at this present moment on
account of a certain project which I have formed, which your influence has no slight share, I imagine, in forming. It is, to work our
passage to Europe, and to walk, work, and beg if needs be, as far
when there as we are inclined to do. We wish to see how it looks, and
to court difficulties; for we feel an unknown depth of untried virgin
strength which we know of no better way at the present time to call
into activity and so dispose of. We desire to go without purse or staff,
depending upon the all-embracing love of God, Humanity, and the
spark of courage imprisoned in us. Have we the will, we have the
strong arms, hard hands to work with, and sound feet to stand upon
and walk with. The heavens shall be our vaulted roof, and the green
earth beneath our bed and for all other furniture purposes. These are
free and may be so used. What can hinder us from going, but our
bodies, and shall they do it? We can as well deposit them there as
here. Let us take a walk over the fairest portions of this planet Earth
and make it ours by seeing them. Let us see what the genius and stu-
pidity of our honored forefathers have heaped up. We wish to kneel
at their shrines and embrace their spirits and kiss the ground which
they have hallowed with their presence. We shall prove the dollar is
not almighty, and the impossible, moonshine. The wide world is before us beckoning us to come, let us accept and embrace it. Reality
shall be our antagonist, and our lives, if sold, not at a good bargain, for
a certainty. How does the idea strike you? I prefer at least to go this
way before going farther in the woods. The past let us take with us;
we reverence, we love it; but forget not that our eyes are in our face,
set to the beautiful unimagined future. Let us be Janus-faced, with a
beard [-ed] and [a] beardless face. Will you accept this invitation?
Let me know what your impressions are as soon as it is your pleasure.

Remember me to your kind family. To-morrow I take the first step
towards becoming a *visible* member of the Roman Catholic Church.
If you and your good family do not become greater sinners, I shall
claim you all as good Catholics, for she claims "all baptized infants, all

innocent children of every religious denomination; and all grownup
Christians who have preserved their baptismal innocence, though they
make no outward profession of the Catholic faith, are yet claimed as
her children by the Roman Catholic Church."

Yours very truly,

ISAAC HECKER.

N. Y., Thursday, *July* 31, 1844.

no. 59 ～

A letter from Henry David Thoreau to Isaac Hecker, here reprinted from E. H. Russell, "A Bit of Unpublished Correspondence between Henry Thoreau and Isaac Hecker," *Atlantic
Monthly,* XC (July-December, 1902), 370-376.

Concord, *Aug.* 14, 1844.

FRIEND HECKER,—I am glad to hear your voice from that populous
city, and the more so for the tenor of its discourse. I have but just returned from a pedestrian excursion somewhat similar to that you propose, *parvis componere magna,* to the Catskill mountains, over the
principal mountains of this State, subsisting mainly on bread and
berries, and slumbering on the mountain tops. As usually happens, I
now feel a slight sense of dissipation. Still, I am strongly tempted by
your proposal, and experience a decided schism between my outward
and inward tendencies. Your method of traveling, especially—to live
along the road, citizens of the world, without haste or petty plans—
I have often proposed this to my dreams, and still do. But [373] the
fact is, I cannot so decidedly postpone exploring the *Farther Indies,*
which are to be reached, you know, by other routes and other methods of travel. I mean that I constantly return from every external enterprise with disgust, to fresh faith in a kind of Brahminical, Artesian,
Inner Temple life. All my experience, as yours probably, proves only
this reality. Channing wonders how I can resist your invitation, I, a
single man—unfettered—and so do I. Why, there are Roncesvalles, the
Cape de Finisterre, and the Three Kings of Cologne; Rome, Athens,
and the rest, to be visited in serene, untemporal hours, and all history
to revive in one's memory, as he went by the way, with splendors too
bright for this world—I know how it is. But is not here too Roncesvalles with greater lustre? Unfortunately, it may prove dull and de-
sultory weather enough here, but better trivial days with faith than

the fairest ones lighted by sunshine alone. Perchance, my *Wanderjahr* has not arrived, but you cannot wait for that. I hope you will find a companion who will enter as heartily into your schemes as I should have done.

I remember you, as it were, with the whole Catholic Church at your skirts. And the other day, for a moment, I think I understood your relation to that body; but the thought was gone again in a twinkling, as when a dry leaf falls from its stem over our heads, but is instantly lost in the rustling mass at our feet.

I am really sorry that the Genius will not let me go with you, but I trust that it will conduct to other adventures, and so, if nothing prevents, we will compare notes at last.

Yrs. etc.,
HENRY D. THOREAU.

no. 60 ～

Letter from Marianne Dwight to Anna Parsons, here reprinted from Marianne Dwight, *Letters from Brook Farm 1844-1847*, edited by Amy L. Reed (Poughkeepsie, N. Y.: Vassar College, 1928), pp. 29-34.

Brook Farm, Friday p.m., August 30, (1844).

DEAREST ANNA,

[31] . . . We have had some pleasant guests since I last wrote. A visit from William H. Channing,[1]—need I tell you how [32] much I enjoyed it? Mr. Alcott[2] has been here too; and today is a sad day with us for we have parted with Mr. Kay and his little girls; with Miss Sophy Jertz,—an intimate friend of Fanny Macdaniel's, a Norwegian lady, one of the sweetest and most harmonious persons I ever met. She has light hair, and earnest mild blue eyes—is well versed in Fourier,— that is to say, she is a *phalansterian;* and better than all, she is inspired with music, it pervades her whole manner, and her voice is music itself, and she performs on the piano-forte, second only to Frederick Rakemann. Then we have had two Frenchmen who came in her train, like-

---

[1] William Henry Channing, nephew of the great champion of Unitarianism, began his own career as a Unitarian minister. About this date he was preaching, whenever and wherever he could, Christian socialism, antislavery, and the upbuilding of the spiritual life. He had eloquence and personal magnetism and a "benign and beautiful presence."

[2] Amos Bronson Alcott made occasional visits and gave "talks" at the Farm.

wise phalansterians, Mons. Bernard, and Mons. Quailke, both men of much depth of mind. Mons. B. could hardly speak a word of English; Mons. Bernard left today with Miss Jertz but will return again on Sunday to stay a little while longer.

And now I must interest you in our fancy group, for which and from which I hope great things.—nothing less than the elevation of woman to independence, and an acknowledged equality with man. Many thoughts on this subject have been struggling in my mind ever since I came to Brook Farm, and now, I think I see how it will all be accomplished. Women must become producers of marketable articles; women must make money and earn their support independently of man. So we, with a little borrowed capital (say twenty-five or thirty dollars; by we, I mean a large part of the women here), have purchased materials, and made up in one week about forty-five dollars worth of elegant and tasteful caps, capes, collars, undersleeves, etc., etc.,—which we sent in to Hutchinson and Holmes, who [33] have agreed to take all we can make. If they find a ready sale, we shall be greatly encouraged,—and be able to go on extending our business, as far as our time and numbers will allow. Of course, if we succeed (and we are determined we will), it will be very desirable for other ladies to come here on purpose to take a part in our fancy work; then our domestic work which now presses too heavily, will get more divided, and we shall each have less housework and more fancy work. By and by, when funds accumulate (!) we may start other branches of business, so that all our proceeds must be applied to the elevation of woman forever. Take a spiritual view of the matter. Raise woman to be the equal of man, and what intellectual developments may we not expect? How the whole aspect of society will be changed! And this is the great work, is it not, that Association in its present early stage has to do? Do, as you love and honor your sex, bear our fancy group in mind, and bring or send us patterns and designs of every sort of thing you see or can conceive of that will be useful to us. We want your mother here. We want your sister Elizabeth; she will come I hope, by and by. For one week I have indulged my passional attraction and painted to my heart's content. Mr. Kay is the patron of our group. I esteem and love him more, the more I know him. Tell Dora, had she been here during his last visit, she could not help loving him. It is my devotion to fancy work and to education that have not left me a minute to spare for writing, reading or thinking on aught else. We are about organizing children into groups for labor and education, a very important step and by no means an easy one. Mr. Orvis is to be the

director for the boys and as they look to me for the girls, it must occupy considerable of my time. [34] You can't think how deeply I
feel my *incompetency* for this work. . . .

Write immediately and tell me that you will come, and if you can,
tell me when. Recollect Parker will be here probably in a week from
tomorrow. Perhaps Hannah Ripley, Dora, etc. will make us the long
talked of visit and bring you with them—in which case they will *not*
take you home with them. Much love to all.

MARY-ANN

no. 61 ~

> Letter from Marianne Dwight to Frank Dwight, here reprinted
> from Marianne Dwight, *Letters from Brook Farm 1844-1847*,
> edited by Amy L. Reed (Poughkeepsie, N. Y.: Vassar College,
> 1928), pp. 40-42.

Thurs, a. m., Sept. 19, '44.

DEAR FRANK,

. . . Yesterday Mr. List and Mr. Reynolds were unanimously ex-
pelled from the carpenter's group in consequence of their being discordant elements.—so they [41] went to the general direction re-
questing to be furnished with work, and that body have set them to
work upon the frame of the Phalanstery,—so they are working right
in the midst of the group, but not of the group, doing just what they
are told to do,—a sort of solitary labor and imprisonment. It is quite
an amusing state of things. The group who thought to get rid of their
company are foiled in that.

It is a most magnificent day—the perfection of autumn, except that
we have needed rain for a long time—And what are you about? The
same old round of labor I suppose, only you may be anxiously laying
new plans. Oh! that we could prepare ourselves to meet all changes
and disappointments without any vexation of spirit, and with a cheerful
trust that all will work out right.—Nay, better, if we could feel that
all is right now! But there is a sense in which all is not right, and perhaps it is this that disturbs us. I wish you were here, Frank, tho' I
don't feel inclined to hurry you. For myself, I would not exchange
this life for any I have ever led. I could not feel contented again with
the life of isolated houses, and the conventions of civilization. I enjoy

here more than I ever enjoyed—and it is true likewise that I have had some very keen suffering—In the present state of Association and with my sensibilities I feel that I must be continually exposed to suffering; —but constant activity is a good counterpoise,—and life is so full and rich here, that I feel as if my experience were valuable, and I were *growing* somewhat faster than when I lived in Boston. We have thought much of your circumstances and long to have you settled here with us, and shall rejoice when you are *ready* to come,—but I repeat we would not hurry you. . . . [42]

Our Fourier class went off finely—some people from the street came over. Hope to go to Boston tomorrow evening, but don't know. If we do, shall stop at E. P. Peabody's I suppose.

Hearing a great hurrah, I have just been to the window, and lo! Martin and a group of boys returning from their work,—little Fourierites, with banners flying. I believe if they have been idle, the banners are not permitted to wave. The boys are really getting to enjoy their work, and these banners are a grand excitement. Probably the fancy group will have to work them a very handsome one. . . .

Yours ever affectionately
MARY ANN

no. 62

From a letter from E. P. Grant (Canton, Ohio) to Osborne Macdaniel (New York), October 14, 1844, printed from the holograph in the *Elijah P. Grant Papers*, Box I, Letterbook III, p. 22, University of Chicago Library.

. . . I will observe in the first place that Mr. Greely [sic] had informed me of your misfortune in being discharged from the Custom House; and if this circumstance should seriously impair your income, as I suppose it probably will, I truly regret it, not only on account of the great cause of Association in which you have been so earnestly and efficiently engaged, but also on account of yourself and your immediate friends. But I am glad to hear, in connexion with this event, that your mother and sisters have connected themselves with the social movement at Brook Farm, and are so well contented there, for I hope they will be speedily relieved, if they are not already, from many of the troubles and anxieties which are so harrassing [sic] in our civilized societies. . . .

no. 63 ❧

Letter from Marianne Dwight to Anna Parsons, here reprinted from Marianne Dwight, *Letters from Brook Farm 1844-1847*, edited by Amy L. Reed (Poughkeepsie, N. Y.: Vassar College, 1928), pp. 44-47.

Brook Farm, Tuesday eve., Oct. 29, 1844

DEAREST ANNA,

. . . It is tea-time. I sit alone in my snug little room. Fred, our "good Fred" has been spending a half hour in [45] relieving me of the head-ache, which has been tormenting me all day, and has positively forbidden me to go down to tea, and engaged to find some one to supply my place in washing cups, etc. after tea. It will not be mother, for she is having a coffee party at the Eyrie, and as our friend Mr. N. is a lover of coffee, undoubtedly he will be a partaker. We have had, what you so much desired, a regular, earnest storm,—a hard rain and plenty of wind. Had quite an exhilarating walk down to breakfast, with Fanny—went from house to house in the consistory; —was asked by C. N.[1] if I had written to you yet,—when I reached the Pilgrim House found Mrs. Hosmer and Fred exchanging rooms; —spent a little time looking on, and assisting John Orvis in putting to rights, for you know he is to room with Fred. Dinner time came ere long—it rained in torrents;—our covered wagon or omnibus drove up to the door to take such passengers as wished to ride down to the Hive, so nine or ten of us packed ourselves into it, and were brought safely home again after dinner. My afternoon has been spent at the Cottage,—so much of the events of the day. For this evening, we are anticipating a dance in Pilgrim Hall in honor of Popleston's departure. The boys have gone to Dedham for a fiddler—I wish *you* were here, I should like so much to have you see one of our dances. I wish, if I feel able, to go down for a short time, as a looker on.

I passed yesterday p. m. in Miss Russell's room, at fancy work—from which I rested about three quarters of an hour, and read to her from Cranch's poems.

I should like to have you peep into my neighbours' room and see the arrangements. The sublime J. O. has a high [46] bedstead which stands directly *over* that of Fred,—who being *small* and young is thus accommodated with a sort of trundle bed to be drawn out at night! Oh! what ingenious beings they are!

---

[1] Charles K. Newcomb.

When I returned to my desolate room on Sunday, after taking leave of you and Dora, you can hardly imagine how I felt,—I knew that I should miss you so much. Fred came in, and brought his grasses, which I fell to helping him arrange. He seemed to be rather blue, and soon his brother Frank joined us. We had a pretty good talk,—some puns and jokes,—among others, Frank brought forward this, which is so good I can remember it. "Where was the first fighting? Ans. In chaos, where *Nihil fit*." I suppose you know Latin enough to understand that, don't you? If you don't, ask some more learned friend to explain. Fred was restored to happiness during the tea hour, by beating his brother at chess.

You see how little material I have to make out a letter with, as I am reduced to the necessity of telling you the merest commonplaces. But then I know that you, who have been here, can look behind these little facts, and see more than they tell to everyone.

The fiddler must have arrived, for I hear the scraping of the fiddle! . . .

I can't very well write more now on account of my head,—perhaps may add a line ere bed-time.

Half past eleven.

The dance is over.—I have been a spectator for two hours. It was a beautiful dance. I was standing near [47] Charlie N., speaking with Amelia, when he went across the room, brought a seat and placed it beside him for me. From *him* I felt the kindness, and we all three sat there together the whole evening.—I wish you could have seen his heavenly smile when I left the room and he bade me good-night. Of course we sat together almost in silence.

And now good night,—I must have sleep and rest.—May you be enjoying the same, and may the spirits of loved ones visit you in your dreams. . . .

Your
MARY ANN

no. 64 ✍

Letter from Marianne Dwight to Frank Dwight, here reprinted from Marianne Dwight, *Letters from Brook Farm 1844-1847*, edited by Amy L. Reed (Poughkeepsie, N. Y.: Vassar College, 1928), pp. 47-48.

Brook Farm, Nov. 1, '44.

DEAR FRANK,

. . . Tuesday evening we had a dance for Popleston's farewell, and Pop has really gone.—I can hardly feel that it is so.—He was so amiable, and such an ornament here, that I hated to have him go. Thursday was appointed for the quarterly Association convention, and delegates were invited from Northampton and Hopedale. The Northamptons didn't come. Six male Hopedales arrived and several women, and we managed to find them each a place to sleep. In the evening we had quite an interesting meeting, tho' nothing remarkable. Mr. Ballou spoke a good deal. But for this meeting we should have had a Shakespeare reading; now I suppose it will come off next Thursday. . . .

Mr. Orvis and Frederick have moved into the next room to mine,— another move in our entry is yet to be made. Oh! when will our habitations be fixed? If it be true, as a favorite writer says, that three removals, for loss, are equivalent to one fire,—then surely B. F. cannot long have [48] much to lose. The move to which I refer is this, —Caspar and Willie[1] are coming into the little room or closet that Anna lately occupied. They don't like the idea much because they can't have any parties (!) in so small a room. I suppose when the Phalanstery is done the expansion will be in proportion to the present cramming or condensation. . . .

Your affectionate
MARY ANN

no. 65 ⚘

"Notice to the Second Edition of the Constitution of the Brook Farm Association," here reprinted from the *Phalanx*, Volume I, Number 20 (Monday, December 9, 1844), p. 305.

NOTICE TO THE SECOND EDITION OF THE CONSTITUTION OF THE BROOK FARM ASSOCIATION.

Since the publication of the first edition of our Constitution and Introductory Statement, the public interest in Association, has greatly increased both in this vicinity, and throughout the country generally. With the conviction now beginning to pervade all classes of society,

---

[1] The Goldermann children, her new charges.

that the incoherence and conflict of interests which characterize civilization, there can be no permanent security either for private rights or public order, the doctrines of social unity, and attractive industry, are taking a sure and deep hold. Already the Phalansterian movement in the United States embraces persons of every station in life, and in its extent, and influence on questions of importance, is fast assuming a national character.

In this state of things, the friends of the cause will [be] gratified to learn, that the appeal in behalf of Brook Farm, contained in our Introductory Statement, has been generally answered, and that the situation of the Association is highly encouraging. In the half year that has elapsed, our numbers have been increased by the addition of many skilful and enthusiastic laborers, in various departments, and our capital has been enlarged by the subscription of about ten thousand dollars. Our organization has acquired a more systematic form, though with our comparatively small numbers we can only approximate to truly scientific arrangements. Still with the unavoidable deficiencies of our groups and series, their action is remarkable, and fully justifies our anticipations of great results from applying the principles of universal order to industry.

In education also, we have succeeded in introducing arrangements of great value, which would be impossible in a society of isolated families; though this, as well as other departments, is still in process of formation.

We have made considerable agricultural improvements; we have erected a workshop sixty feet by twenty-eight, for mechanics of several trades, some of which are already in operation, and we are now engaged in building a section, one hundred and seventy-five feet by forty, of a Phalanstery or Unitary dwelling. Our first object is to collect those who, from their character and convictions, are qualified to aid in the experiment we are engaged in, and to furnish them with convenient and comfortable habitations, at the smallest possible outlay. For this purpose the most careful economy is used, though we are yet able to attain many of the peculiar advantages of the associated household. Still for a transitional society, and for comparatively temporary use, a social edifice cannot be made free from the defects of civilized architecture. When our Phalanx has become sufficiently large, and has in some measure accomplished its great purposes, the Serial organization of labor and Unitary education, we shall have it in our power to build a Phalanstery with the magnificence and permanence proper to such a structure.

Cheering as are the results of our endeavors, we wish to have it distinctly understood that they have been, and for some time must be, merely preparatory labors. We would then again invite the personal cooperation of all suitable persons, and the investment of the funds necessary to a complete application of Fourier's theory of industrial organization.

We call upon the wise and humane to lend their aid to an undertaking which, in the growing insufficiency and insecurity of civilized institutions bases its promise of a better state of things not on mere human wisdom, but on the science of universal laws. We appeal to those who can perceive that the true road to general well-being, is not to be reached by legislative deliberations, or by political or benevolent expedients, but by reverent investigation of the methods of divine order and faithful application of the same to society;—to those who look with alarm upon the growth of pauperism, and civilized slavery; —to those who in despairing sympathy for the masses begin to feel the necessity of an integral philanthropy;—but more than all, to those who are inspired by the sublime ideas of social and universal unity with a deeper faith in God, and a more assured hope of man.

We appeal to them for assistance in the practical demonstration of a scientific theory, which solves the great social problems that have convulsed the world for the last century, and which discloses to man a destiny worthy of his aspirations and energies, and of that beneficent and infinite Being by whom the universe is forever upheld and renewed.

BROOK FARM, Oct. 1844.

no. 66 ⮑

Letter from Marianne Dwight to Anna Parsons, here reprinted from Marianne Dwight, *Letters from Brook Farm 1844-1847*, edited by Amy L. Reed (Poughkeepsie, N. Y.: Vassar College, 1928), pp. 50-52.

Brook Farm, Dec. 14, '44.

DEAREST ANNA

[51] . . . Have I ever told you about our retrenchment, dearest Anna? . . . You know it is one of our rules not to incur any debt, but to pay as we go along—well, we found that we could not be sure of commanding ready money this winter sufficient to pay our ex-

penses, so we agreed to retrench in our table fare, in order to make a saving and come within the means we can command. It was really cheering to see how readily this measure was adopted. We now set one of the long tables in our old style for boarders, scholars and visitors,– and a *few associates* who feel that their *health* requires (!) the use of meat, tea, etc. At the other tables we have no meat, no tea, nor butter, nor sugar. This "retrenchment" has afforded us no little amusement. We are not at a loss for something to eat,–have good potatoes, turnips, squashes, etc., etc., and puddings. At our breakfast table I counted nine different articles this morning; so we can't complain of want of variety. Our New York friends are pitying us very much and wonder what we can have left to eat. For my own part, I think much good will come out of it. I trust our people will find by and by that meat and tea have lost their relish, and that there is something better. Perhaps we shall have fewer head-aches, etc. Charlie N. sat at the *no* retrenchment table at *one* meal, but has come home to us again, and is excepted from the general rule and allowed to have tea and butter brought to him. Our breakfast these short days is ready precisely at seven and, in order to make people punctual, Mr. Capen carries the dishes off at exactly half-past. Here again, friend N. is excepted, as he ought to be. We hear that many small associations are [52] stopped, or will stop soon.–Some good will come of this. *We* only have to *retrench*. Friends of Association in New York and elsewhere are beginning to see the need of concentrating their efforts in some one undertaking, and it is to Brook Farm that they look. Mr. Kay regards our condition as much more prosperous and hopeful than when he was here in the summer. No matter if we are to have a hard winter in some respects, we know how to make sunshine around us and to wear smiling faces. What a hindrance to us is our climate!

I *do* love the country, even in winter. The morning after this snow storm, I went down to the Hive through drifts higher than my head, stepped on a stone wall to get through one. Oh! the snow has been so beautiful and the air and the sky so clear and fine, and everything so much brighter, and more cheerful than winter in Boston. . . .

We had two comedies performed Thursday evening and to admiration. The "dramatic corps" have built a regular stage, and are to have scenery for *Pizarro*[1] three weeks hence. I don't quite approve of their theatricals now, because I think they occupy more time than, in our present state, we can afford to give. I wish you would invite your friend Seth Welles to ride out here with you very soon. I wish you

---

[1] By Sheridan.

would write me something about the trees and flowers. How do pines affect you? How certain flowers? Love to each and all. Hope to see you soon.

Lovingly
MARY ANN

no. 67 ~

From a letter, Marianne Dwight to Anna Parsons, here reprinted from Marianne Dwight, *Letters from Brook Farm 1844-1847*, edited by Amy L. Reed (Poughkeepsie, N. Y.: Vassar College, 1928), pp. 82-85.

Sunday p. m. [March 2, 1845].

DEAREST ANNA,

[85] . . . I told you about the R. L. S. G. (or rejected lover's sympathising group), did I not? Well you can't think how amusing it was, a day or two ago, to hear Charles Dana announce gravely at table, a meeting of the R. L. S. G. to be held at half past ten that evening, in the nursery, a punctual attendance required from all the members and from all those candidates for admission who were expected ere long to become members,—and no one to be admitted without the usual badges—and measures were to be taken for the admission of honorary members. All this was said off very solemnly and created not a little fun and enquiry. . . .

MARY ANN

May I ask of you the favor to lend me Miss Fuller's new work[1] just long enough for perusal after you have done with it yourself?

no. 68 ~

Letter from Marianne Dwight to Anna Parsons, here reprinted from Marianne Dwight, *Letters from Brook Farm 1844-1847*, edited by Amy L. Reed (Poughkeepsie, N. Y.: Vassar College, 1928), pp. 85-87.

Sunday evening, March 9, [1845].

MY DEAR ANNA,

How pleasant and comfortable it is here in my little room this evening, and how clean, for I've had the carpet shaken, windows and paint

---

[1] *Summer on the Lakes,* published late in 1844.

washed, and I do wish you were here with me. I have not been out of the house and scarcely out of the room today, having a very severe head cold, and a strong tendency to ear-ache. I'll tell you how I've passed the day. Mother came up early and brought my breakfast. Then I had just put the room to rights, and sat down, when Fred knocked. . . . After talking awhile, Fred read to me, and thus the whole forenoon passed off, varied only with a call from Amelia and one from M. A. Willard. I was at work, whenever I felt able, painting a picture frame of white wood for Fred. The subject is Pegasus in the stable, drawn by Anna Philbric, and I have surrounded it with a wreath of oak and laurel leaves, with acorns and berries. How I [86] love to be at work for a dear friend!—this occupation has made the whole day pleasant to me. Then came my dinner, then a visit from M. A. Willard (whom I like very much, and who is visiting here) also a visit from John Cheever, who gets attracted here by the *fine arts!* (I hope Dora won't be *jealous.*) They stayed till about tea time. John Cheever brought up my supper, and stayed talking on high and sublime subjects till the present time, and now again I am alone. George Curtis has been here a few days, is now at the Eyrie singing, and were I not afraid to go out I should not now be writing to thee.

Colds are very prevalent here now. Eunice is quite ill—poor thing! She has been made a mummy of,—done up in a wet sheet,—which she thinks a very unpoetical way of getting cured. Brisbane is here, but I scarcely see him. Indeed I'm so busy at my painting that I scarcely see any one,—and I assure you I feel very happy to have such profitable work to do. I have made some improvements in the shades.

I don't know how I feel about Fred and Mary,—glad and happy when I think of them, and yet not wholly confident. There is always in the future so much less of happiness, than is anticipated by these ecstatic lovers. I cannot think of Fred as married,—and *belonging* to any *one.* I don't like to think of myself in the matter at all, and I ought not, but this is human weakness—and I can't help fearing, that, for a while at least he must belong less to *me* than he has done. But I will not contemplate losing so good a friend,—no,—heaven sent him to be my help and strength,—and we have had, and must continue to have no little influence upon each other. Certainly now he is very kind and as friendly as ever. Why do people foolishly [87] want to marry? I am getting to think that Fourier is right, and in full harmony there will be no marriage—at least marriage will be a very different thing from what it now is. Heaven grant that this may be the blessedest thing for Fred! If it prove so then I am sure I shall feel happy,—for he deserves well.

But if the sun of his early and promising life be dimmed, then I am sure I shall feel the shadow. I do trust that this most important step of his life is a right one,—but then he is so young! Oh! it would be sad to be disappointed in him, and I know I shall not be; he must find in Mary his truest help in his onward path. God speed him! I cannot imagine anything that I could not cheerfully sacrifice for his highest good and happiness. . . .

Good-night, dear friend.

Thine in love
MARIANNE

no. 69 ⤸

> Letter from Minot Pratt to George Ripley, April 3, 1845, here reprinted from John Thomas Codman, *Brook Farm, Historic and Personal Memoirs* (Boston: Arena, 1894), p. 150.

DEAR SIR:—In withdrawing from the Association I cannot believe it necessary for me to say to you that I do not cease to feel an interest, a very deep interest, in the success of the cause in which I have in my humble way labored with you for the last few years. The final success of this attempt to live out the great and holy idea of association for brotherly coöperation, will be to me a greater cause for joy than any merely personal benefit to myself could be.

I wished, but could not do it, to say to you and others how much I love and esteem you, and how painful it is for me to leave those to whom I am so much indebted for personal kindnesses. You know me well enough to believe that I feel, more deeply than I can express, pained by this separation. God bless you. God bless and prosper the Association individually and collectively.

Yours truly,
MINOT PRATT.

no. 70 ⤸

> A letter from George William Curtis to John S. Dwight. Here reprinted (in part) from *Early Letters of George William Curtis to John S. Dwight*, edited by George W. Cooke (New York: Harper & Brothers, 1898), pp. 209-210.

Concord, April 5th, 1845

Judge, my unitary friend, how grateful was your letter, perfumed with flowers and moonlight, to an unfortunate up to his ears in manure and dish-water! For no happier is my plight at this moment. I snatch a moment out of the week wherein the significance of that fearful word *business* has been revealed to me to send an echo, a reply to your good letter.

Since Monday we have been moving and manuring and fretting and fuming and rushing desperately up and down turnpikes with bundles and baskets, and have arrived at the end of the week [210] barely in order. Yesterday, in the midst, while I was escorting a huge wagon of that invaluable farming wealth, I encountered Mrs. Pratt and family making their reappearance in civilization. All Brook Farm in the golden age seemed to be strapped to the rear of their wagon as baggage, for Mrs. Pratt was the first lady I saw at Brook Farm, where ladyhood blossomed so fairly. Ah! my minute is over, and I must leave you to lie in wait for another. . . .

G. W. C.

no. 71

From the *Phalanx*, Volume I, Number 22 (Saturday, May 3, 1845), pp. 336-337.

CELEBRATION OF FOURIER'S BIRTH DAY AT BROOK FARM.

The members of the Brook Farm Phalanx commemorated the birth-day [April 7] of Fourier by a festival of unusual interest.

The disciples of Fourier have met for years past in various parts of the world, to commune together and offer up the homage of grateful hearts for his advent upon the earth, and these meetings have been signalized by an atmosphere of lofty and pure sentiment, brilliant wit, and soul-stirring eloquence, seldom if ever excelled on similar occasions; but they were *simplistic* meetings after all—the meetings merely of theorists, of recievers [sic] [337] of a doctrine, who could pay but a *simple* tribute to the memory of Fourier,—the tribute of intellectual conviction; at Brook Farm, however, a practical Association, the meeting assumed a higher and more impressive character. It was a meeting not of theorists alone, convinced of the truth of the doctrine of Association, but of workers who illustrated them in practice; and their offering was a *compound* tribute to the memory of Fourier,—the tribute of the mind and of the hands together. This was the feeling of those who had participated in former festivities, and it was one which deeply impressed all present.

An Association, indeed, seems the only fit place for the celebration of Fourier's birth-day, where old and young, men and women, can join in the delightful service of rendering a respectful and affectionate tribute to his memory; there all can unite in offering up the incense of hearts overflowing with gratitude to him who consecrated his life to the holy purpose of elevating mankind to their destiny on earth, in admiring that exalted genius which has comprehended and revealed the sublimest truths of nature, and in invoking with hope made confident by partial experience, the speedy coming of that era of Harmony and Love and Peace which all the Prophets have announced, and which will be realized in Association.

The company assembled in the evening in the dining-hall of the Association, in which the taste and skill of the members had been displayed in numerous beautiful decorations and appropriate emblems. The ceilings and the walls were festooned with evergreen, and the tables in the centre and corners of the room ornamented with the richest and most fragrant flowers from the green-house of the Association. At one end of the hall stood the bust of FOURIER in plaster lately received from Paris; his brow wreathed with myrtle; and on the wall behind it, extending nearly across the room in large Roman letters of evergreen, was inscribed the name of FOURIER. Under the name the date of his birth, 1772. On each side of this inscription were the emblems of Industry and Hope,—the bee-hive and the anchor. At the opposite end of the room hung the banner of Association, composed of the primary colors, and bordered with white, the emblem of Unity. Over the banner a plain tablet of azure was placed, on which the words UNIVERSAL UNITY, were emblazoned in letters of silvery white. The Lyre, intertwined with flowers, as an emblem of harmony, the frame of which was white, and the strings of the seven prismatic colors, corresponding to the scale of the seven spiritual passions, occupied a conspicuous place on one side of the room; and opposite to it an inscription from the New Testament, containing the promise of the blessed Comforter as confirming the hopes which swell with rapture the breasts of those who have faith that Association will fulfil the glorious prophecies of inspiration, and bring down upon earth the kingdom of Heaven. Another tablet was inscribed with the fundamental law of Fourier, *Les Attractions sont proportionelle aux Destinees.* The tables offered a simple and elegant repast. The scene received an indescribable charm from the perfect social equality of all present, alike of the servers and the served, and the cordial friendship which animated every bosom and sparkled in every eye.

After an hour spent in social converse and enjoyment around the festive board, the President, Mr. Ripley, addressed the company in a short speech, calling their attention to the relation in which, as members of an Association, they stood with regard to Fourier, the discoverer of the laws of Universal Unity. Mr. Ripley gave a rapid sketch of the character of Fourier, his claims to the gratitude and reverence of the world, and the influence he was destined to exert upon the prospects of humanity. He then stated that he should read some select passages from the Scriptures, as being more appropriate to the spirit of the occasion than any language which he could command. These passages, selected from various portions of the Old and New Testament, presented an exalted view of the divine wisdom which was ever flowing into the hearts of the chosen leaders of the human race,—of the assurance of support from the Providence of God to every sincere and faithful effort for the elevation of man,—and of the sublime harmonies which the earth and its inhabitants are destined to enjoy in the progress of the ages.

When Mr. Ripley had concluded, there followed a beautiful chant by the choir, which enlivened the evening by occasional strains of delightful music.

Mr. Brisbane then passed upon Fourier a glowing eulogium, and described in graphic and thrilling language the noble old man as he had personally known him.

Mr. Dana followed in some eloquent and inspiring remarks upon Universal Unity, happily alluding to the tablet on which the words were inscribed.

Speeches and sentiments of great brilliancy were delivered in the course of the evening by Messrs. Ripley, Dana, Orvis, Cabot, Westacott, Allen, Ryckman, and Dwight, members of the Phalanx, and Francis G. Shaw, Brisbane, and Macdaniel, guests.

Before the company separated, they united in singing Old Hundred. The scene altogether was one which will long dwell in our memory.

A GUEST.

no. 72 ～

A notice in the *Phalanx*, Volume I, Number 23 (Wednesday, May 28, 1845), pp. 354-355.

THE HARBINGER

DEVOTED TO SOCIAL AND POLITICAL PROGRESS,

Published simultaneously at New York and
Boston, by the Brook Farm Phalanx.

"All things, at the present day, stand
provided and prepared, and
await the light."

Under this title it is proposed to publish a weekly newspaper, for the examination and discussion of the great questions in social science, politics, literature, and the arts, which command the attention of all believers in the progress and elevation of humanity.

In politics, the *Harbinger* will be democratic in its principles and tendencies; cherishing the deepest interest in the advancement and happiness of the masses; warring against all exclusive privilege in legislation, political arrangements, and social customs; and striving with the zeal of earnest conviction, to promote the triumph of the high democratic faith, which it is the chief mission of the nineteenth century to realize in society. Our devotion to the democratic principle will lead us to take the ground of fearless and absolute independence in regard to all political parties, whether professing attachment to that principle or hostility to it. We know that fidelity to an idea can never be measured by adherence to a name; and hence we shall criticise all parties with equal severity; though we trust that the sternness of truth will always be blended with the temperance of impartial candor. With tolerance for all opinions, we have no patience with hypocrisy and pretence; least of all, with that specious fraud, which would make a glorious principle the apology for personal ends. It will therefore be a leading object of the *Harbinger* to strip the disguise from the pre-[355] vailing parties, to show them in their true light, to give them due honor, to tender them our grateful reverence whenever we see them true to a noble principle; but at all times and on every occasion, to expose false professions, to hold up hollow-heartedness and duplicity to just indignation, to warn the people against the demagogue who would cajole them by honeyed flatteries, no less than against the devotee of mammon who would make them his slaves.

The *Harbinger* will be devoted to the cause of a radical, organic social reform as essential to the highest development of man's nature, to the production of those elevated and beautiful forms of character of which he is capable, and to the diffusion of happiness, excellence, and universal harmony upon the earth. The principles of universal unity as taught by Charles Fourier, in their application to society, we believe, are at the foundation of all genuine social progress; and it will ever be our aim, to discuss and defend these principles, without any sectarian bigotry, and in the catholic and comprehensive spirit of their great discoverer. While we bow to no man as an authoritative, infallible master, we revere the genius of Fourier too highly, not to accept, with joyful welcome, the light which he has shed on the most intricate problems of human destiny. The social reform, of whose advent the signs are every where visible, comprehends all others; and in laboring for its speedy accomplishment, we are conscious that we are devoting our best ability to the removal of oppression and injustice among men, to the complete emancipation of the enslaved, to the promotion of genuine temperance, and to the elevation of the toiling and downtrodden masses to the inborn rights of humanity.

In literature, the *Harbinger* will exercise a firm and impartial criticism, without respect of persons or parties. It will be made a vehicle for the freest thought, though not of random speculations; and with a generous appreciation of the various forms of truth and beauty, it will not fail to expose such instances of false sentiment, perverted taste, and erroneous opinion, as may tend to vitiate the public mind, or degrade the individual character. Nor will the literary department of the *Harbinger* be limited to criticism alone. It will receive contributions from various pens, in different spheres of thought; and free from dogmatic exclusiveness, will accept all that in any way indicates the unity of Man with Man, with Nature, and with God. Consequently, all true science, all poetry and arts, all sincere literature, all religion that is from the soul, all wise analyses of mind and character will come within its province.

We appeal for aid in our enterprise to the earnest and hopeful spirits in all classes of society. We appeal to all who, suffering from a resistless discontent in the present order of things, with faith in man and trust in God, are striving for the establishment of universal justice, harmony, and love. We appeal to the thoughtful, the aspiring, the generous everywhere, who wish to see the reign of heavenly truth triumphantly supplanting the infernal discords and falsehoods, on which modern society is built, for their sympathy, friendship, and practical co-operation, in the undertaking which we announce today.

Among the leading contributors will be Parke Godwin, W. H. Channing, Albert Brisbane, Osborne Macdaniel, and Horace Greeley of New York, George Ripley, Charles A. Dana, John S. Dwight, L. W.

Ryckman, and John Allen of Brook Farm, and Francis G. Shaw of West Roxbury.

The *Harbinger* will be published in New York by Burgess, Stringer, & Co., No. 222 Broadway, and in Boston, by Redding & Col, No. 8 State St.

TERMS.—The price to subscribers will be $2.00 a year, or $1.00 for six months, payable invariably in advance. Ten copies will be supplied for $15.00. Communications and remittances may be addressed to the publisher in New York and Boston, or to the "Editors of the Harbinger," Brook Farm, West Roxbury, Mass.

☞ The subscription lists of the Phalanx and Social Reformer are transferred to the Harbinger. Subscribers to those papers whose terms of subscription have expired, are respectfully requested to renew their subscriptions, and forward the advance payment, as directed above.

☞ Postmasters, regular periodical agents, and friends of the Associative movement are requested to notice our terms. TEN copies for FIFTEEN Dollars, to one address. The cash in all cases to accompany the order.

WEST ROXBURY, May 3, 1845.

NOTICE TO THE SUBSCRIBERS OF THE PHALANX.

Our subscribers will see by the Prospectus that the name of "The Phalanx" is to be changed for that of "The Harbinger," and that the paper is to be printed in future by the Brook Farm Phalanx. The reasons for this arrangement are many and cogent, but to explain them at length seems unnecessary, as we have no doubt the announcement of it will give perfect satisfaction to all.

The *Phalanx* for some time past has been very irregular in its publication, owing to circumstances which could not be controlled, for which we trust our readers will make due allowance. One more number will be published immediately, accompanied by an Index and Title page, which will close the volume. The *Harbinger* will be sent to all our subscribers for the remaining numbers of the paper which may be due them respectively.

Need we appeal to our friends to aid the new enterprize to the utmost of their power by obtaining subscribers to the *Harbinger?* Its success depends in a great measure on their efforts, and we hope they will feel the responsibility which devolves on them. Let every man make a point to get *one* subscriber at least; and let every one whose term expires at the end of the six months' volume renew his subscription immediately, as directed in the Prospectus.

no. 73 ༺

Letter from R. W. Emerson to John Sullivan Dwight, here reprinted from G. W. Cooke, *John Sullivan Dwight . . . A Biography* (Boston: Small, Maynard and Company, 1898), pp. 103-105, where it is printed in part, and without date. This letter is listed, but not reprinted, in *Letters of Ralph Waldo Emerson*, edited by Ralph L. Rusk, III, 289, as having been written in 1845 about June 1.

Your letter was very kind and friendly, and one is always glad that anything is adventured in the midst of so much excusing and impediment; and yet, though I should heartily rejoice to aid in an uncommitted journal,—not limited by the name of any man,—I will not promise a line [104] to any which has chosen a patron. We shall never do anything if we begin with being somebody else. Then, though I admire the genius of Fourier, since I have looked a little into his books, yet it is only for his marvellous tactics. He is another French soldier or rather mathematician, such as France is always turning out; and they apply their wonderful ciphering indifferently to astronomy, chemistry, war, or politics. But they are a sub-type, as modern science now says, deficient in the first faculty, and therefore should never be allowed the lead in grand enterprises, but may very well serve as subordinate coadjutors, where their power as economists will stand in good stead. It seems sadly true that the scholars and philosophers, and I might say also the honest and well-disposed part of society, have no literary organ or voice which is not desperately sectarian; and we are always impelled towards organization by the fear that our little power will become less. But, if things come to a still worse pass, indignation will perhaps summon a deeper-voiced and wiser muse than our cool New England has ever listened to. I am sure she will speak French. But she will, I doubt not, have many wreaths of honor to bestow on you and your friends at Brook Farm; for courage and hope and real performance, God and man and muses love.

You see how little and how much faith I have. As far as your journal is sectarian, I shall respect it at a distance. If it should become catholic, I shall [105] be found suing for a place in it. Respectfully and affectionately yours.

no. 74 ∿

George Ripley, "What Do You Propose?" *The Harbinger*, I (June-December, 1845), 48.

June 28, 1845

WHAT DO YOU PROPOSE?

We have often been asked, What do the friends of Association propose to themselves, in the reform to which they are devoted? Let us answer in a few words,—by the systematic organization of labor, to make it more efficient, productive, and attractive; in this way, to provide for the abundant gratification of all the intellectual, moral, and physical wants of every member of the Association; and thus to extirpate the dreadful inequalities of external condition, which now make many aspects of society so hideous; and to put all in possession of the means of leading a wise, serene and beautiful life, in accordance with the eternal laws of God and the highest aspirations of their own nature. This in modern society is the exception and not the rule, among all classes. Are we not laboring for an end which should command the respect and sympathy of every sincere philanthropist? Is it not worth while for the most cultivated and intelligent minds, at least to look at a remedy which promises to eradicate absolute poverty, do away with the temptations to crime, make the executioner and constable useless functionaries, diffuse inward contentedness and peace, and thus bless the whole population? This reform is based upon the practical application of Christianity to the arrangements of society, under the guidance of an accurate and profound science. To doubt its practicability or its final accomplishment, would be to call in question both science and religion at once.

no. 75 ∿

Two ads from *The Harbinger*. The first issue of *The Harbinger* is dated Saturday, June 14, 1845. *The Harbinger* ad appeared for the first time on the back page of the issue of June 21, 1845. Gerrish's ad appeared for the first time on the back page of the issue of June 28, 1845. Both ads were repeated in almost every issue thereafter until the group at Brook Farm disbanded in 1847.

WEST ROXBURY OMNIBUS!

Leaves Brook Farm at 7 A. M., and 2 1-2 P. M., for Boston, via Spring Street, Jamaica Plains, and Roxbury. Returning, leaves Doolittle's, City Tavern, Brattle Street, at 9 1-2 A. M., and 5 P. M. Sunday excepted.

N. R. GERRISH

June 28, 1845

THE HARBINGER

Is published simultaneously at New York and Boston, by the BROOK FARM PHALANX, every Saturday morning. Office in New York, BURGESS, STRINGER & CO., No. 222 Broadway; and in Boston, REDDING & CO., No. 8 State Street.

TERMS. Two Dollars a year, or One Dollar for six months, payable invariably in advance. Ten copies for Fifteen Dollars.

COMMUNICATIONS
AND REMITTANCES

should be addressed to the publishers in New York and Boston, or to the "Editors of the Harbinger," Brook Farm, West Roxbury, Mass.

☞ Periodical Agents, Post Master, Association Clubs, and all persons wishing to diffuse the principles defended in this paper, by forwarding FIFTEEN DOLLARS, will be supplied with TEN COPIES.

☞ Single copies for sale at the Harbinger Offices, No. 222 Broadway, New York, and No. 8 State Street, Boston, and by booksellers and periodical agents throughout the U. States. Price, 6 1-4 cents.

no. 76 ～

Letter from Marianne Dwight to Anna Parsons, here reprinted
from Marianne Dwight, *Letters from Brook Farm 1844-1847,*
edited by Amy L. Reed (Poughkeepsie, N. Y.: Vassar College,
1928), pp. 114-116.

Brook Farm.—The last day of summer.
[Aug. 31, 1845.]

DEAREST ANNA,

. . . C. P. Cranch is with us now.—Last evening he made for us the
sweetest and most delightful music. Will anything recall the past so
vividly as music? I was carried back to our old home in Boston by
hearing the same songs sung by the same sweet, rich voice. The effect
was strange. All late events, all this life in Association, its aims, its
efforts, its surroundings, seemed to me like a dream, from which I had
just awakened. [115]

Oh! Anna, you ask what is there worth doing? . . . I have often
the same thoughts and feelings.—But this I believe is certain; we trouble
ourselves a great deal too much about what we shall do,—we are not
content to remain in our own spheres, and receive the sunshine and the
dew that heaven sends us,—but must break violently out of them and
go hunting about where we do not belong, and stumbling in paths
where our feet can never walk. It is not so difficult a matter to tell
what to do. I must do the very thing that lies clearly before me to
do this very minute; and that done,—the next minute will bring its
own plain work. If I can see into the past and future and understand
the universal bearing of each action, why!, so much the more interesting; but this is not necessary to keep me in the right path.

Fear not,—our friend[1] shall not have the honor of preventing me
from writing to you. You are marching ahead with your conclusions;
you speak of a crisis of which I do not think—or if such a thought
comes, I banish it. It is not a matter of thought with me,—something
deeper than thought controls here,—but I have nothing new to say—
when I see you we will talk. You careless child, to write as you did,
and send your letter unfastened by the wafer,—don't do so again.

Last evening ten people came to spend Sunday and we have bestowed them all. You will see Mr. Kay next Sunday if you come.
How delightful to hear Mary Bullard sing at our Sunday meeting. . . .

"A new day," yes, that was well said. Channing gave us a pictorial

---

[1] John Orvis.

sermon, a sketch of a temple of worship to be raised here on Brook Farm, as he saw it in his mind's eye.

[116] The picture was real to us, so glowingly was it described. It was sacred and exquisitely beautiful. I never saw anything like it; and there stands that holy temple, I see it yet, of circular form, lighted from above, with its pictures of the infant Jesus, of the crucifixion, and the resurrection—with its white marble altar; that temple where music would rise to heaven and where there would always be flowers. He closed with solemn exhortations to us, to be true, to be earnest, to be wise, etc., etc. It was a comfort to me to feel that he did but repeat to me and renew in me resolutions I had already taken. Would I could be faithful to them!

I miss Mary Lincoln much. The strange child! No one can accuse her of being a civilizee, for she is one of the least civilized beings I have ever met with. I can't help liking her, I believe her aims are high, —but perhaps she is so independent as not to consult sufficiently other people's happiness and convenience—she is very childish—a mere baby in some of her ways; and to this I now attribute many of her odd actions. With much purity, she has, it seems to me, very little delicacy for a woman.

Gossip talks loud at Brook Farm about Charles Dana and Eunice, says they will be united in marriage—perhaps it is not true,—but I do know the symptoms are very strong.

I expect Cranch to paint and draw some whilst here. Mr. Grant is here from the Ohio Phalanx. A Miss Blackwell is with us from Flushing. Mrs. Cote has come back here to board. Sarah W[hitehouse] has gone to New York on a visit. Maria Dana has returned from New Hampshire, is much out of health apparently—I am somewhat anxious about her. . . . Write to me. Give my love to Hingham friends. . . . Adieu, dear friend.

THY MARIANNE.

no. 77 ✒

From John S. Dwight, "Individuality in Association," *The Harbinger,* I (June-December, 1845), 264-265.

October 4, 1845

INDIVIDUALITY IN ASSOCIATION.

The most prevailing fear about Association is on the score of that undefined thing, Individuality. The very vagueness of the term, as used, however, is proof that it covers more than is understood. False Individuality is a thing very well defined; but of true Individuality the scientific account is locked up in the future. Yet it shall soon be unlocked, since this new light has been thrown upon its complement, or true Association. We are prepared to take the ground that there is not and never can be Individuality, so long as there is not Association. Without true union no part can be true. The members were made for the body; if the whole body be incoherent, every member of it will be developed falsely, will become shrunken or overgrown, distorted and weakened, since it will have [265] either more or less than its share, both of duty and of sustenance. Variety itself is dull, if it lack unity; for unity is the beginning and end of variety.

Another fact, the counterpart of that just stated, must be put with it to make up the truth. If we must comprehend the unity of the whole, before we can decide what is due to each component part, if Association only can explain Individuality; so too, on the other hand, our idea of true Association, of the collective destiny of Man, comes mainly from our knowledge of the individual. The rule *"Attractions proportional to Destinies,"* is all the guide we have. Personal peculiarities furnish all the data to any calculation of the true laws of Society. They are troublesome enough now; each demands what no existing society can give; each is strongest where least work awaits him, and most willing where he is not wanted. The "general good" is so abstract, and general measures are so blind, that each is driven even to exaggerated assertion of himself, stands upon "reserved rights," pleads the "law within," grows transcendental, as it were, in self defence, and feverishly afraid of getting swallowed up and lost in that soul-less corporation, called the Whole. The individual sphere protests against the violation to which it is continually liable from any public interest short of that of true integral Association, concentric with the universal unity of all things. Individualism, to be sure, is one-sided, and passions are unreasonable, and characters and tendencies unmanageable, and unavailable, almost, for harmony; and yet they are the only elements given in the problem. Think not to silence them, but study them. They are but so many distracted cries of each one *for his place*. They clamor to fulfil their destiny. We are letters sealed and sent by the hand of the All-Wise; but whither? each is clearly superscribed and directed, could we only read the language; the superscription is our individuality; that we must know, and the general geography of the world, into which we are sent, we must know, to reach our points of delivery respectively. These individualities, well read, are the compass which will conduct us, understandingly, and in harmonic distribution, into all the unexplored ports of the boundless continent of Universal Unity. . . .

no. 78 ~

Letter from Marianne Dwight to Anna Parsons, here reprinted from Marianne Dwight, *Letters from Brook Farm 1844-1847,* edited by Amy L. Reed (Poughkeepsie, N. Y.: Vassar College, 1928), pp. 122-126.

Pilgrim House, Sunday a. m., Oct. 19, '45.

MY DEAR ANNA,

A bright, beautiful Sabbath morning, and *you* in Boston! . . . All the week I have wished to write to you to tell you of last Sunday. It was the busiest day! In the morning, almost everything to do,—in the afternoon a walk to Oak Hill,—then our Eyrie meeting. Channing gave us a very fine address, speaking of the three aspects of Association, the economical, the social, the *religious*, dwelling especially upon the last; he expressed his deep conviction that without the religious element no attempt at Association could possibly succeed, and then he spoke particularly, with much warmth and enthusiasm, much beauty and eloquence, of the religious movement now taking place here. Finally, alluding to the presence of a good many strangers, and of some other persons who take no interest at all in the matter, he proposed that all who felt themselves prepared or in any way interested in the movement, should withdraw to the next room, to take measures for carrying it into execution. About twenty went into the library. I was perplexed, astonished, I expected a full rush of people,—I asked if I were doing right, if we all had done right, to come out of the room. But I saw no way to avoid it. We could not have done otherwise,—it was a necessary step in order to form any organization; with W. H. C. and others I felt sure it grew out of the deepest feeling, and I was with them, because I did not feel that I could [123] be left out. Some who were known to be deeply interested stayed behind and this was not pleasant . . .

Sunday evening. We have had a delightful day. Our meeting was full of interest. Many more joined us. I thought I never had felt my heart so expand with love,—I never had experienced anything so like *social* worship before. Messrs. Ripley, Wolcott, Allen, Orvis and

Kleinstrup were added to our committee. Channing directed his remarks to us to three points. First, that we should avoid rallying around a priest, but should feel that the spirit of Love was the centre of union —that God was with us. 2d, that we should not unite in a creed (for the truth is not yet revealed) but in the spirit of reverence for truth, and in patience waiting for it to come. 3d, that we must exercise charity,—for every resolution we break we must have a new vow, for every fault in another, a new forgiveness.

. . . .

In much love
MARIANNE

no. 79 ～

Letter from Marianne Dwight to Anna Parsons, here reprinted from Marianne Dwight, *Letters from Brook Farm 1844-1847*, edited by Amy L. Reed (Poughkeepsie, N. Y.: Vassar College, 1928), pp. 126-128.

Sunday eve., Nov. 9, '45.

MY DEAR ANNA,

Thanks for your letter. Here are Fanny and I, shut up in our room. Fanny sends her love, and wishes you were in quarantine with us. Such times and such *humbugry* even here in Association! I don't know that anybody has had the small pox yet but little Fred Allen[1] (and his case was slight), but as a precautionary measure the Cottage has been turned inside out, (and our elastic Pilgrim House has swallowed up its contents) and has been made into a hospital, and thither Fred[2] has been carried with his attendants, and Fred's father—who has either slight vareoloid [*sic*] or a cold—I don't know which, and Osborne[3] is imprisoned there as his nurse, and two men, symptomatic people, have been added to the number. Fanny[4] has had for three days one of her old colds, and day before yesterday was quite sick,—today is quite well, only a little headache and weak, and Amelia and Fanny Mac have

---

[1] John Allen did not believe in vaccination. His motherless small boy had the first case of smallpox. There was a serious epidemic but no fatal case.

[2] Fred Allen.

[3] Osborne Macdaniel.

[4] Fanny Dwight.

made a muster, and frightened the folks into thinking it vareoloid. It's the greatest absurdity in the world. So this morning the Archon urged her going to the Cottage. I told him, no—[127] that I would not yield my common sense to other people's absurdities. He said Fanny Mac gave it as her opinion that Fanny had the disease and Amelia was much alarmed. I said Fanny Mac knew nothing about it, and I didn't value her opinion in the matter, the least in the world, and we, knowing very well just Fanny's condition, would not risk sending her where she would be in danger of taking the contagion, unless some physician whose opinion I could respect said she had the symptoms. I told him it was ridiculous, nonsensical, and unreasonable, and that it was no easy matter for me to yield my sense of right to such follies; that if she had the symptoms she would thankfully go, but I would not trust that to any of the girls, for I tho't they were very ignorant in such matters. Finally he tho't she'd better not go to the Cottage, but I must seclude myself as well as her, and stay in our room all day and see what tomorrow would bring forth. I, of course, expressed that this was equally ridiculous and absurd, told him that to allay the panic of the people I would stay up for meals and not go among folks. So I have not seen our glorious Channing. I believe I am a *consummate fool* to have lost this. Oh! I said worse and harder things still to Mr. Ripley, for I knew that the panic, in Fanny's case, was a *got up* fear, and not a natural one. We've had a pretty good day of it. Some folks would come in, in spite of the quarantine, and then I've been to walk in the Phalanstery corridor. I've sewed and read. Fanny is nicely, and it seems to us such a farce, such a sham, that we make ourselves quite merry about it. I don't apprehend that the disease will spread here, to any extent. Many people have colds. Father has quite a severe cold. I don't know but the Cottage may get populous with people so afflicted. . . . [128] I've really raved today,—getting quite mad (John Cheever like) because the other people have gone mad. I'm sure I forgive them with all my heart, am just as friendly as ever, and check, as much as I can, every childish pang at the unfriendliness of some who are dear to me. . . .

Adieu—in love to thee—
MARIANNE

no. 80 ⌐⌐

Letter from Marianne Dwight to Frank Dwight, here reprinted from Marianne Dwight, *Letters from Brook Farm 1844-1847,* edited by Amy L. Reed (Poughkeepsie, N. Y.: Vassar College,

Monday evening, Nov. 10, [1845].

DEAR FRANK,

I keep my promise and send you a bulletin of health. Father is perhaps some better.—I guess he will be pretty well tomorrow,—tho' he
has not been so well as he appeared in the morning. Has kept his bed
nearly all day. Mother is much better, needs rest. Fanny is quite well
—[129] has not been out on account of the high wind. Has a little cold
sore upon her lip, which alarmed Eunice, who called me out to ask if
I was *sure* she had not eruption. I told her I would not listen to any
such nonsense, and afterwards told her from Fanny, that Fanny was
perfectly willing to compare faces with her. I went down to dinner.
Mr. and Mrs. Ripley looked in consternation, but not a word has been
said to me. She had previously told Martin he must not come to our
room, and forthwith he came. I found nobody else alarmed to see me
but all rather glad. And now comes the richest. When in the kitchen
this evening, I heard Amelia was sick. Someone says, "Is she going to
the Cottage?" "Oh yes, if she is not better tomorrow, she *wishes* to."
"Yes," says Maria Dana seeing me, "Miss Russell has *too much sense,*
not to respect people's feelings about it." I could not help saying, "I
hope she has sense enough to *know* whether she has the vareoloid or
not."

After coming home, Maria went in to see Miss Russell. I sent word
to her that if she was ill I would gladly go and see her, and do anything for her I could, provided she was not afraid of me. She sent
word she was not, so I went to her. In came Eunice, "Why Miss R.
are *you* sick?" "Yes, I'm sick." "You don't think it possible you could
have the vareoloid?" "Oh la! no indeed, I've a bad cold, and have a
sick head-ache—shall be well enough in the morning." Rather rich, was
it not? Just what she would not allow to be true of Fanny.

Mrs. Palisse has been on her bed all day. Dr. Stimpson says it's
nothing but a cold. Mr. Blake has a cold,—Kate Sloan has symptoms,
etc., etc. When I entered the kitchen at noon, Ma Ripley called out
very cheerfully, "Hallo, here comes Mary Ann!" "Yes," said I, "Mary
Ann is [130] quite tired of the sham." Nobody feared me, or has
feared Fanny, except Amelia, Mrs. R. and Fanny Mac.

It's a brilliant evening, *perfectly glorious*. I wish you were here. I've
had a fine day's leisure, for I couldn't go into Amelia's room to get my
painting materials. Many people are beginning to laugh at the panic. I
hope you didn't take cold going in. Mr. Dana goes in tomorrow. I do
hope *I* shall not get a cold. I will write you again by the next opportunity, to tell you how father and mother get along.

Your affectionate sister
MARIANNE

All well this a.m.—*Tuesday*.

no. 81 ~

Letter from Marianne Dwight to Frank Dwight, here reprinted from Marianne Dwight, *Letters from Brook Farm 1844-1847*, edited by Amy L. Reed (Poughkeepsie, N. Y.: Vassar College, 1928), pp. 130-132.

Tuesday evening, No. [11,] 1845.

DEAR FRANK,

Have just received your *pleasant* note and now for a little more fun, tho' I am heartily sick of the nonsense, and trust it has now come to an end. This morning as I was waiting on table Mr. Ripley called me to him, and requested that I would not endanger people as I did; it was not safe for one who had been so exposed to come down to the dining-room. I asked him how *exposed?* "Why, you've been much with Fanny." "Well," said I, "*she* hasn't been exposed, more than all of us, and has had no contagious disease, and is coming out herself today." Said he, "It is tho't she has the disease." "Who thinks so?" said I. "Many people have seen her, and no reasonable person thinks she has had anything but a cold." "Why," said he, "there's Miss Mac thinks so." (Fanny Mac and Mrs. R. heard all.) Said I, "I told you, the other day, what I tho't of Miss M.'s opinion. I violated my sense of right [131] and duty by staying away Sunday, and I can on no account consent to act so again. I will use no more needless caution." He requested me not to wait on Mr. Hatch, nor on *his* table, and not to come into the dining-room. I told him it was of no use, I was convinced what I ought to do, and I should do it. He urged very pleasantly all the while, till I told him I'd say no more, I would not waste words with him and walked off. I also told him it was a got up panic, and confined to three or four. Afterwards he came to me again—begged we would be careful and not appear about. I told him Fanny was as well as he. Said he, "You never can tell till the last minute, she may break out yet." I replied, "She is to all appearance, as well as you now. I don't know what she may have by and by, or what you may have. You may break out. Why don't you go and shut yourself up?"—at which he went off laughing. Fanny went to the Eyrie and spent the forenoon. We *all* went down to dinner and to tea, and have heard no more, except that tonight Fanny Mac made an apology to Frances for having made a statement that had given her friends a false impression of her sickness. I think she is well aware of her error. Amelia is still quite ill, tho' better,—much as Fanny was. Dr. Stimpson says it's nothing but a cold—wonder what she thinks of Fanny now! Abby Foord has come home and would stay in spite of her aunt's wishes—says nobody else is half so much afraid as Amelia. The Cottage has two new inmates, Mr. Capen and George Lloyd. The latter I fear is quite ill.

Wed. evening. What strange experiences we go thro' here! The Cottage is filling up. Mr. Monday, the tailor, Cate Sloan, and Mrs. Palisse have gone there today—all [132] plain cases of vareoloid, so say both father and Dr. Stimpson. Maria Dana has been very ill all the afternoon, is now in Amelia's room for the night. She has the symptoms beyond a doubt, and I fear will be severely ill. I've been with her, and with Mrs. Palisse and have sat at table with Mr. Capen. I could not find it in my heart to neglect the sick people in our own house. Amelia is a little better tonight. Hers don't appear to be vareoloid.

Thursday a. m. I will add that Fanny continues very well and is strong as usual and at work. Mother has resumed her duties. Father seems feeble but is about, and has visited all the sick. There never was such a time here—so many people ill. In the pecuniary way, it must be a great loss to us. It is well we find ludicrous things to laugh at, for there is really a dark side to the affair. Still I trust this is the worst of it, and soon all will be better. Write soon.

In haste
MARIANNE

no. 82 ❧

Letter from Marianne Dwight to Anna Parsons, here reprinted from Marianne Dwight, *Letters from Brook Farm 1844-1847*, edited by Amy L. Reed (Poughkeepsie, N. Y.: Vassar College, 1928), pp. 136-139.

Brook Farm, Sunday, Dec. 7, 1845.

MY DEAR ANNA,

I was glad to get even a few lines from you today, and feel prompted to say a great many things to you,—but I do not like to put upon paper what I could say to you upon those subjects now of the deepest moment to me. So I will begin at least with more trifling matters—as this—I think I have about recovered my health,—I was obliged to keep shut up a few days, not because I was really ill, but because I was tormented with the itching and burning of an eruption very similar to erisipelas (I *can't* spell it) or St. Anthony's fire. Now I am quite well except a slight cold. We have had no new cases of small pox for two or three weeks, and have no reason to suppose we shall have any more. Our patients have nearly all left the hospital. They are all quite well excepting Mrs. Palisse, who is recovering fast. She came as near death as possible, and it will be long ere she is quite well. She will be, they say, badly marked. Jenny and little Fred will bear the marks a long time, but I thank Heaven it is no worse. I trust the Cottage will soon be restored to us, then the Hosmers will come back and the Treadwells, and soon Lizzie Curson. You speak of a crisis,—this is one of the things I can't write fully about, and whatever I may say will be confidential. We have reached, I believe, our severest crisis. If we survive it, we shall probably go on safely and not be obliged to struggle thro' another. I think here lies the difficulty,— we have not had business men to conduct our affairs—we have had *no* strictly business transactions from the beginning, and those among us who have some business talents, see this error, and feel that we cannot go on as we have [137] done. They are ready to give up if matters cannot be otherwise managed, for they have no hope of success here under the past and present government. All important matters have been done up in council of one or two or three individuals, and everybody else kept in the dark (perhaps I exaggerate somewhat) and now it must be so no longer;—our young men have started "enquiry meetings," and it must be a sad state of things that calls for such measures. We are perplexed by debts, by want of capital to carry on any business to advantage,—by want of our Phalanstery or the means to finish it. From want of wisdom we have failed to profit by some advantages we have had. And then Brisbane is vague and unsteady; the help he promised us from his efforts comes not—but on the contrary, he and other friends to the cause in New York, instead of trying to concentrate all efforts upon Brook Farm as they promised, have wandered off,—have taken up a vast plan of getting $100,000 and starting anew, so they are for disposing of us in the shortest manner,—would set their foot upon us, as it were, and divert what capital might come to us. What then remains for us, and where are our hopes? I will tell you. We must be independent of the New York friends, and define our position to them, and let them know that we are determined to go on, if we can, and come to *something* (what Heaven wills), if we do not realize a perfect association. Then we must raise some money,—we must have $10,000 at least, before spring, or we may as well die! We can do nothing without it. How shall we get it? We will send out our group of lecturers,—John Allen will go; John Orvis will go, provided the council will take such steps first, that he can in conscience ask people to come here, and put in their money. He would not do it without some [138] change of policy, nor would he, I think be willing to remain. Fred (don't speak of it) has decided, unless he should see reason to change his mind, to leave and go into business awhile. His views and plans are noble,—he means to be working for Association abroad, outside,—and come in, by and by, when he sees a change and bring his earnings. But between you and me, not much would I give for what he will do for Association, if he leaves us— tho' I don't doubt his present intentions. But I look back a year and see what changes have gradually come over his mind, and what influences have been at work upon him, and bro't him to his present convictions,—that Brook Farm cannot succeed. My hopes are here; our council seems to be awake and ready for action; if we get the money, we will finish the building,—then we will enlarge our school, which should bring us in a handsome income. Our sash and blind business is very profitable, and may be greatly enlarged in the spring, the tailor's business is good, the tin block, and why do I forget the printing, and the Farm? Also we shall have together a better set of people than ever before. Heaven help us, and make us wise, for the failure of Brook Farm must defer the cause a long time. This place as it is (take it all in all) is the best place under the sky; why can't people see this, and look upon it hopefully and encouragingly?

J. O. sits with me quietly, reading the President's message. Oh! he is so much more constant and affectionate in his regard for me than I deserve. I believe now I do fully and deeply appreciate all. Announcements? No. All that I have said, I have said to you and to none else. Last evening M. A. Donelly was married to Westcott, and they are to live in Boston. Never did I long more to see you. [139] You would strengthen me and do me a world of good. Can't you come out? Dora must come. I would not have had her lately on any account, for she would have worked herself to death,—but very soon we shall be in a better fix for help in the various departments, so do make her come; she will be of great service to us and we will not quite kill her. . . . I am grieved at W. H. C.'s long illness. Oh! how we need him.

Adieu
MARIANNE

The Whitehouses are discontented at the North American Phalanx. . . .

no. 83 ◁

Letter from Albert Brisbane to George Ripley, here reprinted from John Thomas Codman, *Brook Farm, Historic and Personal Memoirs* (Boston: Arena, 1894), pp. 144-146.

New York, the 9th December, 1845.

MY DEAR RIPLEY:—Yours of the 3d just received, the 5th came to hand yesterday. I note all its contents in relation to your views upon the necessity of developing Brook Farm. The reason why I have spoken in some of my last letters of the best means of bringing Brook Farm to a close, and making preparations for a trial under more favorable circumstances, is this. In the middle of November I received a letter from Charles in which, in speaking of the varioloid, he stated the difficulties you have to contend with, and expressed fears for the future in such a way that I decided you had made up your minds to bring things to a close. I feared that Morton might be foreclosing his mortgage, which would be a most serious affair. This is the cause of my adverting to a possible dissolution and the necessity of looking ahead to meet in the best and most proper manner such a contingency.

As to any opinion of what is to be done, it is easily explained.

First, we must raise a sufficient amount of capital, and the amount must not be small.

Second, when that is secured we must prepare and work out a plan of scientific organization sufficiently complete in its details to serve as a guide in organizing an Association. For my own part, I feel no capability whatever of directing an Association by discipline, by ideas of duty, moral suasion and any other similar means. I want organization; I want a mechanism suited and adapted to human nature, so that human nature can follow its laws and attractions and go rightly, and be its own guide. I might do something in directing such an organization, but would be useless in any other way. As we all like to be active, I would like exceed-[145]ingly to take part in and help construct a scientific organization.

How can we raise the capital necessary to do something effectual? I see but two ways. The first if for C. and I—and if he will not do it, then for you and I, if you would possibly engage in it—to lecture patiently and perseveringly in various parts of the country, having the translation of Fourier with us, *and continue at the work* until we have enlisted and interested men enough who will subscribe each a certain sum sufficient to form the fund we deem necessary. Patience and perseverance would do this. One hundred men who would subscribe one thousand dollars cash, would give us a fine capital. Something effectual, I think, might be done with such an amount; less than that would, I fear, be patchwork.

Second, if C. or you cannot engage in this enterprise, then I shall see what I can do alone. I shall make first the trial of the steel business —that will now soon be determined, probably in a few weeks. There are chances that it may be a great thing; if that turns out nothing, then

I shall take Fourier's work and do something of what I propose you or C. and I should do together.

If the capital can be had, where shall we organize you will ask? That is a thing to be carefully considered, and which we cannot decide at present.

Placed under the circumstances you are, all these speculations will appear foreign to the subject that interests you, and useless. You want capital, and immediately, for Brook Farm. Now it seems to me a problem as perplexing to get fifteen thousand dollars for Brook Farm as it does to raise one hundred thousand dollars. Where can it be had? The New Yorkers who have money, G., T., S., etc., are all interested in and pledged to raise ten thousand dollars for the North American Phalanx, to pay off its mortgage. You might [146] as well undertake to raise dead men, as to attain any considerable amount of capital from the people here; I have tried it so often that I know the difficulties.

The fact is, we have a great work to accomplish, that of organizing an Association, and to do it we must have the means adequate to the task, and to get these means we must make the most persevering and Herculean efforts. We must go at the thing in earnest, and labor until we have secured the means. I really see no other way or avenue to success; if you do, I should be glad to hear your explanation of it. Fifteen thousand dollars might do a great deal at Brook Farm, but would it do the thing effectually—would it make a trial that would impress the public? And for anything short of that, none of us, I suppose, would labor.

We are surrounded by great difficulties. I see no immediate chance of obtaining a capital sufficient for a good experiment, and until we have the capital to organize upon quite a complete scale, I should say that it would be a very great misfortune to dissolve Brook Farm. No uncertain prospects should exercise any influence; the means must be had in hand before we made any decisive movement towards a removal or organizing in a more favorable location, even if you were perfectly willing to leave New England and the neighborhood of Boston. As I said I spoke of it, and should be urged to make at once the greatest efforts to obtain capital only under the fear that circumstances might force a crisis upon you.

I have touched merely upon generalities to-day; after further correspondence I will write you more in detail. I will also come on and see you if you deem it advisable. The other experiment keeps me here at present; I think that next week I shall test it. I am greatly rejoiced to hear that you are getting on well with the translation.

A. Brisbane.

no. *84* ～

Letter from Marianne Dwight to Anna Parsons, here reprinted from Marianne Dwight, *Letters from Brook Farm 1844-1847*, edited by Amy L. Reed (Poughkeepsie, N. Y.: Vassar College, 1928), pp. 139-142.

Friday, Dec. 12, 1845.

MY DEAR ANNA,

I have been so constantly occupied with various matters this week, that I scarcely remember what I said in my last letter to you; probably it was rather dismal and cheerless; but now we stand in clearer light, and I can give you a more encouraging statement. I have made C. K. N. promise to call and see you tomorrow, as he earnestly wishes to do, and I intend he shall be the bearer of this letter with its good tidings. We are not dead here, but live—our hearts are firm and true, our courage good, and our hands ready for action. I wish I could remember what I told you in my last,—it must have been the dark side of our affairs, I think, for then, I looked to the future with fear and trembling. We have had a most cheering meeting of the association on Wednesday evening. Fred was absent. Every one present was firm and determined, and *full of confidence* that we *shall* and *will* bring Brook Farm to success. There is no word of discouragement from anyone,—no thought [140] of anything but going on together with our best efforts,—there was one heart, one soul, one opinion, and all the strength and hope that comes from such union. And yet our position was carefully and candidly examined in its worst aspects; every argument that had been heard against our success was brought up and looked at. How small and insignificant they all seemed compared with the great ends we have in view! We felt that to be influenced by them would be treachery to the cause. I do not believe a man or woman here (of any value to the cause) would leave Brook Farm now, excepting Fred. Our dear, good warm-hearted, devoted Fred, for whose stability we would once have wagered everything valuable to us,— "our Fred," as we loved to call him,—has (not in wisdom as I think, but in weakness) yielded to the influences that have been so long and steadily and resolutely at work upon him, yielded even to the changing of his convictions. Still he calls himself an Associationist—still declares that in civilization he shall work only for the cause,—but he says Brook Farm *must* come to naught,—he believes it is not founded on so high a basis as something else will be, and he will wait and work for that something. Oh! it is sad to see him so deluded. I tell him he is deceiving himself—that when he quits Brook Farm he will soon cease to work for the movement,—he will be chained faster and firmer in a civilized hell. Has he not chosen sadly? Does not your heart ache for him?

To return to our meeting. It was glorious. Everything was asked and answered in good spirit. Mr. Ripley read a letter which he had written to Mr. Brisbane, defining our position; and declaring our intention to go on here, on this spot, and our reasons therefor, which letter gave us much [141] satisfaction. Then J. S. D. set forth clearly and at length, our present case, and the course of action the council had decided it would be best to pursue. He looked fearlessly at the strongest arguments which had been brought up in private conversation of late, against our chance of success, and showed how little they were really worth; that we must look at this movement in a higher point of view than a merely mercantile one, and be willing to be sustained by faith until the time comes when we shall be able to realize pecuniary success. After all this had been fully talked over, we had some very interesting conversation about the social atmosphere of the place,—the difficulty and importance of a cordial hospitality to strangers and newcomers,—the importance of cultivating a warm, genial, social feeling towards all. The tone of the meeting inspired us all, and especially our lecturers, John Orvis and Allen, who were to set off the next morning, for a fortnight's tour thru' Lynn, Marblehead, Gloucester, etc., with a view to procuring subscribers for the *Harbinger*, and ascertaining the amount of interest in the cause that may be relied on in that region. They will return at Christmas time, spend three or four days with us, then off again for many weeks, in another direction. May God inspire them, that their golden lips may utter divine words to the people, and kindle a fire in many hearts!

What a magnificent evening! I wonder how you are passing it. These are heavenly clear days that shine upon us now, are they not? How is it with you in Boston? Are you almost frozen? Our greenhouse is the most charming little spot that ever was. I wish more of the rich people in Boston would order bouquets now; Mr. K. could furnish really magnificent ones. It is a treat to go in there and enjoy one's self among the birds and flowers, and with the [142] conversation of Mr. K., the presiding genius. I passed an hour there the other evening by moonlight, with the flowers. Our sickness seems to be all over. Mrs. P.[1] leaves the Cottage tomorrow.

---

[1] Mrs. Palisse.

I regret C. K. N.'s[2] departure more than I can tell. He has been always a conspicuous, or rather an important object in the picture to me. I can hardly think of Brook Farm without him. The sweet, sad youth! He will feel the change still more than we. Think of him in a city life, if you can. Oh! it will kill him, soul and body. Wherever he is, may God bless him and cheer him. I hope you will have a pleasant call from him. When shall I see Dora, when thee? Do write.

Ever yours
MARIANNE

no. 85 ⚬

George Ripley, "Life in Association," *The Harbinger*, II (December 13, 1845-June 6, 1846), 32.

December 20, 1845

LIFE IN ASSOCIATION

The highest life, of which the nature of man is capable, is rarely witnessed, and then forms a signal exception to the general rule.

It is no wonder that theologians have so generally maintained the doctrine of innate, hereditary depravity. This was the only way, by which they could account for the universal prevalence of limited, distorted, noxious forms of character. The idea, on which their dogma was based, sprung from experience, from observation, from a correct knowledge of human action.

For what is every man soon taught by the intercourse of life? Certainly, the subjection of the world to the dominion of evil. He learns to calculate on selfishness, more or less disguised, on falsehood, however glossed over with the appearance of truth, on fraud, which though in fear of public opinion, is always ready to entrap the heedless.

It is an easy inference, that these monstrous evils are the true growth of human nature, that they belong to man as man, that they will never cease while his passions and propensities remain unchanged. A more profound view, however, shows us that the fault is not in the intrinsic elements of human nature, but in the imperfect institutions under which that nature is trained and developed.

The savage is not guilty of the frightful acts of cruelty, which make our eyes start from their sockets, because there is a necessary tendency to brutal ferocity in human nature, but because all the influences that have acted on him, all the excitements that have been applied to his passions, have been adapted to cherish the warlike spirit, to give him

2 Newcomb.

a taste for blood, to make revenge a deep joy to his soul, to convert all the sweet emotions of humanity into the spirit of the tiger and wolf. Place the savage in a different situation; let the first words that fall upon his ear be those of Christian gentleness and peace; let him be surrounded by generous and loving hearts; another spirit will be manifested; and you would almost say that he had been endowed with another nature.

The man who is so devoted to gaining wealth, that he appears on 'Change like a walking money-bag, with no ideas beyond his ledger and cash-book, with no hope but that of becoming a millionaire, and no fear but that of being surpassed in property by his more lucky neighbor, was not born to be a muck-worm; if he has not the faculties of an archangel, as some one has said, folded up within his bosom, he has the elements of goodness, disinterestedness, a sincere devotion to the common weal, and under more favorable influences, might have been a worthy, useful, and happy man, instead of being a little above the vilest reptile.

We cannot believe that the selfishness, the cold-heartedness, the indifference to truth, the insane devotion to wealth, the fierce antagonisms, the painted hypocrisies, the inward weariness, discontent, apathy, which are everywhere characteristic of the present order of society, have any permanent basis in the nature of man; they are the poisonous weeds that a false system of culture has produced; change the system and you will see the riches of the soil; a golden fruitage will rejoice your eye; but persist in the mode, which the experience of a thousand years has proved defective, and you can anticipate no better results. Men do not gather grapes of thorns, nor figs of thistles. But if you would rear the vine, and the fig-tree, so that you may enjoy their products in full luxuriance and beauty, you must not plant them in the hot sand, deprive them of the rain and dew of heaven, expose them to destructive insects, or violent animals; but ascertain the cultivation which is adapted to their nature, and surround them with the influences, which God who made the vine and the fig-tree, made also essential to their perfection.

So with the influences of modern society. They do not give fit nutriment to the noblest forms of character. They do not make man what he is intended to be by the constitution of his nature. They help him not to fulfil the destiny which is assigned to him by the Creator. It is because we are convinced that the Associative Order is the Divine Order, that life in Association is the only true life of the soul, just as harmony with outward nature is essential to the true life of the body, that we are unwilling to give sleep to our eyes or slumber to

our eyelids till we witness the commencement of the great and solemn
work, which is to emancipate man from the terrible scourges of a
false order of society, and reinstate him in the glorious life for which
a benignant Providence has adapted his nature.

no. 86 ❧

From John Sullivan Dwight, a review of *Oliver Cromwell's Letters
and Speeches: with Elucidations,* by Thomas Carlyle, *The Harbinger,* II (December 13, 1845-June 6, 1846), 56-59.

January 3, 1846

[57] . . . The fault we find with all his comments is, that in Cromwell, as in all his heroes, Mr. Carlyle makes one or two virtues stand
for all. If Cromwell was sincerely bent on having a reign of justice
established in England, if he had faith in the word of God, if he could
give his whole strength unwaveringly to one end, if he was clear-
sighted enough to see through the pedantic formulas of the Presby-
terian party, and not stay his arm till the principle was acknowledged
in its length and breadth, the principle of civil and religious liberty
(of liberty to do right however, not to do wrong!)—yet was not he
sufficiently narrow in his ideas of right? did he extend liberty to
Papists? and was he not unscrupulous of measures and of consequences
in the energy with which he did his work? The "Cromwell Curse"
can never be forgotten in Ireland; though Mr. Carlyle may deem it
proof of a strong stomach and a clear head, that he did not attempt
to sprinkle "rose-water upon the wounds of that bleeding country,
but had force of character enough to resort to more terrible surgery."
    Then again, the absorbing of everything around the hero into
him, as if he were it all, is an interesting art of effect, which will hardly
stand the test of reason. Your hero, according to this, is the one believing man, the one that has got a meaning in him, and proceeds by
God's impulse to act it out. These, however, are very rare, one or
so, only, in an age. Yet does not all the virtue of it in these one or two,
reside in the fact, that it ought also to be the virtue of all men? You
call them manly! How, O Thomas Carlyle? Was it, then, the design
of Providence that there should be only one man, the rest not men, but
shams, or good, easy, simple, faithful followers of that one, to be always rebuked contemptuously, or praised contemptuously, by history,
if history be of thy mind? Here is the danger of Hero-Worship. It
ends in something too like contempt for Humanity, . . .

                    . . . .

no. 87 ～

An ad from *The Harbinger*, January 17, 1846.

NEW ENGLAND FOURIER SOCIETY.

The Annual Meeting of the NEW ENG-
LAND FOURIER SOCIETY will be held in
BOSTON, on TUESDAY, January 27, at ten
o'clock, A. M. The friends of Industrial Reform, and the public generally, are invited to
attend. Distinguished speakers from different
parts of the country, are expected to address
the meeting.

GEORGE RIPLEY, *Pres't.*
J. BUTTERFIELD, *Sec'y.*
Jan. 17, 1846.

---

no. 88 ～

From a letter from E. P. Grant to James D. Thornburg (Pitts-
burgh, Pa.), printed from the holograph in the *Elijah P. Grant
Papers*, Box I, Letterbook III, pp. 42-45, University of Chicago
Library.

Mill Brook Con Jan. 28, 1846.

FRIEND THORNBURG.

I did not *forget* my promise to write you after I had been two or
three weeks at Brook Farm—and when I made the promise I sincerely
expected to fulfil it. But after inspecting the arrangements at that place
I was so disheartened at their prospects and the prospects of Association generally that I had no heart to write about the subject. I did
not expect perfection there—on the contrary I looked for much im-
perfection, accompanied with scanty means—but the appearance of
things was so much more unsatisfactory than I expected that I was
completely discouraged. My depression of spirits was aggravated by
the consideration that so many interesting and devoted people were
laboring and sacrificing themselves to so little purpose.

I have not been at B. F. since about the middle of October nor
heard from there except in a general way. They have suffered from
having had the small pox and varioloid among them, and I am told

are obliged to live very scantily in respect to food {,} clothing and fuel, for want of means to provide these necessaries abundantly. In fact their industrial operations are and ever have been, for the most part, miserably unproductive and unprofitable, and the place has been mainly supported by its school, its boarders, transient guests, and similar sources of revenue. The publication of the Harbinger is now beginning to pay a handsome profit, as I am informed. But an Association resting upon such foundations can never amount to much—at all events can never be an Association in the true sense of that word. A Phalanx must support itself by its manual *industry* before it can attain the *lowest* form of success.

I have also visited the North American Phalanx, but have not examined it so thoroughly as Brook Farm. My visit there was about the 20th October. Mrs. Blanche and Mrs. Renshaw were there, though they had but recently arrived. I suppose they remain there still, though I have not heard from them for some time. Their manual industry appeared to be much more productive than at B. F. and I thought their business arrangements rather superior—while the leading men and women at the latter place were vastly superior in intelligence and refinement to any at the former. As far as I could judge the members of the N. A. P. were supporting themselves by their labor, and at the same time lived comfortably—but their organization is so wretched that they must some time fail, if they do not change it, or if they do not fail their condition will be worse than isolation—as in fact I think it is already.

You will readily infer that I find no place in any of these Associations in which I think I could make myself useful, and that I shall join none of them. In my opinion the subject of Association is very little understood even among the more intelligent associationists of the East. Mr. Brisbane understands portions of the theory well, but in the practical parts I think him deficient. I think that both he and Mr. Ripley and Mr. Dana misapprehend some points of great practical importance; and as to Mr. Godwin he has paid little attention to the subject except in its purely theoretical aspects. It is my opinion that the subject of practical Association imperiously requires to be adjusted and systematized anew, and must be before experiments will be anything better than gropings in the dark. I do not see clearly that I can do anything for the cause of Association in its present condition, and shall therefore most likely *go back to civilization*, that is, resume my profession or resort to some other civilized mode of getting a living. I think it probable I shall go to Ohio again—and at all events I expect to visit Ohio the coming spring.

no. 89 ～

An ad in *The Harbinger*, II (December 13, 1845-June 6, 1846),
192. This ad, with sundry modifications, appeared frequently in
The Harbinger.

no. 90 ～

From George Ripley, "Association in This Country," *The Harbinger*, II (December 13, 1845-June 6, 1846), 189-190.

February 28, 1846

ASSOCIATION IN THIS COUNTRY

It was the desire of Fourier, to the latest day of his life, to induce some wealthy capitalist to engage in a practical experiment for the realization of his ideas in Social Science. His works contain many powerful appeals, addressed to men of this class, showing the facility with which the enterprise could be accomplished, its freedom from hostility towards existing interests, and the momentous benefits that would accrue to Humanity from its successful prosecution. This was no doubt the most judicious course which he could pursue, in his situation and circumstances. He had no intelligent middling classes, accustomed to exertion and self-reliance, possessing a moderate share of wealth [190] accumulated by their own industry, prepared to take part in an intellectual and social movement of the most profound character, to whom he could explain his sublime conceptions of human destiny, and on whom he could depend for cooperation. The masses in France were not sufficiently enlightened to be relied on for devotion to a work, which required wisdom, address, and a strenuous adherence to an ideal purpose. Hence, he addressed himself exclusively to men of wealth and intelligence, and sought the aid of capital only from the higher ranks of society.

The case is entirely different in our own country. It is not necessary with us to court the favor of enormous capitalists, who, with the rarest exceptions, are the last men to approve of novel movements for the general good. We need not wait for the advent of some great potentate of the money-bags, who shall be such an anomaly in natural history, as to prefer the progress of humanity to the conservation of his gains; but, without looking for any such miraculous interposition, we may cheerfully pursue our task of unfolding the doctrines of Association, with an undoubting faith that they will be embraced by a sufficient number of the mass of the people, to ensure the ultimate triumph of the movement. We depend on the intelligence, the sense of justice, the faith in progress, the practical skill and energy, and the material resources, which will be consecrated to this cause, by the great middling classes of American society. . . .

no. 91 ∾

Letter from James Kay, Jr., Philadelphia, March 2, 1846, to John Sullivan Dwight, here reprinted from Zoltan Haraszti, *The Idyll of Brook Farm* (Boston: Public Library, 1937), pp. 36-37.

The introduction of the people into the practical administration of the government, the restoration of education in its widest meaning to its paramount position; the reform of the abuses which have made your agriculture an infinite loss; and the obvious policy of expelling, as far as may be, and unexceptingly rejecting all who cannot demonstrate their ability to support themselves, are measures which are primary and preliminary. For the rest, I never have seen any great difficulty in the way of providing support so unpretending, for a number of consumers so small. . . .

It is my firm belief, that precisely the persons whom I saw at Brook Farm in September last are able to demonstrate the untruth of a statement made in my hearing aloud and at Brook Farm by one of your neighbors—that you have not for a single day paid your way, and have throughout the whole experiment been dependent on (what he termed) the charity of others. But in order to do this, you must abandon every other object beside that of calling into profitable action the talents of every person in the institution. In some way and by some means, no talent must be allowed to lie dormant. And this, *directly and by a blessed unconsciousness, would be Association*. Then all feuds would cease . . . Then my best friends, Mr. and Mrs. Ripley, Mr. Dana and Mr. Dwight, forgetting how frequently and strongly they had announced their want of qualification and taste for the arduous and beautiful work of instruction, would discover that it was their providential occupation. Then the experienced and the aged would take the place of Jonathan Butterfields and John Orvis in the management of the practical matters . . . And then the impure, especially the children, would be ejected—no longer defended by the unnatural union of the Phalansterians and Spiritualists . . .

Fred Cabot told me that you had run behind $400 in six months— at least such is my recollection, as I have not his letter at hand. I do not [37] consider this statement deplorable, nor did I expect to receive a worse one. The education must be your chief source of income; and all other pursuits must be contingent and subsidiary. With a successful school, other occupations will become profitable chronologically and by imitation. I cannot object to propagandism, as it

will furnish excitement that may be desirable, even indispensable; but
the backbone of success is quiet assiduous labour in obvious and practicable pursuits . . .

no. 92 ～

Letter from Marianne Dwight to Anna Parsons, here reprinted
from Marianne Dwight, *Letters from Brook Farm 1844-1847*,
edited by Amy L. Reed (Poughkeepsie, N. Y.: Vassar College,
1928), pp. 145-149.

Brook Farm, Wed. a.m. March 4, '46.

DEAREST ANNA,

I requested Frank to show you a hasty note I sent in to him this
morning, announcing the burning of our Phalanstery, and as I know
you are anxious for further particulars, I must with what poor words
I can, attempt to put you in possession of them. The council meeting
had just appointed a committee to superintend the finishing of the
Phalanstery and had dispersed, when Mr. Salisbury, passing the building, saw a light in the upper part, and put his head into a window to
learn the cause thereof. (Men had been at work there all day, and a
fire kept up in the stove.) He found the room full of smoke, and ran
instantly to the Eyrie and told Mr. Ripley, who was the first on the
spot. Then came the sudden, earnest cry, "Fire! the Phalanstery!" that
startled us all, and for a moment made every face pale with consternation. I was in my room, just about writing to Dora. I ran to the front
of the house. Flames were issuing from one of the remote windows,
and spreading rapidly. It was at once evident that nothing was to be
[146] done. It seemed but five minutes when the flames had spread
from end to end. Men ran in every direction, making almost fruitless
attempts to save windows and timber. The greatest exertions were
made to save the Eyrie, which at one time was too hot to bear the
hand, and even smoked. Our neighbor, Mr. Orange, went first upon
the roof and worked like a hero, and not in vain. But the scene! Here
words are nothing—Why were you not here? Would I could convey
to you an idea of it. It was glorious beyond description. How grand
when the immense heavy column of smoke first rose up to heaven!
There was no wind, and it ascended almost perpendicularly,—sometimes
inclining towards the Eyrie,—then it was spangled with fiery sparks,
and tinged with glowing colors, ever rolling and wreathing, solemnly
and gracefully up—up. An immense, clear blue flame mingled for a

while with the others and rose high in the air,—like liquid turquoise
and topaz. It came from the melting glass. Rockets, too, rose in the
sky, and fell in glittering gems of every rainbow hue—much like our
4th of July fire-works. I looked upon it from our house till the whole
front was on fire,—that was beautiful indeed,—the whole colonnade
was wreathed spirally with fire, and every window glowing. I was
calm, felt that it was the work of Heaven and was good; and not for
one instant did I feel otherwise. Then I threw on my cloak and
rushed out to mingle with the people. All were still, calm, resolute, un-
daunted. The expression on every face seemed to me sublime. There
was a solemn, serious, reverential feeling, such as must come when we
are forced to feel that human aid is of no avail, and that a higher power
than man's is at work. I heard solemn words of trust, cheerful words
of encouragement, of resignation, of gratitude [147] and thankfulness, but not one of terror or despair. All were absorbed in the glory
and sublimity of the scene. There was one minute, whilst the whole
frame yet stood, that surpassed all else. It was fire throughout. It
seemed like a magnificent temple of molten gold, or a crystallized fire.
Then the beams began to fall, and one after another the chimneys. The
end, where the fire took, being plastered, held out the longest, but in
less than an hour and a half the whole was leveled to the ground. The
Phalanstery was finished! Not the building alone, but the scenery
around was grand. The smoke as it settled off the horizon, gave the
effect of sublime mountain scenery; and during the burning, the trees,
the woods shone magically to their minutest twigs, in lead, silver and
gold. As it was to be, I would not have missed it for the world. I
wanted here you and Channing, Frank, Orvis and Allen, Mary B. and
Helen and all the absent who belong to us. You know not what you
have lost. And I do assure you, the moral sublimity with which the
people took it was not the least part of it. The good Archon was like
an angel. Mrs. Ripley alone was, for half an hour, too much overcome
to look upon it. People walked here from Roxbury, Dedham, Boston
and Cambridgeport. Engines could not help us much. There was such
a rush of the world's people to the Hive! We gave them what we
could—made hot coffee, brought out bread and cheese and feasted
about 200 of the fatigued, hungry multitude. Mr. Orange brought us
provisions from his house and ran thro' the street for milk.

About midnight I wrote letters to Orvis and Allen, for I thought
they would be in agony for us, if they did not get their first intelligence directly from home. I had one short, [148] sound sleep and was up
early writing to Frank. I looked at the bare hill this morning, I must
say, with a feeling of relief—there was an incumbrance gone. Heaven

had interfered to prevent us from finishing that building so foolishly undertaken, so poorly built and planned, and which again and again some of us have thought and said we should rejoice to see blown away or burned down. It has gone suddenly, gloriously, magnificently, and we shall have no further trouble with it. Just what the effect will be to us, it is impossible now to tell. The contract was lately given into our own hands, and I suppose ours must be the loss. About $7000 had been spent on it. We must take deep to heart a good lesson. We have been thro' almost every other trial; now we have been thro' the fire. We needed this experience, and I pray we may come from it like pure gold. It leaves us no worse off than before we began it, and in some respects better. May Heaven bless to us the event. I feared it would look ugly, dismal and smutty this morning, but the ruins are really picturesque. A part of the stone foundation stands like a row of grave stones,—a tomb of the Phalanstery—thank God, not the tomb of our hopes! Charles Dana returned from New York an hour since, and I am happy to say, takes it as cheerfully as the rest of us. We breakfasted an hour later than usual today, and our hired carpenters have gone back to Dedham and I see no other change. The day is calm and beautiful, all goes on as usual. We look towards the hill and all seems like a strange dream. You can't think how it struck me last night towards the close of the fireworks when, after watching the constantly rolling, changing flames, for two hours, I looked up to the sky and saw Orion looking down so steadily, so calmly, reminding me of the unchanging, the eternal. I [149] fear you can hardly read this, I have been obliged to scribble so fast.

Ever your loving friend
MARIANNE

P. S. If Frank don't come out tonight please show this to him.

no. 93 ～

> Letter from Anna Q. T. Parsons to Marianne Dwight, here printed (in part) from a true copy of the holograph in the Abernethy Library of American Literature, Middlebury College, Middlebury, Vermont. The true copy was supplied by the courtesy of Miss Mary Noel, Curator of the Abernethy Library.

Wednesday March 4th 1846

God be with you—guard & guide you all, my own dear Marianne— What can I say to you that you do not know how we have thot of

you—felt for you—hoped for you—prayed for you the livelong day—
Marianne—how is this event to affect you—who owns -[?]- owned the
Phalanstery—Was it insured? How did it happen? We have all day
been tortured by suspense—As I went to history class "fire—fire—fire"
an invisible spirit whispered & it seemed to suffocate me—A few minutes after I went in an editor came to the door to enquire "if Miss P
knew anything of the particulars of the burning of the Phalanstery"
—Do you think I passed much of the morning in Ancient Greece? I
was rather stunned and then I was relieved—so often have I seen the
flames pouring from those windows—so strongly have I felt that it must
be a prey to fire—Have I not said so to you—& it was a relief that it
shld have gone before any farther expense was put upon it & before
it was inhabited. What wd. I not give to see you—to know how you
are feeling & what thinking. It seems to me—to all outward appearance
that this must be a death blow to you & yet I cannot feel deeply
depressed about it—I am anxious—but only for the present—for the
immediate effect—so sure am I that you have placed your hands firmly
in the hand of the all loving & all powerful that I can have no fears
no doubts as to the ultimate result—

. . . .

no. 94 〜

From a letter from John Allen to Marianne Dwight, here printed
from a true copy of the holograph in the Abernethy Library of
American Literature, Middlebury College, Middlebury, Vermont.
The true copy was supplied by the courtesy of Miss Mary Nocl,
Curator of the Abernethy Library.

North Bennington March 9 (9½ o'clock P.M.) 1846

My very dear, dear friends,—doubly dear in our afflictions, *one* in the
bonds of eternal friendship and devotion, and never, never to be separated on earth nor in heaven. I know it cannot be. Fire may burn our
dwellings, floods destroy our provisions, foes without, and *within* if
possible, may war upon us but the gates of hell, the maddened elements, the concentrated selfishness and ferocity of civilisation cannot
prevail against us. Under God we will triumph yet. Today at noon I
received your letter, Marianne. When I open [*sic*] it and my eye fell
upon the announcement of our loss,—that the home of so many of our
cherished friends, who were *of* us, and waiting to be *with in labor and
life*, as they were in spirit, was destroyed in an hour, my heart sunk

within me and my hands dropped down in despair. A friend who was with me said I became as pale as a corpse, and looked as though every friend on earth had been taken from me. But as I read the letter, the words of Marianne were so full of heroism and determined courage, of Christian trust and enduring hope, that I exclaimed, "We cannot be separated." "We are not crushed." "We shall yet succeed." Separated! What could we do in civilisation—in isolation now? I am entirely unfitted to live in the Egypt we have left behind us. And unless we can be one, and live for each other, in this enjoyment of the friendship that we had begun to realise, that we have achieved, life is a failure—I am a used up man. I am good for nothing out of Association—I must live for that idea, and in the spirit thereof, and with the high and holy aims that have made *us one* in this sublime work or I cannot *live*, though my body were *breathing* and *walking* above ground. We have tasted of the fruit from the tree of unity, of the milk and honey which the spies have brought from the promised land, and flames or floods shall not prevent our entering there. We shall succeed! If not on that spot, on another that God shall lead us to. And I feel like saying, do for us and with us, O Father, what seemeth good in thy sight. If it is not ours to realise the sublime hopes we have cherished, allow us to tread the wilderness of transition towards our promised destiny; and like the *"forlorn hope"* if need be, allow us to bridge over with our bodies the ravine between civilized falseness and universal truth, that the army of progress may pass on to victory & dominion.

. . . .

no. 95 ⟞

George Ripley, "Fire at Brook Farm," *The Harbinger*, II (December 13, 1845-June 6, 1846), 220-222.

March 14, 1846

FIRE AT BROOK FARM

Our readers have no doubt been informed before this, of the severe calamity with which the Brook Farm Association has been visited, by the destruction of the large unitary edifice which it has been for some time erecting on its domain. Just as our last paper was going through the press, on Tuesday evening the 3d inst., the alarm of fire was given at about a quarter before nine, and it was found to proceed from the "Phalanstery;" in a few minutes, the flames were bursting through the doors and windows of the second story; the fire spread with almost incredible rapidity throughout the building; and in about an hour and a half the whole edifice was burned to the ground. The members of the Association were on the spot in a few moments, and made some attempts to save a quantity of lumber that was in the basement story; but so rapid was the progress of the fire, that this was found to be impossible, and they succeeded only in rescuing a couple of tool-chests that had been in use by the carpenters.

The neighboring dwelling-house called the "Eyry" was in imminent danger, while the fire was at its height, and nothing but the stillness of the night, and the vigilance and activity of those who were stationed on its roof preserved it from destruction. The vigorous efforts of our nearest neighbors, Mr. T. J. Orange, and Messrs. Thomas and George Palmer were of great service in protecting this building, as a part of our force were engaged in another direction, watching the workshops, barn, and principal dwelling house.

In a short time, our neighbors from the village of West Roxbury, a mile and [221] a half distant arrived in great numbers with their Engine, which together with the Engines from Jamaica Plain, Newton, and Brookline, rendered valuable assistance in subduing the flaming ruins, although it was impossible to check the progress of the fire, until the building was completely destroyed. We are under the deepest obligation to the Fire Companies, which came, some of them, five or six miles, through deep snow on cross roads, and did every thing in the power of skill or energy, to preserve our other buildings from ruin. Many of the Engines from Boston came four or five miles from the city, but finding the fire going down, returned without reaching the spot. The engines from Dedham, we understand, made an unsuccessful attempt to come to our aid, but were obliged to turn back on account of the condition of the roads. No efforts, however, would have probably been successful in arresting the progress of the flames. The building was divided into nearly a hundred rooms in the upper stories, most of which had been lathed for several months, without plaster, and being almost as dry as tinder, the fire flashed through them with terrific rapidity.

There had been no work performed on this building during the winter months, and arrangements had just been made to complete four out of the fourteen distinct suites of apartments into which it was divided, by the first of May. It was hoped that the remainder would be finished during the summer, and that by the first of October, the edifice would be prepared for the reception of a hundred and fifty persons, with ample accommodations for families, and spacious and convenient public halls and saloons. A portion of the second story had been set apart for a Church or Chapel, which was to be finished in a style of simplicity and elegance, by private subscription, and in which it was expected that religious services would be performed by our friend William H. Channing, whose presence with us, until obliged to retire on account of ill health, has been a source of unmingled satisfaction and benefit.

On the Saturday previous to the fire, a stove was put up in the basement story for the accommodation of the carpenters, who were to work on the inside; a fire was kindled in it on Tuesday morning, which burned till four o'clock in the afternoon; at half past eight in the evening, the building was visited by the night watch, who found every thing apparently safe; and at about a quarter before nine, a faint light was discovered in the second story, which was supposed at first to have proceeded from a lamp, but on entering, to ascertain the fact, the smoke at once showed that the interior was on fire. The alarm was immediately given, but almost before the people had time to assemble, the whole edifice was wrapped in flames. From a defect in the construction of the chimney, a spark from the stove pipe had probably communicated with the surrounding wood work; and from the combustible nature of the materials, the flames spread with a celerity that made every effort to arrest their violence without effect.

This edifice was commenced in the summer of 1844, and has been in progress from that time until November last, when the work was suspended for the winter, and resumed, as before stated, on the day in which it was consumed. It was built of wood, one hundred and seventy-five feet long, three stories high, with spacious attics, divided into pleasant and convenient rooms for single persons. The second and third stories were divided into fourteen houses, independent of each other, with a parlor and three sleeping rooms in each, connected by piazzas which ran the whole length of the building on both stories. The basement contained a large and commodious kitchen, a dining-hall capable of seating from three to four hundred persons, two public saloons, and a spacious hall or lecture room. Although by no means a model for the Phalanstery, or unitary edifice of a Phalanx, it was well adapted for our purposes at present, situated on a delightful eminence which commanded a most extensive and picturesque view, and affording accommodations and conveniences in the Combined Order, which in many respects, would gratify even a fastidious taste. The actual expenditure upon the building, including the labor performed by the Associates, amounted to about $7,000, and $3,000 more, it was estimated, would be sufficient for its completion. As it was not yet in use by the Association, and until the day of its destruction, not exposed to fire, no insurance had been effected. It was built by investments in our loan stock, and the loss falls upon the holders of partnership stock and the members of the Association.

It is some alleviation of the great calamity which we have sustained, that it came upon us at this time rather than at a later period. The house was not endeared to us by any grateful recollections; the tender and hallowed associations of home had not yet begun to cluster around it; and although we looked upon it with joy and hope as destined to occupy an important sphere in the social movement to which it was consecrated, its destruction does not rend asunder those sacred ties, which bind us to the dwellings that have thus far been the scene of our toils and of our satisfactions. We could not part with either of the houses in which we have lived at Brook Farm, without a sadness like that which we should feel at the departure of a bosom friend. The destruction of our edifice makes no essential change in our pursuits. It leaves no family destitute of a home; it disturbs no domestic arrangements; it puts us to no immediate inconvenience. The morning after the disaster, if a stranger had not seen the smoking pile of ruins, he would not have suspected that anything extraordinary had taken place. Our schools were attended as usual; our industry in full operation; and not a look or expression of despondency could have been perceived. The calamity is felt to be great; we do not attempt to conceal from ourselves its consequences; but it has been met with a calmness and high trust, which gives us a new proof of the power of Associated life to quicken the best elements of character, and to prepare men for every emergency.

We shall be pardoned for entering into these almost personal details, for we know that the numerous friends of Association, in every part of our land, will feel our misfortune, as if it were a private grief of their own. We have received nothing but expressions of the most generous sympathy from every quarter, even from those who might be supposed to take the least interest in our purposes; and we are sure that our friends in the cause of Social Unity will share with us the affliction that has visited a branch of their own fraternity.

We have no wish to keep out of sight the magnitude of our loss. In our present infant state, it is a severe trial of our strength. We cannot now calculate its ultimate effect. It may prove more than we are able to bear; or like other previous calamities, it may serve to bind us more closely to each other, and to the holy cause to which we are devoted. We await the result with calm hope, sustained by our faith in the Universal Providence, whose social laws we have endeavored to ascertain and embody in our daily lives.

It may not be improper to state, as we are speaking of our own affairs more fully than we have felt at liberty to do before in the columns of our paper, that, whatever be our trials of an external character, we have every reason to rejoice in the internal condition of our Association. For the few last months, it has more nearly than ever approached the idea of a true social order. The greatest harmony prevails among us; not a discordant note is heard; a spirit of friendship, of brotherly kindness, of charity, dwells with us and blesses us; our social resources have been greatly multiplied; and our devotion to the cause which has brought us together, receives new strength [222] every day. Whatever may be in reserve for us, we have an infinite satisfaction in the true relations which have united us, and the assurance that our enterprise has sprung from a desire to obey the divine law. We feel assured that no outward disappointment or calamity can chill our zeal for the realization of a divine order of society, or abate our efforts in the sphere which may be pointed out by our best judgment as most favorable to the cause which we have at heart.

PART FOUR ~~~

The Last Days

~~~ *1846–1847*

Editor's Preface

The secret of Charles Dana's marriage provided a bitter disappointment for Marianne Dwight. Marianne loved to keep secrets. She kept them so arduously that no one could overlook her possession of them.—And then, after all, to learn that she had been keeping the wrong secret! It was too much. No wonder she had harsh things to say about the charming Eunice Dana.

But for reasons much more serious than any that romance could afford, these were vexing days at the Farm. None of the Farmers wished to confront the end of their venture. Each sought for a way to avert disaster. And in the urgency of their search they argued, differed, set out on new lines of hopeful activity.

In emergency the true character of an institution, as well as of a man, most clearly shows itself. The emergency of the fire displays the character of Brook Farm. In the letters and *The Harbinger*'s of these final months one can see each man's conception of himself, and of the community that had been his home. Some of them, a few, had been there from the outset. Others had lived there for longer than the four years a student spends at college. It was a trying time.

But for modern students the problem now becomes more clearly defined. It is possible at last to answer some of the questions that Ripley evaded in 1841.

What happens when cultivated, dedicated people band together to live simply by the products of their communal labor? How may they best order their affairs? Will they succeed or fail? If they succeed, what will be the true nature of their success?

Permanent, absolute answers to such questions will continue to elude us. But we can see what happened once, at Brook Farm.

no. 96 ~

Letter from Charles A. Dana, Brook Farm, (March, 1846), to John Sullivan Dwight, in New York; here reprinted from Zoltan Haraszti, *The Idyll of Brook Farm* (Boston: Public Library, 1937), pp. 38 and 41.

You ought to be at home on Thursday evening. I never wanted you and indeed all of you, Godwin, Macdaniel, Brisbane so much. It is the [41] evening of my wedding party and not one of the inner circle at least ought to be absent. But as it is we can only regret it, and make you all as real to us as we can when you are not here.

You will be surprised at this, and indeed when you left it was entirely unexpected to me. The marriage itself took place in New York before I came home, but for obvious reasons connected with Eunice's private movements, which then seemed to require her to stay for some time in New York, it was entirely private. Only Osborne, Brisbane, Mr. D. and Sarah Whitehouse were present. We designed to make it known when Eunice came home, which was to have been in the summer; but as the present crisis in Brook Farm affairs brought her home, it is made public of course. These explanations are for yourself and not for the world in general . . .

We are pretty much agreed to call together the creditors and holders of loan stock and lay the case before them. If they will do nothing to diminish the weight of interest we now have to pay, we shall have to go through bankruptcy, in which case they will get nothing at all; while if they will relax somewhat of their demands, their claims will be worth something at least.

Should we be compelled to adopt the former alternative and go through bankruptcy which I trust we may not, we must still keep together and carry on the movement. In that case, we may be able to rent the place at a reasonable rate and continue with a modified organization, the plan of which some hint has been given by Frank Shaw. This is, however, all subject to future discussion in which you will participate. The conference with the creditors, I presume, will take place before long. It will probably be decided upon at the meeting to-night. These hints are unsatisfactory enough, but the best time will permit.

no. 97 ✑

Letter from Marianne Dwight to Anna Parsons, here reprinted from Marianne Dwight, *Letters from Brook Farm 1844-1847*, edited by Amy L. Reed (Poughkeepsie, N. Y.: Vassar College, 1928), pp. 151-152.

Tuesday eve, March 17, [1846].

DEAREST ANNA,

I find so many of the friends who are most interested in the events of next Thursday evening, are so particularly desirous of your presence here, that I write again to urge it. Perhaps W. H. C. may have told you, if not I will tell you now a secret. It is to be an important evening. Keep it to yourselves, you and Helen and Mary, for the parties concerned do not wish it known here until the time comes. I invite you to a wedding. So I suppose, for Fanny Macdaniel, when she told me the party was to be for Eunice, and earnestly asked me to get you and Helen and Mary here (all, if possible, but especially you), said I might guess what I pleased but not tell anybody but you. I expect we shall have a fine time. Give my love to Helen and Mary. Tell them about it, and how very, very delightful it will be to us all to have you all here, for we feel that you are all identified with us. Can't you manage all to be here? We can find some sleeping place for you all, and you can come out in the omnibus. I am looking for you, Anna, all the time,—perhaps I shall see you tomorrow.*

Mr. Ripley had a pleasant and bright, cheering letter from "Our John" [John S. Dwight] today. He says he has told the *exact truth* to the New York friends and they don't think our case nearly as bad as they expected; think we *must go on,*—relinquish readily whatever stock they have,—and are [152] ready to assist by a subscription as soon as our plan is struck. And I suppose it soon will be. Come as soon as you can, and again I ask that, if possible, you will all three be with us on Thursday evening. Tell Mary she promised me to come on all great occasions.

Yours lovingly
MARIANNE

I don't know that this secret has been revealed to mother or Fanny, so you must recollect when you come out, not to mention it.

---

* Please *all* count the *alls*.

no. 98 ❧

Letter from John Sullivan Dwight, New York, to George Ripley, Brook Farm (March, 1846); here reprinted from George Willis Cooke, *John Sullivan Dwight . . . A Biography* (Boston: Small, Maynard and Company, 1898), pp. 111-114.

My days are crowded full; and I get little time for writing, even on my lectures. At the first lecture there were about one hundred and twenty persons present, some of the subscribers failing on account of short notice and other accidental reasons. [112] The impression was far better than I had hoped. I believe it gave universal satisfaction to those who heard, although I extemporized association at the end of it. Dr. Dewey was highly delighted, and has paid me much attention. On Saturday the weather was so unpromising I was advised to postpone. By this I gained time to see our association friends. I had quite a talk with Greeley. He wrote upon the paper which I took with me, 'I give up all my stock unconditionally, and will subscribe, besides, the first $100 I get which does not belong to somebody else.' Marcus Spring gives up his, and expresses a wish to subscribe something. He says that he has got something which he is holding in reserve to aid this cause; but he fears that Brook Farm, in its present locality, cannot do much. I convinced him, I think, that it is indispensable for us to go on, and to go on where we are for some years more, at least. He says he will aid, but he does not wish to encourage any large expenditure on our present operations. He believes that we Brook Farmers are the real and only nucleus of the association to be first realized in this country.

I met him again at Miss Lynch's party in the evening, and had more talk. The result was to invite me over to Brooklyn last night (Sunday) to meet the Christian Union people. So, after holding private matins with Fred Rackemann, who opened to me the gospels according to Beethoven, Mendelssohn, and other minor prophets, and after [113] dining with George Curtis, and attending 'Vespers' at the Catholic church, and walking six or seven miles, I (with Cranch) arrived at Marcus Spring's, and took tea and had music. Then we adjourned to Mr. Manning's, where some thirty people were assembled. I held forth for the whole evening on the history and condition and prospects of Brook Farm, answering everybody's questions, and going very fully into the matter. I told the strict truth, and found that to most people it was not near so bad as they had expected. Every one seemed deeply interested, and anxious that Brook Farm should go on.

Mr. Hicks relinquishes his stock. Mr. Manning gives his to Channing, to dispose of as he pleases. Mr. Hunt is willing to do anything; and Mr. Benson, of his own accord, said that some effort must be made in New York to help out the subscription in Boston. Tweedy seems deeply interested, and is more and more a Fourierist, having attained to it by much the same internal process that I did. He is a man much after my own heart. You may consider the whole of the stock held in New York as cancelled. As soon as a clear plan shapes itself on our part, there will be something done here.

I talk association everywhere. Everybody questions me, and I have removed prejudices from a good many minds. With Mr. and Mrs. Bellows I have talked hours and hours,—in fact, all the time,—and think they entertain the idea rather more [114] willingly. Of gastrosophic adventures I have too much to tell: that shall be for Brook Farm evening chats. Parties, music, dinings out and in, and hosts of visitors, besides the tremendously long walks, and hitherto unfortunate attempts to write on my last lectures, crowd my days to the fullest. Every day I am belated, run away with, lost, and wearied. But I can stand it some time longer; and it is wholly profitable, I think I have had real pleasure in Dr. Dixon and lady, and mellifluous Rev. Mr. Hart; so, too, in Kempel, who is extravagantly delighted with my lecture. Had a beautiful evening also at Godwin's, where were Miss Sinclair, Margaret Fuller, Mrs. Kirkland, Dewey and daughter, etc.

no. 99 ~

Letter from Sophia Ripley, Brook Farm, to John Sullivan Dwight, New York (March, 1846); here reprinted from G. W. Cooke, *John Sullivan Dwight . . . A Biography* (Boston: Small, Maynard and Company, 1898), pp. 115-117.

And so my estimate of your lectures was not one of my exaggerations, after all! . . . Tributes to the merits of the first one are coming in upon us; and yet I cannot think the audience, unaccustomed to your mode of expression, to your somewhat associative dialect, can have gone into the depths of the thought. I feel as if a repetition of them would be demanded, and am trying to get used to the thought of a slightly prolonged absence on your part. I wish you could have seen the group in the reading-room last evening after supper, the tall ones stooping over and the short ones standing tiptoe to read the notice of you in the *Tribune*. Can I tell you the pleasure with which your letter was received? Your description of the luxuries of civilization seemed very like a story I once read of Aladdin's wonderful lamp, and your deep sense of the more abundant wealth to be found in the circle of pure Phalansterians was most cordially responded to. What a rich and varied life you are at once drawn into! and, in the midst of it you find your home circle of every-day Brook Farm friends. You have an unusually grand standpoint from which to speak to the public. [116]

Thank you for Mr. King's letter. That little sentence in which he speaks of our loss as bringing us again into harmony with universal laws is worth all he has written for months. How true, too, that we can see a Providential guidance in our all being led back to our primitive occupations, and having somewhat collected our scattered forces and brought them to bear on definite objects of real value, before we were thrown into dismay by our calamity! We had in some sort, and almost unconsciously, planned our new mode of life before we were burned out of the old one.

We earnestly wish for you back at every moment and every turn; and yet, surely, this is a better time for your absence than later. Everything now is preliminary. The general council meets every night. They have been reviewing all departments, looking over accounts, etc., I think all minds tending towards the decision that it will be best to give up our property and begin anew (this, of course, entirely private), let school, paper, painting and domestic industry necessarily connected with them, constitute the associative centre, and our band of farmers (stanch and noble-minded yeomen as they are) take the farm under some new arrangement, including more responsibility on their part. Mr. Shaw says the school and paper must not be given up for a single week. His interest is reviving under the light of a new hope, and he comes with cheerful spirits almost every day. Mr. Russell is much engaged about the school, and says he can do something for it . . . [117]

Mr. Orvis came home Tuesday, rather worn down and disappointed, but with undying hope, faith, and devotion. He went to town yesterday to make some more active arrangements about the subscription. Much can be done if we are in a situation to avail ourselves of it, which we are not just at present. One thing you will be glad to know, —that all minds in the least degree capable of it are thinking and deciding for themselves. There is no crushing influence bearing upon them. I never knew them more free. Last night a grand letter came from John Allen, full of glowing love, expressed in his primitive style.

no. 100 ~

Letter from Marianne Dwight to John Sullivan Dwight, here reprinted from Marianne Dwight, *Letters from Brook Farm 1844-1847*, edited by Amy L. Reed (Poughkeepsie, N. Y.: Vassar College, 1928), pp. 152-155.

Brook Farm, Tuesday eve, Mar. 17, '46.

MY DEAR BROTHER,

Your letters are very delightful, especially the one Mr. R. received today, and we rejoice that you are having so rich a time, but take care you don't get quite used up, or annihilated in that great City. You must have received Mrs. R.'s. letter ere this, which I suppose gave you an account of the state of things here. I feel that we grow stronger and firmer all the time and are coming near to a decision upon our future plans. Probably the creditors will very soon be called together, and a settlement offered them. We shall tell them as the Archon says, that we are an obstinate set of chaps,—that they may, if they wish, take the property and sell it, but that this will not be for their interest, as we are determined to make it go yet, and believe that we can do it. We have men here willing to be responsible for the farm, men willing to be responsible for the shop, and so on, and we do mean, if it is a human possibility, to come to some success here. Charles still talks long in council, maintaining his view that it will be impossible to [153] carry on any mechanical branches or agriculture, or to make any attempt towards an association. He would dismiss all but about twenty people, and have only a school and the Harbinger. Miserable! I wonder at the patience with which others can listen to it. I am told he is alone in his views, but I think he must hinder and perplex the council; I should like to have him take a journey for a few weeks and return when we got matters well settled. The probability is that we shall retain the sash and blinds, and the farm, and Harbinger, and get a good School. But upon what plan they will be retained is, as far as I can learn, yet unsettled.

. . . .

no. 101 ~

Letter from George Ripley, Brook Farm (March 19, 1846), to John Sullivan Dwight in New York, here reprinted from Zoltan

Haraszti, *The Idyll of Brook Farm* (Boston: Public Library, 1937), p. 38.

We can decide on nothing definite as yet, with regard to our course. . . . Everything I consider to be precarious in the highest degree. We need your presence constantly and I trust you will not fail to be with us as soon as you can leave New York without sacrificing something more important. I hope Mr. Kay will come back with you; we need him too; I can scarce do without him . . . It occurs to me that a successful effort might be made for *The Harbinger*, apropos to your lectures. Would it not be well to consult Osborne and Greeley, and see what they think of making a direct application for subscribers on the strength of its musical merits?

The people are all firm and cheerful as usual. Several plans are proposed; the Council meets about every night; the discussions are harmonious; we all agree as to what we want, more than we can see the means of accomplishment. They all want if possible to hold on to the industry in every branch, and feel sanguine that it will be more successful than ever before . . .

Have you heard the news, even the marriage of Charles and Eunice which took place in New York just before he left? It is announced today for the first time, and tonight a social reunion takes place for its celebration. As you may suppose, the whole matter calls forth some amazement and the people are not altogether well pleased at the mystery in which it has been kept. It was an injudicious step on the part of Charles, I am sure, and I fear the influence of it will not be pleasant on his relation to the Association.

no. 102 ∾

Letter from Marianne Dwight to Anna Parsons, here reprinted from Marianne Dwight, *Letters from Brook Farm 1844-1847*, edited by Amy L. Reed (Poughkeepsie, N. Y.: Vassar College, 1928), pp. 155-158.

Sat. eve., [Spring, 1846].

My dear Anna,

I begin on this little piece of paper, because it is all my mother can find for me, and the storm drove me to the Eyrie, instead of to the Pilgrim, and what is more, it sent me around by way of the Cottage!

Of all things I should love to have you here to talk with this evening. How much better it would be than this writing! The storm reconciles me somewhat to your absence, whilst it makes me desire your presence. The general council are in session and Channing with them. Every evening they hold deliberative meetings, and will continue to do so till they have agreed upon a course of action, when it will be proposed to the association. John Orvis says there is a deep hope in his [156] heart that all will come out well; he gave me a full account today of their last evening's discussion, and really it promises well. I think we shall decide upon combining a thorough educational course with some industrial departments, printing the Harbinger, farming, etc. We shall get upon a sure basis yet. It is true our affairs don't stand so well, by a great deal, as we could desire, but we hope to find they are not past mending.

. . . .

[157] With regard to Fred—Too much has perhaps been said and too much notice taken of so small a matter—for it really *is* small, tho' his imagination has made a mountain of a mole hill. As I said before, Fred knows Charles D.'s manner too well to care one iota for it, and it is little in him to be so aggrieved by anything Charles could or did say. Mrs. Ripley, John and others regretted that Charles wrote the letter, because they did not like the tone of it,—still they did not think it a matter of great importance as it contained the truth, tho' boldly stated. I believe that all you write me of Fred is no more than I have heard him say. You see he quibbles more than he reasons,—his mind is diseased on the subject and most sincerely do I pity him. I am sorry to hear that he sent a long document to the Council last evening, which Mr. R. tells me is very insulting—I have not yet seen it. He sent to John O. with a few lines to him, saying that he sent it to him because he was determined to have the Council hear it, and he was afraid that if he sent to Mr. R. he would pocket it and not be willing to produce it before the Council. What think you [158] of this? Poor Fred! I believe the less said to him the better. Every word exasperates him more. If his mind could only rest awhile upon something else, it might do him good. John O. says he will write him a good loving letter.

And now shall I tell you something of a certain deep joy there is in my heart, giving a tone and strength to all my other emotions? Or shall I wait till I see you. Oh! I will *wait*, for you are coming out here this very week. . . . All that I have been writing to you comes so far short of the whole that is to be said, that it seems one sided as I

read it over—we must talk. I cannot find that anyone here has any ill
feeling or any exasperation whatever towards Fred. He has himself
created a great hubbub about his own ears—we don't make it—we believe that when left to himself he will come to his senses and be as
much ashamed of the steps he has taken, and the hue and cry he is
making, as his friends here are now ashamed of him. We pity him and
are sorry to have him so unhappy, and I would gladly see him more
manly and noble than to fight so hard for his rights, were he ever so
right. But I repeat, he would not be so inconsistent, so contradictory,
so unjust, so unfriendly, so revengeful, if he knew what he is about.
He has worked himself up to a pitch of insanity on this point, and I
can't see that we could have helped it and we, of course, blame him. I
see he has influenced you somewhat, but I shall tell you the whole
when we meet,—and I beg of you to consider if he will not be soonest
cured by having his mind led off in another direction for awhile. It
seems to me even loving words (as is usual in insanity) have made
him worse. . . .

[The end of this letter is missing]

no. *103* ❧

Letter from Marianne Dwight to Anna Parsons, here reprinted
from Marianne Dwight, *Letters from Brook Farm 1844-1847*,
edited by Amy L. Reed (Poughkeepsie, N. Y.: Vassar College,
1928), pp. 159-162.

Brook Farm, Sunday. Mar. 22, 1846.

[159]

MY DEAR ANNA,

It has been quite a trial to me to get along all this while without
seeing you. All the letters I have written have been so entirely unsatisfactory to me, that each one has but made me long the more to
have a talk with you. However, written words, are to me far better
than none. My note, inviting you to the wedding, went to Boston in
Mr. Monday's pocket, and came back to me yesterday. He forgot to
deliver it,—no wonder you was puzzled at the one that followed it!
The party—the wedding party went off very well—very pleasantly
indeed. I think about a dozen of our best people preferred to stay
away. Others of us felt and thought, that altho' the privacy of the
wedding and other circumstances were unpleasant, or perhaps worse

than that, this public announcement was, at least, a right step; it was best to go, and in kindness and justice make it as agreeable as we could. I had a little talk with W. H. C. He did not seem to see any cause for our feeling as we do about it,—said he knew all the circumstances, etc. Well,—I doubt if he does know all,—at any rate, he don't know Eunice, tho' I would not tell him this. Fanny M. has put me in possession of the whole, as she understands it, and gives me liberty to tell *you*,—but I will not write it. Wait till we meet. I am glad, as it was to be, that they are married,—for they seem very happy; Charles now talks brightly and cheeringly of Brook Farm. This wedding party, and the Hive party I mentioned were one and the same thing.

. . . . . .

Your affectionate
MARIANNE

no. 104 ❧

Letter from John S. Dwight to Mary Ann Dwight, here printed from a true copy of the holograph in the Abernethy Library of American Literature, Middlebury College, Middlebury, Vermont. The true copy was supplied by the courtesy of Miss Mary Noel, Curator of the Abernethy Library.

New York March 25, 1846

DEAR MARY ANN

Thank you for your noble letter! I got it Sunday noon, & should have answered it before, but I have been ill, & though I am better, I still cannot venture out in this equinoxial storm. The consequence is, I shall not get away quite so soon as I had hoped. I have not yet met Mr Kay. I expect him here tomorrow or next day with Ally, who is to accompany me to B. F. I shall leave Saturday if possible, but perhaps not till Monday.

My lectures *in one sense* were very successfull [*sic*]; that is, they produced a deep impression, & were even received with enthusiasm. But pecuniarily the result will not be what I expected. I shall hardly realize over *one hundred* dollars, instead of *two*. This is owing to the great expence [*sic*] of hall & advertising. The audience was doubled on the second night, & shrank a *little* after that. It was owing partly to the inertness of very enthusiastic friends about noticing in the newspapers. The associationists (Foster excepted) did in fact nothing. God-win wrote one or two moderate notices in his own paper. But it will be a fine opening, I think, for another time. More of this, when I get home.

What you tell me of the spirit of the Brook-farmers, of Channing, & of the tendency of affairs towards a settlement is highly cheering. I think Charles cannot be so far from your view as you imagine, by what he wrote me. So you have had a wedding-festival, & I not there to rejoice with you all! That was shameful. I had a letter from Charles on the morning of the day of the party, confessing the whole matter, & regretting my absence. I was taken wholly by surprise. Though I can see no good in the secresy [sic] with which the marriage was ac-complished, yet I am glad it has taken place & wish you to offer my kind congratulations & assurances of friendship & respect to the parties. I should have written to Charles & Eunice immediately; but was then head & ears in the lecture business & since then sick. I hope to hear about the party.

Mr Kay writes: "In regard to making up my proportionate share of your loss, I need scarcely state my entire willingness provided that it should be deemed wisest. Pecuniary interest in the business will have no weight with me." "I doubt my ability to contribute additionally."

The storm prevents everything today. Tomorrow, if I am well, I shall see Mr Spring & try to put the subscription in train. Something, not much, doubtless can be realized. I must also try to go to Brooklyn again. Tell Mr Kleinstrup that Mr Hicks promised to look up some seeds for him. I shall go there if I get time. I met Mr Ryckman yester-day—just returned from his tour—he looks remarkably well—is all absorbed in the National Reform business & expects some permanent agency. He inquired with warm interest after all Brook-Farmers.

I have had a wonderfully fine time socially. Wm. Story & a party of friends from Boston have been here some days. We all met, with Cranch & his wife, at Mrs Child's on Sunday evening. Mrs C's en-thusiasm about my lectures is unbounded—she presented me a beauti-ful bouquet at the close of the last & says they have given her the only fresh feeling of interest since Ole Bull. On the subject of that gentle-man we frankly differ but she tolerates my heresy.

Thank Mrs Ripley for her very kind & agreeable letter. Give my love to mother & father, Fanny, Frank & all—Also remind Fanny McDaniel of her promise to write, though I know she is perplexed and preoccupied against her will. Tell Charles & Archon that the last Harbinger is capital.

I do not despair yet of bringing Mr Kay on with me, & have today written him an urgent appeal on that point. So, if there is to be a meeting of the creditors &c, it would be well perhaps to wait for him.

Yours affectionately
J. S. D.

. . . .

no. 105 ⤙

> From William H. Channing, an announcement in *The Harbinger*, III (June 13, 1846-December 5, 1846), 14-16.

TO THE ASSOCIATIONISTS OF THE UNITED STATES

BRETHREN:

Your prompt and earnest cooperation is requested, in fulfilling the design of a Society organized May 27, 1846, at Boston, Mass. by a General Convention of the Friends of Association. This design may be learned from the following copy of its

CONSTITUTION.

I. The name of this Society shall be the AMERICAN UNION OF ASSOCIATIONISTS.

II. Its purpose shall be the establishment of an order of Society based on a system of

> Joint-Stock Property;
> Co-operative Labor;
> Association of Families;
> Equitable Distribution of Profits;
> Mutual Guarantees:
> Honors according to Usefulness;
> Integral Education;
> UNITY OF INTERESTS:

which system we believe to be in accordance with the Laws of Divine Providence, and the Destiny of Man.

III. Its Method of operation shall be the appointment of agents, the sending out of lecturers, the issuing of publications, and the formation of a series of affiliated societies, which shall be auxiliary to the parent Society, in holding meetings, collecting funds, and in every way diffusing the Principles of Association; and preparing for their practical application.

IV. Any person may become a member of this society by signing its Constitution, or that of any affiliated society.

V. An Anniversary meeting of this Society shall be held at times and places duly appointed, when officers shall be chosen for the ensuing year.

VI. The Officers shall be a President, five or more Vice Presidents, two Corresponding Secretaries, one Domestic and one Foreign,—a Recording Secretary, a Treasurer, and seven Directors, who shall constitute the Executive Committee of the Society, and shall be responsible for its general management; it shall also be their duty to fill all occasional vacancies in the offices of the Society.

VII. This Constitution can be amended at any anniversary meeting, by a vote of two-thirds of the members present.

The officers appointed to give an impulse to the operations of this Society, and to take the general management of its affairs for the first year, are

PRESIDENT.
HORACE GREELEY, New York

VICE PRESIDENTS.
PELEG CLARKE, Coventry, R. I.
FREDERIC GRAIN, New York.
E. P. GRANT, Canton, O.
JAMES KAY, JR., Philadelphia.
CHARLES SEARS, N. Am. Phalanx.
BENJAMIN URNER, Cincinnati.
H. H. VAN AMRINGE, Pittsburg, Pa.

DOMESTIC CORRESPONDING SECRETARY.
WILLIAM H. CHANNING, Brook Farm.

FOREIGN CORRESPONDING SECRETARY.
PARKE GODWIN, New York.

RECORDING SECRETARY.
James T. Fisher, Boston.

TREASURER.
Francis Geo. Shaw, West Roxbury.

DIRECTORS.
George Ripley, Brook Farm.
Charles A. Dana, Brook Farm.
Albert Brisbane, New York.
Osborne Macdaniel, New York.
Edmund Tweedy, New York.
John Allen, Brook Farm.
John S. Dwight, Brook Farm.

The plan is a simple one, and its advantages are obvious. We wish to secure unity, concentration and energy in the efforts of Associationists throughout the country. There are thousands of believers in an Order of Society founded upon the Laws of Divine Wisdom, now scattered abroad, whose zeal and influence are dissipated for want of concert of action. Henceforth let us be united. We have a solemn and glorious work before us,—

1. To indoctrinate the whole People of the United States, with the Principles of Associative Unity;

2. To prepare for the time, when the Nation like one man, shall reorganize its townships upon the basis of perfect Justice.

This work is an arduous one, and will demand of us lives of devoted labor for its accomplishment; prejudices are to be removed,—changes wrought in the habits of thinking of all classes,—a new spirit of Trust in Providence and of Brotherhood awakened,—and a band of high-minded, judicious, and efficient persons enlisted to give their talents and means to the practical application of the sublime truths of Universal Unity. We have no time to lose, no strength to waste. Providence, the Age, and the state of the Nation summon us; and with concert of action, patience and firmness, we cannot fail.

. . . . . .

[15] . . . *Peaceful Revolution,*—let us emphasize each word; because there is imminent danger, that one of these two events will happen; either (1), that the Productive Classes,—feeling themselves entangled in an inextricable web of injustice, conscious that their labor is the

source of the very riches, in which they are denied participation, and which flow by them in tantalizing streams, maddened by the constant contrast of their own want, care, toil, with their employer's wealth, leisure, ease,—will league together in an outbreak of destructive radicalism, such as earth has never seen; or (2), that, heart-broken, dispirited, and weak in body, having no confidence in themselves or one another, distrusting leaders who have always betrayed them, awed by the superior qualifications of those who hold and enjoy the privileges of life, crowded upon by eager hosts of fellow sufferers, and driven each day and hour by the cutting lash of necessity, they will, with dogged apathy, submit to their fate, and in a voluntary servitude more degrading and brutalizing than savage and barbarous societies have ever witnessed, underbid each other, and sell themselves and families for the poor chance of bread, shelter, and rags. From this horrible destiny which awaits the Working-Man, in his hopeless contrast with Machinery moved by Capital, we say there is no escape except by Peaceful Revolution. Destructive radicalism will but ensure a wider wo; and passive submission will but hasten the fast coming era of the reign of Money over Men.

. . . . . .

[16] The *measures* which you are now requested, at once and energetically to carry out, are the three following:

I. Organize AFFILIATED SOCIETIES, to act in concert with the *American Union of Associationists;* wherever it is possible and as soon as possible, summon the Friends of Association in your vicinity, and adopt a Constitution harmonizing in its main provisions with the Constitution of the Parent Society . . .

II. *Circulate* the HARBINGER, and other papers devoted to Association,—procure for them *subscribers,*—and obtain *insertions of articles and extracts* from them in the most influential presses.

. . . . . .

III. Collect *Funds,* for the purpose of defraying the expenses of *Lectures and Tracts.* It is proposed in the autumn and winter to send out lecturers, in bands and singly, as widely as possible. In proportion to the means, can be the extent and duration of this effort. Henceforth let a system of lecturing be steadily pursued; in this way only can the people be aroused to the importance of the Unitary Reform, to which we are devoted. . . . Be in earnest Friends. Let us work while it is day.

Our White Flag is given to the breeze. Our three-fold motto,
Unity of *Man with Man* in true Society:
Unity of MAN WITH GOD in true Religion:
Unity of Man with Nature in creative Art and Industry:
Is blazoned on its folds. Let hearts, strong in the might of Faith and
Hope and Charity, rally to bear it on in triumph. We are sure to con-
quer. God will work with us; Humanity will welcome our word of
Glad Tidings. The Future is Ours. On! in the Name of the Lord.

WILLIAM HENRY CHANNING,
Domestic-Corresponding Secretary of the
American Union of Associationists.

Brook Farm, West Roxbury,
    June 6th, 1846.

no. 106 ❧

From George Ripley, "The Working Men's Movement," *The
Harbinger*, III (June 13, 1846-December 5, 1846), 30.

June 20, 1846

THE WORKING MEN'S MOVEMENT.

We wish to neglect no opportunity of declaring our earnest sympathy with the principles and objects of the Reform movement by the
Workingmen of New England. It has always given us the liveliest
pleasure to co-operate with its advocates, whenever it has been in our
power, and although we were unable to attend its recent meeting in
Boston, we rejoice in the spirit of union and determined zeal which
it exhibited, and would fain express our hearty good wishes for the
accomplishment of the objects, which it brought forward.

The movement among the Workingmen is a proof among ten
thousand others, of the correctness of the views of social progress set
forth by the immortal Fourier. He shows, with the clearness, as it
were, of anatomical demonstration, the successive phases of society,
the elements contained in its progressive development, and the different means by which an escape can be made from the miseries of the
present order, called Civilization. Every thing he maintains is now
tending to Commercial Feudalism, that is, the dominion of moneyed,
trading corporations, over the industrial, productive masses; the pres-

ent age, as he declared, was to witness a struggle between these two interests, unless prevented by the speedy establishment of Domestic and Agricultural Association; and the first symptoms of attempting a better order of society would be found in the formation of a system of mutual guarantees, to take the place of the competition and universal antagonism of commercial relations.

The present movement of the Workingmen is a fulfilment of these predictions, uttered nearly fifty years since, before the first note of remonstrance had been sounded against the tyranny of capital, and at a time when the horrors of war had shed a disastrous eclipse on every prospect of social advancement. The Workingmen are now demanding a system of practical guarantees; they protest against the usurpations of the moneyed influence; they call upon each other for mutual protection against the sovereignty of combined capital; and with a strong instinct, if not a clear consciousness of the strength of union, are forming systematic organizations, with a view to a more efficient and thorough maintenance of their undeniable rights. This is the secret of the movement in which they are now engaged. We need not say that we wish for it the most complete success. We do more. We are devotedly attached to the movement ourselves. We would labor, night and day, summer and winter, by word and by deed, for the realization of its objects. They are all good, all holy, all adapted to win the support of every true man. They are an important step in the progress of Humanity towards its destined goal. In the present state of things, they are necessary to the attainment of still higher good. They are the first bugle notes, summoning the army of the faithful to take up their march, not to a war of devastation, rapine, and bloodshed, but to the defence of the inborn rights of man, and the conquering for the race of the fair heritage of material prosperity, industrial attraction, leisure for intellectual culture, and the consequent social harmony which a beneficent Providence has ordained as the certain destiny of Humanity.

· · · · · · ·

no. *107* 〜

Letter from Marianne Dwight to Frank Dwight, here reprinted from Marianne Dwight, *Letters from Brook Farm 1844-1847*, edited by Amy L. Reed (Poughkeepsie, N. Y.: Vassar College, 1928), pp. 169-170.

Brook Farm, Tuesday evening, [July 28, 1846].

DEAR FRANK,

I get no time to write by daylight, and find myself too tired, or lamp-light too uncomfortable to undertake it in the evening. . . . There is little to tell you by way of news. Tomorrow Mr. Kleinstrup and Mr. Palisse start for N. Y., and will visit the North American Phalanx. Mr. K is really determined to leave. I fear the Palisses will soon go, and the Mondays,—tho' they don't say anything about it. I must tell you, with a deep feeling of disappointment, (tho' I believe we are in God's hands and feel resigned to what must come) that I see little reason to hope for any success here. I think we might have it, if the people were persistent,—but there is a general discouragement and want of hope,—a willingness, it seems to me to let the thing come to naught so far as an industrial association is concerned. It seems to me that our secret central council, our leaders here, don't even care to have an industrial association,—don't believe it can be, and aim only to carry on the school and the Harbinger. I don't believe the school and Harbinger will support the place, if people enough remain to make the life anything like as associative as it has been. They want to let out the farm. Well—I don't [170] know—my hope all along has been in the people; if the wise, the good and true think it their duty to quit, how or what shall I hope for Brook Farm? Oh! there is something rotten in Denmark depend upon it. I do what I can now—what my duty may be ere many weeks I know not. You may think this desponding. I am not so. I don't mean to be so even if I see this beloved Brook Farm, this adopted home, draw to an end,—but enough of this. . . .

With much love
MARIANNE

no. 108 ❧

Three "fillers" printed in *The Harbinger*, III (June 13, 1846- December 5, 1846), 96.

July 18, 1846

☞ The "AEgis" published at Worcester, Mass. has an article on Association occasioned by the recent lectures of Messrs. CHANNING, BRISBANE, and DANA at that place. Fair or

even decent criticism we are always ready to reply to, but the tone and manner of the "AEgis"
preclude all argument.

☞ The New York Express of July 9, has an
article on "Fourierism," which in all the qualities
in general so abundantly displayed in its writings
on that subject, somewhat exceeds the less practised "AEgis;" what these qualities are, no one
who has ever seen the Express, will need to be
informed.

☞ A company in London offers to insure
against loss by failure of harvests. What next?—
Worcester Transcript.

Why the next thing is to apply the principle of
Mutual Insurance to the whole of society, and to
convert every community into an Association for
that purpose. A principle found to be so beneficial
ought to have a more extended operation. Let
"Mutual Guarantees" be instituted in all the relations of men; that is "what next."

---

no. 109 ⌇

Letter from Marianne Dwight to Frank Dwight, here reprinted
from Marianne Dwight, *Letters from Brook Farm 1844-1847*,
edited by Amy L. Reed (Poughkeepsie, N. Y.: Vassar College,
1928), pp. 173-174.

[October 17, 1846]

DEAR FRANK,

The greatest objection to our having company on Sunday is that we
have so little opportunity for any talk with you,—we enjoyed Harriet's
visit very much, but felt that we had scarcely seen *you*. I thought certainly to have written to you this week, but the days have been busy
with the autumn leaves, and painting rather more steadily than of late
has affected my eyes so that I have not dared to write in the evening,
lest I should be obliged to be idle the next day. The country is magnificent, I never knew it more so, and the weather fine. I only wish you

could be out here all the time just now, to enjoy with us the beauties of the dying year. I have gathered fine leaves on Oak Hill this week, (hope we shall go there tomorrow) and have met with very good success (for me) in painting them. Mr. Monday, Mother and I went one day after cranberries,—found them in great abundance but were hurried home by approaching rain, with about 6 quarts apiece.

And now Frank, as I have come to the clear conviction that it is a real fact, and no imagination of mine, I will tell you that I am actually thinking of perpetrating marriage about Thanksgiving or Christmas time (probably the latter). I do wish most sincerely that this information may give you real pleasure, and if you look at it in its true light, I have not any doubt but it will. It would have seemed to me, a year and a half ago, the strangest thing that could have happened on the face of the earth,—now, it seems to me the most natural, and a step so clearly directed by [174] Heaven, made so plainly the path of duty, that it seems to me inevitable. We know of no reason that could be urged for deferring it, except the unsettled state of things here, and poverty. It has been already deferred from these reasons and we think it should not be so any longer.—Matters will very likely be always unsettled here, so long as Brook Farm exists, and as to poverty, that ought not to be made an obstacle to a true relation. It is a very different thing from what it would be, if one or both of us were incapable of taking care of themselves. I have no fear on that score. We shall not need much money to start with. Shall be content if we can furnish our room, and have everything of our own, however plain or humble. John will have (probably) about $75.00 and I shall make by my paintings a small sum for myself, and we calculate that about $100 will fit us out very comfortably for Brook Farm. Of course the future is quite uncertain, the fate of Brook Farm is uncertain. What John will conclude to do in the spring, I do not yet know. He has two or three plans. This winter, he will probably be gone considerably on lecturing tours, —and feels very unwilling to go off again as a single man. He wants the settled, home feeling that marriage will give. It has not been from secretiveness or want of confidence that I have said nothing of all this before. It has been partly from our unsettled plans, and partly from the fact that the relation between John and myself has grown up so gradually, that there have never been any crises to date from. Moreover I believe that such things tell themselves.—My time grows short, and I must wind up my letter rather reluctantly. . . .

Affectionately your sister
MARIANNE

no. 110 ～

From John Sullivan Dwight, "How Stands the Cause?" *The Harbinger*, III (June 13, 1846-December 5, 1846), 348-351.

November 7, 1846

How Stands the Cause?

Since the first flush of enthusiasm with which the idea of Association was newly received in this country, by so many earnest seekers after light respecting the true social destiny of man; since the first memorable conventions in New York and Boston, and the impulse thereby given to thousands who rushed into practical experiments in various parts of the land; much, no doubt, has happened to moderate expectations, much has been suffered, and a new aspect has come over the movement which it requires some insight to define. Practical trials in almost every instance have been failures, as those best acquainted with the true principles and conditions of the associative organization could have predicted and indeed did predict. But Association is like Christianity itself, it triumphs in its failures; where it is trampled upon, there it most effectually plants itself, and its seeds are now silently taking root even in the hearts of those who outwardly reject it. The world has been gradually growing up to this conviction, reached it may be by but few minds now; while *all* minds, consciously or unconsciously, are on the way to it. . . .

[349] The movement, then, is going on. It *is* a movement—every day more widely recognized, more deeply felt. There is earnest thinking on this subject where but a little while ago there was undisturbed persuasion of the impossibility of mending or improving the existing order, or where there were only sneers and passing smiles at the idle, amiable vision. It enters largely into the conversation of all thinking circles. It has become the life-long hope and study of some who have everything personally to hope from the present form of society, except that which only truth can give. It forces itself upon the attention of the working classes, who are rising in their turn, as the middling classes rose before them, to constitute the soul of society and settle the destiny of nations. It is the freshest subject on the carpet, and yet not the newest; it still justifies consideration and still demands it, where the political and other interests and hobbies of the day, and even other schemes of reform, have ceased to promise anything. It still rings out livelily and clearly to the blow, where these have long since returned nothing but a flat and

deadened sound.—And now what for action? And where stands the movement? If there is not a fully organized Association for us to go into, or an attempt at one of sufficient magnitude and promise to warrant the concentration of all the means and energies of all friends of the cause upon it, yet there is no necessity for standing utterly aloof; there are channels opened into which belief may flow to feel the gratifying sense of action; there are nuclei of permanent and useful measures formed, about which Associationists may gather and feel their strength not lost. There is enough to do, the worth of which and way to which can be made plain. We will mention three things, which we trust it will become the settled policy of all Associationists to regard and aid as most important agencies, and as mutually dependent branches of the movement. We think the relation which they sustain each to each must soon be seen by all, as it is seen by us, and then we shall not longer feel that we are waiting and wandering in the dark, but travelling by routes agreed upon and definite to the same definite end.

1. In the first place we have overstated the failure of actual attempts at Association. The North American Phalanx, the Wisconsin and several other Phalanxes at the West, still exhibit decided symptoms of progress. Their industry, organized so far as it can be with small numbers on Associative principles, proves abundantly productive; and social harmony, though without the full accords of more varied elements of character and culture, rewards their faithful efforts. . . .

[350] 2. There is at the same time a tendency to the opposite mode of realization, or what may be called the Analytic, which enumerates and provides beforehand all the elements, constructs the scales of industrial and passional varieties, contrives the various affinities and contrasts, of the complete model Phalanx, and having first cast the material mould, then introduces the life and sets it all in motion. The elements are brought together in proper proportions and varieties, and the whole is then left to attraction as in the coalescing of any chemical compound. For the laws of passional attraction are strictly analogous to those of material attraction. Given the right circumstances, and instantly the social elements will disengage themselves from artificial and constrained combinations, and flow together into willing harmony and beauty. There is truth in this also; but the greatest hope is in the meeting of both these counter-processes. Nature's methods are composite and not simple; and these many ways are leading to the same result. . . .

3. We believe it to be essential to the cause that there should be an associative home and rallying-point, an intellectual and moral nucleus of the faith, preserved at Brook Farm. Many speculations and inquiries

are afloat respecting the condition and probable fate of this earliest and most cherished little associative institution. Reports of its failure and approaching dissolution are by no means unfrequent. We cannot say that as an Industrial Association it has succeeded, or offers at the present time much promise of success. Its position is ambiguous and precarious. Yet there is the strongest clinging to the life among those of its members who have been enabled to remain, and it is felt to be like death to give it up. There is a feeling, both within and without the institution, that it is thus far the sacred citadel of the Associative cause, humble as may be its importance in other points of view; that if it should be abandoned, the most devoted advocates and soldiers of the cause would be scattered, there would be no constant reunion of so many of them again, where they could meet each other upon true associative ground and inspire each other to the study and diffusion of the doctrine; and that the sympathies of Associationists generally would find no common spot to rest upon; the cause would be identified no longer with a society, a life, which, notwithstanding business mistakes and failures, has been a beautiful and hope-sustaining thing, more beautiful in all its poverty than aught which civilization can afford.

What has been the mission of Brook Farm, and is that mission yet accomplished? These are the questions which we wish to have considered.

It is almost needless to review the history of this institution. Originally commenced without any purpose of Association on a large scale, without capital and in debt, its experience daily proved the need of organization like that in the mind of Fourier; then it partook of the first enthusiasm of the Associative movement to which we have referred above, and set to work with zeal to enlarge its industry and expand into a great industrial Phalanx. In this it failed; and it now is held in existence only by the considerable reduction in its numbers to which it has submitted, and by a modification of its internal arrangements, whereby every branch of business, and indeed every member, is made responsible for self-support, until there shall be nothing left that does not pecuniarily aid the institution. In this way so far as it goes, it must be sound; whether it will survive, however, remains to be seen. Of course we cannot enter here into all the details of its present arrangements and workings. But what is the motive which makes this life so clung to, in spite of so many discouragements and losses? It is the conviction of the important influence which it has always had upon the cause. How much of the impulse which has been given to the whole movement, by lectures, publications, discussions, conversations, has proceeded from this centre! It has been the nursery and school of Associationists; the social centre and strong-hold of those who are engaged in the great work of propagation. This it may yet be; and while we would do nothing to preclude any possibilities of enlarged and various industry, on associative principles, still we think that the peculiar providential mission of Brook Farm has been, to be the intellectual and moral centre of the movement. This has been the essential and central fact of its existence; and all the rest should always have been considered incidental. The [351] outward husk, the incidental part has failed; but the essential *fact* survives; the inspiring and uniting influence which may still proceed from this little school or centre, will be greater and better than ever, provided only that its true character and worth be generally recognized by all friends of the cause. We do not ask for it any pecuniary aid; we simply ask that it shall not be *considered* a failure, because in one point of view it has failed; we ask that its true importance to the movement may be understood and recognized, and that it be not judged by any false standard. If it should be dissolved tomorrow, would not our plans for propagation, to be at all efficient, instantly demand the establishment of another such centre? And could another be created in years which would have the sacredness, the wealth of experience and of cherished associations, and that binding power between many souls, which this has?—At present the only printed organ which we have, proceeds from this place, and would cease with it; it is an educational resort also to young and old, who breathe here the hopeful spirit of humanity amid all their lessons of literature and science; it has sent forth nearly every lecturer, and been the main-spring of nearly every meeting and convention from which the cause has gained new impulse; it has brought together manual industry with refined scholarship and culture, and taught the two elements to live and share together in equal honor; and even in its lowest estate, amid its worst embarrassments as a pecuniary and business operation, there is a feeling, so long as it lasts, that the cause of Association is not without "a local habitation and a name;" is not without its holyland, where pilgrimages may be made, with hope of more than the imaginary influence of seeing the spot where the dead Lord was laid, but of being quickened by a living spirit, warmed to a new hope, and filled with a clearer light, about the destinies of society and the duty of each towards so great a movement.

We can but hint at this idea, and here we can leave it for the present, the earnest and candid consideration of all who work and pray with us for the coming of the great day of Unity.

no. 111 〜

Letter from John Orvis, Middlebury, Vermont, December 9, 1846, to John Sullivan Dwight at Brook Farm, here reprinted from Zoltan Haraszti, *The Idyll of Brook Farm* (Boston: Public Library, 1937), pp. 44-45.

You are wondering why the subscriptions to the *Harbinger* do not come pouring in, and most of all, perhaps, that the money for such as have subscribed has not been forwarded. In the first place, there have not been many subscribers obtained, and in the next place, I thought it better to keep the money until I got home, rather than run the risk of a safe transmission by mail . . .

My lectures at Brandon were not largely attended owing to the conservative bigotry of the Churches, but they were perfectly successful upon all who were there—and among them the best people of the place. I formed a Union which adopted the weekly subscription. The number of members and the weekly amount of their subscriptions I could not obtain as I was obliged to leave before all had signed the pledge; and the secretary said he knew of many who would esteem it a privilege to sign it who were not present and whom he wished to see. He will transmit a copy of the names with the same pledge to Brook Farm by Christmas. The same was the case with the Pittsford and Clarendon meetings. The formations of affiliated Unions will be a decidedly popular thing, judging from our experiments thus far. From Brandon, I went to Middlebury and lectured all day and evening Sunday, and Monday evening. John Allen continued there last evening, and he was going to form a Union and do what he could for subscribers.

The meetings were large and intensely interesting. But only the proportion of the weekly subscription will test the depth of the interest. I offered to put the Harbinger at $1.37½ per each copy for 12 copies to one address. If this is not right, I will make it so. But it is not as yet certain that any will be obtained even at that rate.

I lectured in Middlebury Village last evening to only a small audience. The County Court is in session and is the grand scene of interest for the time; and owing to the badness of weather, and the impossibility [45] of getting the bell rung, I gave up the idea of continuing them here. It is the very citadel of conservative Congregationalism, of Vermont Chronicles, New York Observerism in this State. There is nothing so detestable as the two-penny piety and six-penny aristocracy

of an insignificant country village—especially if it has made a successful
failure to sustain a college. The influence of such a village in Vermont
is worse than any possible opposition in the cities. There is such a
contemptible aping of what they cannot reach that one heartily sickens
and blushes that he belongs to a species of apes, after all his aspiration
for freedom and noble independence . . .

no. 112 ~~

> Final actions of the Association. Here reprinted from O. B.
> Frothingham, *George Ripley* (Boston: Houghton Mifflin Com-
> pany, 1882), pp. 194-195.

Brook Farm, March 4, 1847

Minutes of a meeting held this day pursuant to a call in writing,
through the post-office to each of the stockholders and creditors of
the Brook Farm Phalanx. The following persons being present, namely,
G. Ripley, J. M. Palisse, Jno. Hoxie, Francis G. Shaw, Geo. R. Russell, S. Butterfield, N. Colton, P. N. Kleinstrup. G. Ripley in the chair.
J. M. Palisse was chosen Secretary.

After a verbal statement from G. Ripley respecting the present condition of the Phalanx, it was voted unanimously, that Geo. Ripley
be authorized to let the Farm for one year from March 1st, for $350;
and the Keith lot for $100 or more, with such conditions and reserva-
tions as he may deem best for the interest of the stockholders.

Adjourned.

J. M. PALISSE, *Secretary*.

Brook Farm, August 18, 1847

Minutes of a meeting of the stockholders and creditors of the Brook
Farm Phalanx, held pursuant to due notice given to all parties by
George Ripley. Present: Geo. Ripley, Theodore Parker, Samuel Teal,
P. N. Kleinstrup, A. Kay, J. M. Palisse, Amelia Russell, Mary Ann
Ripley.

J. M. Palisse was appointed Secretary of the meeting. Theodore
Parker read a letter from G. R. Russell, authorizing the former to
represent him and vote at this meeting. It was then voted unanimously:
that the President of the Phalanx be, and [195] is hereby authorized,
to transfer to a Board of Three Trustees the whole property of the
Corporation for the purpose and with power of disposing of it to the
best advantage of all concerned.

Voted unanimously, that Messrs. T. Parker, G. R. Russell, and Samuel P. Teal compose that Board of Trustees.

Voted unanimously, that said Board of Trustees has power to add Mr. Francis Jackson or some suitable person to its number, or employ him as its agent in the management of the business confided to its care.

Adjourned.

J. M. PALISSE, *Secretary.*

no. 113

From a letter from John Orvis to Marianne Dwight Orvis, here printed from a true copy of the holograph in the Abernethy Library of American Literature, Middlebury College, Middlebury, Vermont. The true copy was supplied by the courtesy of Miss Mary Noel, Curator of the Abernethy Library.

Edgartown Marthas Vineyard
March 8th 1847.

. . . I have spent a long time with a young man this morning from Charleston S. C. who ran away from the whale-ship Florida at the Sandwich Islands. You know that is the ship which Frank Cabot is on board of—He left the Florida & secreted himself on the ship York which was bound home. When the York was well out to sea he came from his hiding place. He is college educated is a passionate lover of music, & plays with a great deal of appreciation Beethoven Mozart Rossini & Tholberg. I was much pleased with his intelligence, but I think he has been a hard case. He is undoubtedly a talented fellow with a good share of vanity. He left all his clothing except the coarse sailor suit which he had on. Here he goes round from house to house in his horrible dress & is welcomed by all. He gave me a whalebone [?] with a California pearl set. I suppose it is of no value, nor is there any beauty about it except in the pearl. But I like it. He gave me a very pleasant account of Frank, saying that he was well & happy, & well liked by the captain & officers. He speaks well of all the crew—says they all have some gentility in their manners & are as active a crew as he ever saw. He thinks Frank will do well—says he has a friend on board by the name of Somers who is his most intimate friend. This young man's name is Berlin (?) and left the ship last September. The Florida had then but a very small part of her cargo. He thinks that Frank will leave, if she does not complete the cargo, this year. But he does not know anything about it. This will be pleasant news to the

Cabots. I learned all this by accident. I was conversing with the mate of the York on the subject of whaling & mentioned that I had a friend on board the Florida. He then told me of this young man & this morning I looked him up.

I dont think I ever made a more unpleasant tour than this has been in many things. At Mattapoisett we were bored to death by a ninny of a universalist minister, who was anxious to redeem himself in our estimation by acting the pliant fool for having represented me as an infidel after my first lectures there. We had no peace with him for he would have us stop with him & his tongue was busy with idle clatter. I tried to read Don Quixote which I found among his books & told him he must excuse my reading it for it was new to me & I was intensely interested. So on leaving his house he offered to lend his Quixote, two volumes of which I took, & you cant imagine what a comfort they have been to me in the general dearth of society, & dour & stormy weather which I have met with. It is really one of the most interesting books that I have read. Cervantes was really a prodigy. Don Quixote & his esquire Sancho were as great curiosities as the Egyptian mummies. I spend what little time I can get in the study of the great chivalrous characters of that notable knight of the sorrowful countenance. Thus you see that my vagrant life is not wholly diverted from literature. How accomplished I shall soon become under my present favorable circumstances will be matters of conjecture in various quarters. How do you get on in the study of Fourier? It is too bad that I am denied all the pleasure of your reading. I dont see but banishment is my sentence. It is a hard fate, but I will show that it can be endured if so it be. You may be assured that I am growing unbearably homesick & shall be on my way home as soon as I can persuade myself that I can in conscience. Isn't that a pretty speech?

. . . .

It is clearing up. I hope we shall have fair weather yet. At any rate it is fair within. Be careful of your health—your eyes—your head & in due time, hope to see me. Meanwhile I fling you a kiss, in the welcome of the spring. Flora will soon bring you her magical laughing flowers. We will have a stroll when I see you, if the weather is fine. I have many a fine walk by the sea—I meet you always there & in all great & pure thoughts. Give my love to all our dear folks You can scarcely tell how I long to see them—Be with me in the real life.

Ever thine own
JOHN.

no. *114* ～

Letter from Marianne Dwight to Anna Parsons, here reprinted
from Marianne Dwight, *Letters from Brook Farm 1844-1847*,
edited by Amy L. Reed (Poughkeepsie, N. Y.: Vassar College,
1928), pp. 176-178.

Brook Farm, Sat. eve., Mar. 29, (1847).

DEAREST ANNA,

. . . [177] Oh, Anna! It is sad to think of the greenhouse plants
being sold off. It is sad to see Brook Farm dwindling away, when it
need not have been so. How it has struggled against all sorts of dis-
eases and accidents, and defects of organization! With what vitality
it has been endowed! How reluctantly it will give up the ghost! But
is it not doomed to die by and by of consumption? Oh! I love every
tree and wood haunt—every nook and path, and hill and meadow. I
fear the birds can never sing so sweetly to me elsewhere,—the flowers
can never greet me so smilingly. I can hardly imagine that the same
sky will look down upon me in any other spot,—and where, where in
the wide world shall I ever find warm hearts all around me again? Oh!
you must feel with me that none but a Brook Farmer can know how
chilling is the cordiality of the world.

But I am ready for anything that must be. I can give all up, knowing well that a more blessed home than we can [178] imagine will yet
be prepared for humanity. No words can tell my thankfulness for
having lived here, and for every experience here, whether joyful or
painful. It certainly is very unusual for me, and I think it may be
quite wrong, to look for less in the future than we have derived from
the past, but it does seem as tho' in this wide waste of the world, life
could not possibly be so rich as it has been here. This is a fact, however, that tho' our state here for some months past, has been on many
accounts, very disagreeable, and very little to my taste, yet life is
more rich to me at this very time than ever; my inner life is more true
and deep,—but I want a field for external action, a very small and
humble one, of course, but I want something. I wait very patiently,
however, and certainly find enough to be busy about . . .

Dearest, believe me ever your friend
MARIANNE

no. 115 ~

A letter from George William Curtis to John S. Dwight. Here
reprinted (in part) from *Early Letters of George William Curtis
to John S. Dwight*, edited by G. W. Cooke (New York: Harper
& Brothers, 1898), pp. 265-273.

Naples, April 27th, 1847

MY DEAR FRIEND, . . . [272] I have heard various rumors of Brook
Farm, [273] none agreeable. I feel as if my letter might not find you
there; but what can you be doing anywhere else? I have received no
letter from you, no direct news from Brook Farm, except through
Lizzie Curzon and Geo. Bradford. But it floats on in my mind, a sort
of Flying Dutchman in these unknown seas of life and experience,
full of an old beauty and melody. I know how your time is used, and
am not surprised at any length of silence. We go into the beautiful
country about us for a fortnight, to Salerno, Sorrento, Pestum, and
Capri, afterwards Rome again. Florence, the Apennines, Venice, Milan,
Como, the Tyrol, Switzerland, and Germany lie before us. What a
spring which promises such a summer! You will still go with me as
silently as before.

At this moment I raise my eyes to Vesuvius, which is opposite my
window, and the blue bay beneath. I can see the line of the Mediter-
ranean blending with the sky, and remember that you are at the other
side. I write as if Brook Farm still was there, and am more than ever

Yr Friend
G.W.C.

no. 116 ~

From a letter from John Orvis to Marianne Dwight Orvis, here
printed from a true copy of the holograph in the Abernethy
Library of American Literature, Middlebury College, Middlebury, Vermont. The true copy was supplied by the courtesy of
Miss Mary Noel, Curator of the Abernethy Library.

Rochester Aug 31, 1847.

. . . The prospect for meetings in this city is less favorable than that
of any place which we have previously visited. It is the nest wherein

was hatched that anomalous brood of birds, called the "Godut (?) Boy Phalanx" the "Clarkson Phalanx" the "Bloomfield Phalanx" & the "Manchester Union" The very name of Association is odious with the public and the unfortunate people who went into these movements, in such mad haste, have been ridiculed till endurance is no longer possible; & they are slunk away from the sight & knowledge of their neighbors. There are some who always were & will be so poor as to have nothing to sacrifice that are still as open before the world as they can be, & there are two or three families however, of those whose circumstances command their influence, that are steadfast Associationists. We shall make an effort to give two lectures here & afterwards determine what else is to be done in the premises.

PART FIVE

Brook Farm Remembered

～～ 1847–1928

Editor's Preface

The materials of this part were written or published after Brook Farm had been abandoned. Some of them are the work of "principals," like Hawthorne and Emerson; others, especially the later ones, are by students at the Farm whose names, at most, are barely mentioned in the contemporary record.

As these people grew older they learned that as veterans of Brook Farm they had a notable distinction. Perhaps they had not been aware at the time that what they were doing was so very remarkable. It appears that some of them were influenced by the reputations that fellow Farmers had won since 1847. A number of them display a remarkable acuteness in remembering Hawthorne, who at the Farm was no more than a rather taciturn and shy young man unknown to the world at large.

In short, the testimony of the memory is never quite so accurate as that of immediate observation. And yet, after immediate observation, it is the next best thing.

In another sense, the testimony of memory is especially useful, for it represents a selection, deliberate or otherwise, from the welter of experience. It reflects judgment. And what the people of the Farm chose to remember about it is perhaps as good an indication as any of what George Ripley really accomplished. He would be surprised, no doubt, if he could read what Cedar Sears has to say about the Farm. And yet, he might also be pleased.

The materials of Part Five contribute to the flavor of the story. Here and there a genuine fact appears, and sometimes a palpable contradiction of fact. But without reminiscence there can be no history. This Part deserves a close and careful reading.

Additional Books

Nathaniel Hawthorne. *The Blithedale Romance,* from *The Complete Writings of Nathaniel Hawthorne.* Boston: Houghton Mifflin Company, 1900. Volume VIII.

R. W. Emerson, W. H. Channing, and J. F. Clarke. *Memoirs of Margaret Fuller Ossoli.* 3 volumes. London: Richard Bentley, 1852.

John Sullivan Dwight. "Music as a Means of Culture," *Atlantic Monthly,* XXVI (July-December, 1870), 321-331.

Amelia Russell. "Home Life of the Brook Farm Association," *Atlantic Monthly,* XLII (July-December, 1878), 556-563.

Complete Works of Ralph Waldo Emerson. Edited by E. W. Emerson. 10 volumes. Boston: Houghton Mifflin Company, 1904.

Georgiana Bruce Kirby. *Years of Experience.* New York: G. P. Putnam's Sons, 1887.

Ora Gannett Sedgwick. "Girl of Sixteen at Brook Farm," *Atlantic Monthly,* LXXXV (1890), 394-404.

Arthur Sumner. "A Boy's Recollections of Brook Farm," *New England Magazine,* X, New Series (March-August, 1894), 309-313.

John Van Der Zee Sears. *My Friends at Brook Farm.* New York: Desmond, Fitzgerald, 1912.

no. 117 ⮂

Letter from F. L. Macdaniel to E. P. Grant (Canton, Ohio), printed from the holograph in the *Elijah P. Grant Papers,* Box II, Folder 13, University of Chicago Library.

No 1 Central Court. Boston.
Dec. 12th, '47.

MR. GRANT.

MY DEAR SIR,

I do not know that I may be allowed the name of correspondent, so long has it been that I have allowed your kind letter to remain unanswered. There have been many reasons for it, not one however which has affected my desire and intention when the right moment should come to atone for my remissness. The seperation [*sic*] from Brook-Farm has been one of so many personal regrets to me, that it has taken, and will take me for some time longer much patience and courage to accept Life in its new forms. That however I shall do.

I feel myself now however in a position to weigh the great truths of our doctrine, more by the actual wants of the world, and as I do so my enthusiasm loses none of its power, and I gain much in sober determination. I have been since I left Brook Farm (one month ago), tarrying in this good city of Boston.—My mother still remaining at Brook Farm—one of the houses being occupied by Mrs. Codman, with whom she boards. We prefer staying in this part of the country—to returning to New York City—although there are inducements for our doing so—from Eunice and Osborne being there. But we are enabled to gain for ourselves, here, a material independence, which it might be more difficult for us to do there. Such then being our locale, I will proceed to give you some of my thoughts and feelings in a more universal sphere.

I have been since I came to the city, much connected with the Associationists of the Boston Union—and were it not that the American Union fails to unite all with whom I have a bond in the Cause, my hopes for the future could know of no check—so earnestly and truly do I find persons alive to the truths of the doctrine. And the Doctrine —direct and pure from Fourier. I look with the greatest solicitude to the further action of the American Union and Mr. Brisbane. That thro' Mr. Brisbane the great channel for reception—has been opened in this country, we all acknowledge—and no one more loyally than myself. An organization or School which does not make him one of the integral elements fails to place itself on a legitimate foundation. To do that however I know is a point not easily attained—Mr. B. offering many causes in himself, of prevention. With this Country, arousing as it is to conviction—the time cannot be far distant however when there will be demanded a scientific centre which will have elements enlarged enough to place all in their true spheres—without any individual juxtaposition. I look to you My friend, as one of the chosen persons to give some of the essential formulas for such a demand.

It cannot but be that every one, from a conviction—even in *Time*, will be called to give their experience and consequent action for the true understanding and realization of these great Truths.—You are to me one of the first in Time—as well as in a pure adherence to fundamental points. You will pardon me for daring to make out a scale, my love of unity must be my excuse for the presumption. I know that you do not accept much that is bread and wine to me, but that does not prevent me, from intuition perceiving, that you are true to points which are necessary to support and protect this bread and wine of mine. The *church* for instance which I am Idealizing even in Civilization you would leave for a creation of the Future.

Will you not my friend, now that I have given you the sign of Brotherhood—let me know some of your views of this great thought of Universal Unity, and your tendencies for the formation of a perfectly United Band. My Brother's plan for the South, I understood met with your approbation—but how is it to be put in practise?—I would not have it an individual undertaking. If there is any thing in this quarter of intellectual activity of which I can keep you informed—for the further good of the cause, always hold me in readiness to do so.

With my regards to Mrs. Grant—through your introduction.—Beleive [*sic*] me in the Bonds of Faith

Yours truly

F. L. MACDANIEL.

no. 118 ～

Nathaniel Hawthorne, "Author's Preface" to *The Blithedale Romance*, here reprinted from *The Complete Writings of Nathaniel Hawthorne* (Boston: Houghton Mifflin Company, 1900), VIII, xxix-xxxii.

AUTHOR'S PREFACE

In the "Blithedale" of this volume many readers will, probably, suspect a faint and not very faithful shadowing of Brook Farm, in Roxbury, which (now a little more than ten years ago) was occupied and cultivated by a company of socialists. The author does not wish to deny that he had this Community in his mind, and that (having the good fortune, for a time, to be personally connected with it) he has occasionally availed himself of his actual reminiscences, in the hope of giving a more life-like tint to the fancy sketch in the following pages. He begs it to be understood, however, that he has considered the institution itself as not less fairly the subject of fictitious handling than the imaginary personages whom he has introduced there. His whole treatment of the affair is altogether incidental to the main purpose of the romance; nor does he put forward the slightest pretensions to illustrate a theory, or elicit a conclusion, favorable or otherwise, in respect to socialism.

In short, his present concern with the socialist community is merely to establish a theatre, a little removed from the highway of ordinary [xxx] travel, where the creatures of his brain may play their phantasmagorical antics, without exposing them to too close a comparison with the actual events of real lives. In the old countries, with which fiction has long been conversant, a certain conventional privilege seems to be awarded to the romancer; his work is not put exactly side by side with nature; and he is allowed a license with regard to every-day probability, in view of the improved effects which he is bound to produce thereby. Among ourselves, on the contrary, there is as yet no such Faery Land, so like the real world, that, in a suitable remoteness, one cannot well tell the difference, but with an atmosphere of strange enchantment, beheld through which the inhabitants have a propriety of their own. This atmosphere is what the American romancer needs. In its absence, the beings of imagination are compelled to show themselves in the same category as actually living mortals; a necessity that generally renders the paint and pasteboard of their composition but too painfully discernible. With the idea of partially obviating this difficulty (the sense of which has always pressed very heavily upon him), the author has ventured to make free with his old and affectionately remembered home at Brook Farm, as being certainly the most romantic episode of his own life,—essentially a day-dream, and yet [xxxi] a fact, —and thus offering an available foothold between fiction and reality. Furthermore, the scene was in good keeping with the personages whom he desired to introduce.

These characters, he feels it right to say, are entirely fictitious. It would, indeed (considering how few amiable qualities he distributes among his imaginary progeny), be a most grievous wrong to his former excellent associates, were the author to allow it to be supposed that he has been sketching any of their likenesses. Had he attempted it, they would at least have recognized the touches of a friendly pencil. But he has done nothing of the kind. The self-concentrated Philanthropist; the high-spirited Woman, bruising herself against the narrow limitations of her sex; the weakly Maiden, whose tremulous nerves endow her with Sibylline attributes; the Minor Poet, beginning life with strenuous aspirations which die out with his youthful fervor,—all these might have been looked for at Brook Farm, but, by some accident, never made their appearance there.

The author cannot close his reference to this subject without expressing a most earnest wish that some one of the many cultivated and philosophic minds, which took an interest in that enterprise, might now give the world its history. Ripley, with whom rests the honorable paternity of the institution, Dana, Dwight, [xxxii] Channing, Burton, Parker, for instance,—with others, whom he dares not name, because they veil themselves from the public eye,—among these is the ability to convey both the outward narrative and the inner truth and spirit of the whole affair, together with the lessons which those years of thought

and toil must have elaborated, for the behoof of future experimental-
ists. Even the brilliant Howadji [G. W. Curtis] might find as rich a
theme in his youthful reminiscences of Brook Farm, and a more novel
one,—close at hand as it lies,—than those which he has since made so
distant a pilgrimage to seek, in Syria and along the current of the
Nile.

Concord, Mass., *May*, 1852.

no. 119 ∾

From Nathaniel Hawthorne, "A Modern Arcadia," Chapter VIII
of *The Blithedale Romance,* here reprinted from *The Complete
Writings of Nathaniel Hawthorne* (Boston: Houghton Mifflin
Company, 1900), VIII, 84-91.

. . . Emerging into the genial sunshine, I half fancied that the labors
of the brotherhood had already realized some of Fourier's predictions.
Their enlightened culture of the soil, and the virtues with which they
sanctified their life, had begun to produce an effect upon the material
world and its climate. In my new enthusiasm, man looked strong and
stately,—and woman, oh, how beautiful!—and the earth a green garden,
blossoming with many-colored delights. [85] Thus Nature, whose laws
I had broken in various artificial ways, comported herself towards me
as a strict but loving mother, who uses the rod upon her little boy for
his naughtiness, and then gives him a smile, a kiss, and some pretty
playthings to console the urchin for her severity.

   In the interval of my seclusion, there had been a number of recruits
to our little army of saints and martyrs. They were mostly individuals
who had gone through such an experience as to disgust them with
ordinary pursuits, but who were not yet so old, nor had suffered so
deeply, as to lose their faith in the better time to come. On comparing
their minds one with another they often discovered that this idea of
a Community had been growing up, in silent and unknown sympathy, for years. Thoughtful, strongly lined faces were among them;
sombre brows, but eyes that did not require spectacles, unless prematurely dimmed by the student's lamplight, and hair that seldom showed
a thread of silver. Age, wedded to the past, incrusted over with a stony
layer of habits, and retaining nothing fluid in its possibilities, would
have been absurdly out of place in an enterprise like this. Youth, too,
in its early dawn, was hardly more adapted to our purpose; for it
would behold the morning radiance of its own spirit beaming over

the very same spots of withered [86] grass and barren sand whence most of us had seen it vanish. We had very young people with us, it is true,—downy lads, rosy girls in their first teens, and children of all heights above one's knee; but these had chiefly been sent hither for education, which it was one of the objects and methods of our institution to supply. Then we had boarders, from town and elsewhere, who lived with us in a familiar way, sympathized more or less in our theories, and sometimes shared in our labors.

On the whole, it was a society such as has seldom met together; nor, perhaps, could it reasonably be expected to hold together long. Persons of marked individuality—crooked sticks, as some of us might be called—are not exactly the easiest to bind up into a fagot. But, so long as our union should subsist, a man of intellect and feeling, with a free nature in him, might have sought far and near without finding so many points of attraction as would allure him hitherward. We were of all creeds and opinions, and generally tolerant of all, on every imaginable subject. Our bond, it seems to me, was not affirmative, but negative. We had individually found one thing or another to quarrel with in our past life, and were pretty well agreed as to the inexpediency of lumbering along with the old system any further. As to what should be substituted, there was much less [87] unanimity. We did not greatly care—at least, I never did—for the written constitution under which our millennium had commenced. My hope was, that, between theory and practice, a true and available mode of life might be struck out; and that, even should we ultimately fail, the months or years spent in the trial would not have been wasted, either as regarded passing enjoyment, or the experience which makes men wise.

Arcadians though we were, our costume bore no resemblance to the beribboned doublets, silk breeches and stockings, and slippers fastened with artificial roses, that distinguish the pastoral people of poetry and the stage. In outward show, I humbly conceive, we looked rather like a gang of beggars, or banditti, than either a company of honest laboring-men, or a conclave of philosophers. Whatever might be our points of difference, we all of us seemed to have come to Blithedale with the one thrifty and laudable idea of wearing out our old clothes. Such garments as had an airing, whenever we strode afield! Coats with high collars and with no collars, broad-skirted or swallow-tailed, and with the waist at every point between the hip and arm-pit; pantaloons of a dozen successive epochs, and greatly defaced at the knees by the humiliations of the wearer before his lady-love,—in short, we were a living epitome [88] of defunct fashions, and the very raggedest presentment of men who had seen better days. It was gentility in tatters. Often retaining a scholarlike or clerical air, you might have taken us for the denizens of Grub Street, intent on getting a comfortable livelihood by agricultural labor; or Coleridge's projected Pantisocracy in full experiment; or Candide and his motley associates at work in their cabbage garden; or anything else that was miserably out at elbows, and most clumsily patched in the rear. We might have been sworn comrades to Falstaff's ragged regiment. Little skill as we boasted in other points of husbandry, every mother's son of us would have served admirably to stick up for a scarecrow. And the worst of the matter was, that the first energetic movement essential to one downright stroke of real labor was sure to put a finish to these poor habiliments. So we gradually flung them all aside, and took to honest homespun and linsey-woolsey, as preferable, on the whole, to the plan recommended, I think, by Virgil,—"*Ara nudus; sere nudus*,"—which as Silas Foster remarked, when I translated the maxim, would be apt to astonish the women-folks.

After a reasonable training, the yeoman life throve well with us. Our faces took the sunburn kindly; our chests gained in compass, and our shoulders in breadth and squareness; [89] our great brown fists looked as if they had never been capable of kid gloves. The plough, the hoe, the scythe, and the hay-fork grew familiar to our grasp. The oxen responded to our voices. We could do almost as fair a day's work as Silas Foster himself, sleep dreamlessly after it, and wake at daybreak with only a little stiffness of the joints, which was usually quite gone by breakfast-time.

To be sure, our next neighbors pretended to be incredulous as to our real proficiency in the business which we had taken in hand. They told slanderous fables about our inability to yoke our own oxen, or to drive them afield when yoked, or to release the poor brutes from their conjugal bond at nightfall. They had the face to say, too, that the cows laughed at our awkwardness at milking-time, and invariably kicked over the pails; partly in consequence of our putting the stool on the wrong side, and partly because, taking offence at the whisking of their tails, we were in the habit of holding these natural fly-flappers with one hand and milking with the other. They further averred that we hoed up whole acres of Indian corn and other crops, and drew the earth carefully about the weeds; and that we raised five hundred tufts of burdock, mistaking them for cabbages; and that by dint of unskilful planting few of our seeds ever came up at all, or, if they [90] did come up, it was stern-foremost; and that we spent the better part of the month of June in reversing a field of beans, which had thrust themselves out of the ground in this unseemly way. They quoted it as nothing more than an ordinary occurrence for one or other of us to crop off two or three fingers, of a morning, by our clumsy use of the hay-cutter. Finally, and as an ultimate catastrophe, these mendacious rogues circulated a report that we communitarians were exterminated, to the last man, by severing ourselves asunder with the sweep of our own scythes!—and that the world had lost nothing by this little accident.

But this was pure envy and malice on the part of the neighboring farmers. The peril of our new way of life was not lest we should fail in becoming practical agriculturists, but that we should probably cease to be anything else. While our enterprise lay all in theory, we had pleased ourselves with delectable visions of the spiritualization of labor. It was to be our form of prayer and ceremonial of worship. Each stroke of the hoe was to uncover some aromatic root of wisdom, heretofore hidden from the sun. Pausing in the field, to let the wind exhale the moisture from our foreheads, we were to look upward, and catch glimpses into the far-off soul of truth. In this point of view, matters did not turn out quite so well as we [91] anticipated. It is very true that, sometimes, gazing casually around me, out of the midst of my toil, I used to discern a richer picturesqueness in the visible scene of earth and sky. There was, at such moments, a novelty, an unwonted aspect, on the face of Nature, as if she had been taken by surprise and seen at unawares, with no opportunity to put off her real look, and assume the mask with which she mysteriously hides herself from mortals. But this was all. The clods of earth, which we so constantly belabored and turned over and over, were never etherealized into thought. Our thoughts, on the contrary, were fast becoming cloddish. Our labor symbolized nothing, and left us mentally sluggish in the dusk of the evening. Intellectual activity is incompatible with any large amount of bodily exercise. The yeoman and the scholar—the yeoman and the man of finest moral culture, though not the man of sturdiest sense and integrity—are two distinct individuals, and can never be melted or welded into one substance.

· · · · · · ·

no. 120 ➳

From R. W. Emerson, W. H. Channing, and J. F. Clarke, *Memoirs of Margaret Fuller Ossoli*, 3 volumes (London: Richard Bentley, 1852), II, 268-275. The passage here quoted from the

Memoirs is in the *Memoirs* quoted from Margaret Fuller's journals. The dates of Miss Fuller's composition of the passages are
not recorded.

"My hopes might lead to Association, too,—an association, if not of
efforts, yet of destinies. In such an one I live with several already, feeling that each one, by acting out his own, casts light upon a mutual
destiny, and illustrates the thought of a master mind. It is a constellation,
not a phalanx, to which I would belong."

"Why bind oneself to a central or any doctrine? How much nobler
stands a man entirely unpledged, unbound! Association may be the
great experiment of the age, still it is only an experiment. It is not
worth while to lay such stress on it; let us try it, induce others to try
it,—that is enough."

"It is amusing to see how the solitary characters tend to outward-
ness,—to association,—while the social and sympathetic ones emphasize
the value of solitude,—of concentration,—so that we hear from each the
word which, from his structure, we least expect." [269]

"On Friday I came to Brook Farm. The first day or two here is desolate. You seem to belong to nobody,—to have a right to speak to nobody; but very soon you learn to take care of yourself, and then the
freedom of the place is delightful.

"It is fine to see how thoroughly Mr. and Mrs. R. act out, in their
own persons, what they intend.

"All Saturday I was off in the woods. In the evening we had a general conversation, opened by me, upon Education, in its largest sense,
and on what we can do for ourselves and others. I took my usual
ground: The aim is perfection; patience the road. The present object
is to give ourselves and others a tolerable chance. Let us not be too
ambitious in our hopes as to immediate results. Our lives should be
considered as a tendency, an approximation only. Parents and teachers
expect to do too much. They are not legislators, but only interpreters
to the next generation. Soon, very soon, does the parent become merely
the elder brother of his child;—a little wiser, it is to be hoped. —— differed from me as to some things I said about the gradations of [270]
experience,—that 'to be brought prematurely near perfect beings
would chill and discourage.' He thought it would cheer and console.
He spoke well,—with a youthful nobleness. —— said 'that the most perfect person would be the most impersonal'—philosophical bull that, I
trow—'and, consequently, would impede us least from God.' Mr. R.

spoke admirably on the nature of loyalty. The people showed a good deal of the *sans-culotte* tendency in their manners,—throwing themselves on the floor, yawning, and going out when they had heard enough. Yet, as the majority differ from me, to begin with,—that being the reason this subject was chosen,—they showed, on the whole more respect and interest than I had expected. As I am accustomed to deference, however, and need it for the boldness and animation which my part requires, I did not speak with as much force as usual. Still, I should like to have to face all this; it would have the same good effects that the Athenian assemblies had on the minds obliged to encounter them.

"Sunday. A glorious day;—the woods full of perfume. I was out all the morning. In the afternoon, Mrs. R. and I had a talk. I said my [271] position would be too uncertain here, as I could not work. ——— said:—'They would all like to work for a person of genius. They would not like to have this service claimed from them, but would like to render it of their own accord.' 'Yes,' I told her; 'but where would be my repose, when they were always to be judging whether I was worth it or not. It would be the same position the clergyman is in, or the wandering beggar with his harp. Each day you must prove yourself anew. You are not in immediate relations with material things.'

"We talked of the principles of the community. I said I had not a right to come, because all the confidence in it I had was as an *experiment* worth trying, and that it was a part of the great wave of inspired thought. ——— declared they none of them had confidence beyond this; but they seem to me to have. Then I said, 'that though I entirely agreed about the dignity of labour, and had always wished for the present change, yet I did not agree with the principle of paying for services by time; neither did I believe in the hope of excluding evil, for that was a growth of [272] nature, and one condition of the development of good.' We had valuable discussion on these points.

"All Monday morning in the woods again. Afternoon, out with the drawing party; I felt the evils of want of conventional refinement, in the impudence with which one of the girls treated me. She has since thought of it with regret, I notice; and, by every day's observation of me, will see that she ought not to have done it."

"In the evening, a husking in the barn. Men, women, and children, all engaged. It was a most picturesque scene, only not quite light enough to bring it out fully. I stayed and helped about half an hour, then took a long walk beneath the stars."

"Wednesday. I have been too much absorbed to-day by others, and

it has made me almost sick. Mrs. —— came to see me, and we had an
excellent talk, which occupied nearly all the morning. Then Mrs. ——
wanted to see me, but after a few minutes I found I could not bear
it, and lay down to rest. Then —— came. Poor man;—his feelings and
work are wearing on him. He looks really ill now. Then —— and I
went to walk in the woods. I was deeply interested in all she told me.
If I were to write down all she and [273] four other married women
have confided to me, these three days past, it would make a cento, on
one subject, in five parts. Certainly there should be some great design
in my life; its attractions are so invariable."

"In the evening, a conversation on Impulse. The reason for choosing this subject is the great tendency here to advocate spontaneous-
ness, at the expense of reflection. It was a much better conversation
than the one before. None yawned, for none came, this time, from
mere curiosity. There were about thirty-five present, which is a large
enough circle. Many engaged in the talk. I defended nature, as I always do;—the spirit ascending through, not superseding, nature. But
in the scale of Sense, Intellect, Spirit, I advocated to-night the claims
of Intellect, because those present were rather disposed to postpone
them. On the nature of Beauty we had good talk. —— spoke well. She
seemed in a much more reverent humour than the other night, and
enjoyed the large plans of the universe which were unrolled. ——,
seated on the floor, with the light falling from behind on his long gold
locks, made, with sweet, serene aspect, and composed tones, a good
exposé of his way of viewing things." [274]

"Saturday. Well, good-bye, Brook Farm. I know more about this
place than I did when I came; but the only way to be qualified for a
judge of such an experiment would be to become an active, though
unimpassioned, associate in trying it. Some good things are proven,
and as for individuals, they are gainers. Has not —— vied, in her deeds
of love, with 'my Cid,' and the holy Ottilia. That girl who was so
rude to me stood waiting, with a timid air, to bid me good-bye. Truly,
the soft answer turneth away wrath.

"I have found myself here in the amusing position of a conservative.
Even so is it with Mr. R. There are too many young people in proportion to the others. I heard myself saying, with a grave air, 'Play out
the play, gentles.' Thus, from generation to generation, rises and falls
the wave."

Again, a year afterward, she writes:—
"Here I have passed a very pleasant week. The tone of the society

is much sweeter than when I was here a year ago. There is a pervading spirit of mutual tolerance and gentleness, with great sincerity. There is no longer a passion for grotesque freaks of liberty, but a disposition, [275] rather, to study and enjoy the liberty of law. The great development of mind and character observable in several instances, persuades me that this state of things affords a fine studio for the soul-sculptor. To a casual observer it may seem as if there was not enough of character here to interest, because there are no figures sufficiently distinguished to be worth painting for the crowd; but there is enough of individuality in free play to yield instruction; and one might have, from a few months' residence here, enough of the human drama to feed thought for a long time."

no. 121 ~

From John Sullivan Dwight, "Music as a Means of Culture," *Atlantic Monthly*, XXVI (July-December, 1870), 321-331.

[September 1870]

. . . .

[322] Then came the Brook Farm experiment, and it is equally a curious fact, that music, and of the best kind, the Beethoven Sonatas, the Masses of Mozart and Haydn, got at, indeed, in a very humble, home-made, and imperfect way, was one of the chief interests and refreshments of those halcyon days. Nay, it was among the singing portion of those plain farmers, teachers, and (but for such cheer) domestic drudges, that the first example sprang up of the so-called "Mass Clubs," once so much in vogue among small knots of amateurs. They met to practise music which to them seemed heavenly, after the old hackneyed glees and psalm-tunes, though little many of them thought or cared about the creed embodied in the Latin words that formed the convenient vehicle for tones so thrilling; the *music* was quite innocent of creed, except that of the heart and of the common deepest wants and aspirations of all souls, darkly locked up in formulas, till set free by the subtile solvent of the delicious harmonies. And our genial friend who sits in Harper's "Easy-Chair" has lately told the world what parties from "the Farm" (and he was "one of them") could come to town to drink in the symphonies, and then walk back the whole way, seven miles, at night, elated and unconscious of fa- [323] tigue, carrying home with them a new good genius, beautiful

and strong, to help them through the next day's labors. Then, too, and among the same class of minds (the same "Transcendental set"), began the writing and the lecturing on music and its great masters, treating it from a high spiritual point of view, and seeking (too imaginatively, no doubt) the key and meaning to the symphony, but anyhow establishing a vital, true affinity between the great tone-poems and all great ideals of the human mind. In the "Harbinger," for years printed at Brook Farm, in the "Dial," which told the time of days so far ahead, in the writings of Margaret Fuller and others, these became favorite and glowing topics of discourse; and such discussion did at least contribute much to make music more respected, to lift it in the esteem of thoughtful persons to a level with the rest of the "humanities" of culture, and especially to turn attention to the nobler compositions, and away from that which is but idle, sensual, and vulgar. . . .

no. 122 ～

From Amelia Russell, "Home Life of the Brook Farm Association," *Atlantic Monthly*, XLII (July-December, 1878), 458-466, 556-563.

(November 1878)

II

. . . . . .

[562] The Pilgrim House was placed in a very barren spot, with no trees near it, and altogether the change was not pleasant to me. I had always lived at the Cottage, which was in itself a beautiful little home, and I had become attached to it. Of course I must yield my own personal comfort for what was thought to be advantageous for the good of the whole. The educational plan was to be remodeled, at least so far as concerned the smaller pupils on the place, who before had never been strictly confined to hours and rules. This was evidently a very good move, as it had always appeared wonderful to me how they had ever gained any book knowledge at all, and a more systematic course would certainly be an advantage to them, if it were only for the sake of acquiring orderly habits, which are a great help in the routine of common life. The Cottage was looked upon as the proper building to be appropriated to educational purposes. As it was decidedly the prettiest house on the place, it was thought the youthful mind

would be impressed by it and lessons become easier; and it was held that every means should be employed to make the hours of school discipline pleasant, so that the pupils should forget it was not an agreeable recreation. This view is delightful in theory, but in my compulsory move I could not help remembering the state of the desks in a school-room; as well as the more immovable parts of the apartment, such as I had seen in my youth when attending an academy for both sexes. However, go I must, and I was soon domiciled in my new apartment. The new Fourierite system began to be organized, and the poetry of our lives vanished in what we hoped would prove more substantially advantageous.

no. 123 ⌇

R. W. Emerson, "Historic Notes of Life and Letters in New England," (in part). First published in the *Atlantic Monthly* for October 1883, here reprinted from the *Complete Works of Ralph Waldo Emerson*, ed. by E. W. Emerson (Boston: Houghton Mifflin Company, 1904), X, 359-369.

Brook Farm

[359] The West Roxbury Association was formed in 1841, by a society of members, men and women, who bought a farm in West Roxbury, of about two hundred acres, and took possession of the place in April. Mr. George Ripley was the President, and I think Mr. Charles Dana (afterwards well known as one of the editors of the New York Tribune) was the Secretary. Many members took shares by paying money, others held shares by their labor. An old house on the place was enlarged, and three new houses built. William Allen was at first and for some [360] time the head farmer, and the work was distributed in orderly committees to the men and women. There were many employments more or less lucrative found for, or brought hither by these members,—shoemakers, joiners, sempstresses. They had good scholars among them, and so received pupils for their education. The parents of the children in some instances wished to live there, and were received as boarders. Many persons, attracted by the beauty of the place and the culture and ambition of the community, joined them as boarders, and lived there for years. I think the numbers of this mixed community soon reached eighty or ninety souls.

It was a noble and generous movement in the projectors, to try an experiment of better living. They had the feeling that our ways of

222

living were too conventional and expensive, not allowing each to do what he had a talent for, and not permitting men to combine cultivation of mind and heart with a reasonable amount of daily labor. At the same time, it was an attempt to lift others with themselves, and to share the advantages they should attain, with others now deprived of them.

There was no doubt great variety of character and purpose in the members of the community. [361] It consisted in the main of young people,—few of middle age, and none old. Those who inspired and organized it were of course persons impatient of the routine, the uniformity, perhaps they would say the squalid contentment of society around them, which was so timid and skeptical of any progress. One would say then that impulse was the rule in the society, without centripetal balance; perhaps it would not be severe to say, intellectual sans-culottism, an impatience of the formal, routinary character of our educational, religious, social and economical life in Massachusetts. Yet there was immense hope in these young people. There was nobleness; there were self-sacrificing victims who compensated for the levity and rashness of their companions. The young people lived a great deal in a short time, and came forth some of them perhaps with shattered constitutions. And a few grave sanitary influences of character were happily there, which, I was assured, were always felt.

George W. Curtis of New York, and his brother, of English Oxford, were members of the family from the first. Theodore Parker, the near neighbor of the farm and the most intimate friend of Mr. Ripley, was a frequent visitor. Mr. Ichabod Morton of Plymouth, a plain man for-[362]merly engaged through many years in the fisheries with success, eccentric,—with a persevering interest in education, and of a very democratic religion, came and built a house on the farm, and he, or members of his family, continued there to the end. Margaret Fuller, with her joyful conversation and large sympathy, was often a guest, and always in correspondence with her friends. Many ladies, whom to name were to praise, gave character and varied attraction to the place.

In and around Brook Farm, whether as members, boarders or visitors, were many remarkable persons, for character, intellect or accomplishments. I recall one youth of the sublest mind,[1] I believe I must say the subtlest observer and diviner of character I ever met,

---

[1] Readers who have questions concerning the character and the life of Charles King Newcomb may find answers in *The Journals of Charles King Newcomb*. Edited with a biographical and critical introduction by Judith Kennedy Johnson. Providence: Brown University, 1946. HWS

living, reading, writing, talking there, perhaps as long as the colony held together; his mind fed and overfed by whatever is exalted in genius, whether in Poetry or Art, in Drama or Music, or in social accomplishment and elegancy; a man of no employment or practical aims, a student and philosopher, who found his daily enjoyment not with the elders or his exact contemporaries so much as with the fine boys who were skating and playing ball or bird-hunting; forming [363] the closest friendships with such, and finding his delight in the petulant heroism of boys; yet was he the chosen counsellor to whom the guardians would repair on any hitch or difficulty that occurred, and draw from him a wise counsel. A fine, subtle, inward genius, puny in body and habit as a girl, yet with an *aplomb* like a general, never disconcerted. He lived and thought, in 1842, such worlds of life; all hinging on the thought of Being or Reality as opposed to consciousness; hating intellect with the ferocity of a Swedenborg. He was the Abbé or spiritual father, from his religious bias. His reading lay in Aeschylus, Plato, Dante, Calderon, Shakspeare, and in modern novels and romances of merit. There too was Hawthorne, with his cold yet gentle genius, if he failed to do justice to this temporary home. There was the accomplished Doctor of Music, who has presided over its literature ever since in our metropolis. Rev. William Henry Channing, now of London, was from the first a student of Socialism in France and England, and in perfect sympathy with this experiment. An English baronet, Sir John Caldwell, was a frequent visitor, and more or less directly interested in the leaders and the success.

Hawthorne drew some sketches, not happily, [364] as I think; I should rather say, quite unworthy of his genius. No friend who knew Margaret Fuller could recognize her rich and brilliant genius under the dismal mask which the public fancied was meant for her in that disagreeable story.

The Founders of Brook Farm should have this praise, that they made what all people try to make, an agreeable place to live in. All comers, even the most fastidious, found it the pleasantest of residences. It is certain that freedom from household routine, variety of character and talent, variety of work, variety of means of thought and instruction, art, music, poetry, reading, masquerade, did not permit sluggishness or despondency; broke up routine. There is agreement in the testimony that it was, to most of the associates, education; to many, the most important period of their life, the birth of valued friendships, their first acquaintance with the riches of conversation, their training in behavior. The art of letter-writing, it is said, was immensely cultivated. Letters were always flying not only from house to house, but from room to room. It was a perpetual picnic, a French Revolution in small, an Age of Reason in a pattypan. [365]

In the American social communities, the gossip found such vent and sway as to become despotic. The institutions were whispering galleries, in which the adored Saxon privacy was lost. Married women I believe uniformly decided against the community. It was to them like the brassy and lacquered life in hotels. The common school was well enough, but to the common nursery they had grave objections. Eggs might be hatched in ovens, but the hen on her own account much preferred the old way. A hen without her chickens was but half a hen.

It was a curious experience of the patrons and leaders of this noted community, in which the agreement with many parties was that they should give so many hours of instruction in mathematics, in music, in moral and intellectual philosophy, and so forth,—that in every instance the newcomers showed themselves keenly alive to the advantages of the society, and were sure to avail themselves of every means of instruction; their knowledge was increased, their manners refined,—but they became in that proportion averse to labor, and were charged by the heads of the departments with a certain indolence and selfishness.

In practice it is always found that virtue is [366] occasional, spotty, and not linear or cubic. Good people are as bad as rogues if steady performance is claimed; the conscience of the conscientious runs in veins, and the most punctilious in some particulars are latitudinarian in others. It was very gently said that people on whom beforehand all persons would put the utmost reliance were not responsible. They saw the necessity that the work must be done, and did it not, and it of course fell to be done by the few religious workers. No doubt there was in many a certain strength drawn from the fury of dissent. Thus Mr. Ripley told Theodore Parker, "There is your accomplished friend ——: he would hoe corn all Sunday if I would let him, but all Massachusetts could not make him do it on Monday."

Of course every visitor found that there was a comic side to this Paradise of shepherds and shepherdesses. There was a stove in every chamber, and every one might burn as much wood as he or she would saw. The ladies took cold on washing-day; so it was ordained that the gentlemen-shepherds should wring and hang out clothes; which they punctually did. And it would sometimes occur that when they danced in the evening, clothespins dropped plentifully [367] from their pockets. The country members naturally were surprised to observe that one man ploughed all day and one looked out of the window all day, and perhaps drew his picture, and both received at night the same wages.

One would meet also some modest pride in their advanced condition, signified by a frequent phrase, "Before we came out of civilization."

The question which occurs to you had occured much earlier to Fourier: "How in this charming Elysium is the dirty work to be done?" And long ago Fourier had exclaimed, "Ah! I have it," and jumped with joy. "Don't you see," he cried, "that nothing so delights the young Caucasian child as dirt? See the mudpies that all children will make if you will let them. See how much more joy they find in pouring their pudding on the table-cloth than into their beautiful mouths. The children from six to eight, organized into companies with flags and uniforms, shall do this last function of civilization."

In Brook Farm was this peculiarity, that there was no head. In every family is the father; in every factory, a foreman; in a shop, a master; in a boat, the skipper; but in this Farm, no authority; each was master or mistress of his or [368] her actions; happy, hapless anarchists. They expressed, after much perilous experience, the conviction that plain dealing was the best defence of manners and moral between the sexes. People cannot live together in any but necessary ways. The only candidates who will present themselves will be those who have tried the experiment of independence and ambition, and have failed; and none others will barter for the most comfortable equality the chance of superiority. Then all communities have quarrelled. Few people can live together on their merits. There must be kindred, or mutual economy, or a common interest in their business, or other external tie.

The society at Brook Farm existed, I think about six or seven years, and then broke up, the Farm was sold, and I believe all the partners came out with pecuniary loss. Some of them had spent on it the accumulations of years. I suppose they all, at the moment, regarded it as a failure. I do not think they can so regard it now, but probably as an important chapter in their experience which has been of lifelong value. What knowledge of themselves and of each other, what various practical wisdom, what personal power, what studies of character, what [369] accumulated culture many of the members owed to it! What mutual measure they took of each other! It was a close union, like that in a ship's cabin, of clergymen, young collegians, merchants, mechanics, farmers' sons and daughters, with men and women of rare opportunities and delicate culture, yet assembled there by a sentiment which all shared, some of them hotly shared, of the honesty of a life of labor and of the beauty of a life of humanity. The yeoman saw refined manners in persons who were his friends; and the lady or the romantic scholar saw the continuous strength and faculty in people who would have disgusted them but that these powers were now spent in the direction of their own theory of life.

no. 124 ❧

From Georgiana Bruce Kirby, *Years of Experience* (New York: G. P. Putnam's Sons, 1887), p. 105.

It was easy to discriminate between members of the association—boarders, half-boarders, and pupils—by the air of business or leisure observable in each. Mr. Charles N., for instance, whose room adjoined mine at the Eyrie, was a full boarder. I was sure of this from his habit of reading Greek aloud long after the working members of the household had retired, and not infrequently breaking out solemnly with the church litany in the middle of the night. The walls of the rooms were not so thick but his invocations were audible through them. He was a young man with large, devout eyes, which had an absorbed expression. There was a want of firmness in his gait, and his long black curls deserved more care than he bestowed on them. Mr. N. was highly esteemed by Emerson because of his rare intuitiveness and his love of nature. He stayed at the community to escape the distractions and formalities of society. He had a genius for penetrating to the very core of a subject, so that a few words from him often impressed his hearers more than an hour's talk with one more healthily balanced. In every way he was eccentric.

no. 125 ❧

From Ora Gannett Sedgwick, "A Girl of Sixteen at Brook Farm," *Atlantic Monthly*, LXXXV (1890), 394-404.

．　．　．　．　．　．

[395] . . . The Hive was the Ellis farmhouse, one of the lovely old New England houses with a broad hall running through the whole length, and having a door at each end. From the left side of this hall, as you entered, a staircase went straight up to the second floor. The walls of the hall were lined with open bookshelves filled with rare English, French, and German books, belonging to Mr. Ripley, who had, I imagine, one of the finest libraries in Boston at that time, especially in foreign works. After the Eyrie was built the Hive be-

came merely the working headquarters, and this library was removed to the new building; but the books were always free to all, a fact which showed the real generosity of Mr. Ripley.

There was a comfortable sofa in the hall, under the stairs, on which Nathaniel Hawthorne, who then occupied the front room at the right, used to sit for hours at a time, with a book in his hand, not turning a leaf, but listening with sharp ears to the young people's talk, which he seemed to enjoy immensely, perhaps with the satisfaction of Burns's "Chiel amang ye takin' notes." It is, however, but just to Mr. Hawthorne to say that, whatever use he made in Blithedale Romance of the scenery and "romantic atmosphere" of Brook Farm, he cannot be accused of violating the sanctities of the home and holding up to public observation exaggerated likenesses of his associates there. I spent some delightful hours with him the winter he died, when he assured me that Zenobia represented no one person there. . . .

[396] As I remember our meals, they were most delightful times for talk, humor, wit, and the interchange of pleasant nonsense. When our one table had grown into three, Charles A. Dana, who must have been a very orderly young man, organized a corps of waiters from among our nicest young people, whose meals were kept hot for them, and they in their turn were waited on by those whom they had served. I have seen Mr. Dana reading a small Greek book between the courses, though he was a faithful waiter. The table talk was most delightful and profitable to me. Looking back over a long and varied life, I think that I have rarely sat down with so many men and women of culture, so thoroughly unself-[397]ish, polite, and kind to one another, as I found at those plain but attractive tables. All seemed at rest and at their best. There was no man, tired with the stock market and his efforts to make or to increase a big fortune, coming home harassed or depressed, too cross or disappointed to talk. There was no woman vying with others in French gowns, laces, and diamonds. The fact that all felt that they were honored for themselves alone brought out more individuality in each, so that I have often said that I have never elsewhere seen a set of people of whom each seemed to possess some peculiar charm.

I do not recollect Hawthorne's talking much at the table. Indeed, he was a very taciturn man. One day, tired of seeing him sitting immovable on the sofa in the hall, as I was learning some verses to recite at the evening class for recitation formed by Charles A. Dana, I daringly took my book, pushed it into his hands, and said, "Will you hear my poetry, Mr. Hawthorne?" He gave me a sidelong glance from his very shy eyes, took the book, and most kindly heard me. After that he was on the sofa every week to hear me recite.

One evening he was alone in the hall, sitting on a chair at the farther end, when my roommate, Ellen Slade, and myself were going upstairs. She whispered to me, "Let's throw the sofa pillows at Mr. Hawthorne." Reaching over the banisters, we each took a cushion and threw it. Quick as a flash he put out his hand, seized a broom that was hanging near him, warded off our cushions, and threw them back with sure aim. As fast as we could throw them at him he returned them with effect, hitting us every time, while we could hit only the broom. He must have been very quick in his movements. Through it all not a word was spoken. We laughed and laughed, and his eyes shone and twinkled like stars. Wonderful eyes they were, and when anything witty was said I always looked quickly at Mr. Hawthorne; for his dark eyes lighted up as if flames were suddenly kindled behind them, and then the smile came down to his lips and over his grave face.

My memories of Mr. Hawthorne are among the pleasantest of my Brook Farm recollections. His manners to children were charming and kind. I saw him one day walking, as was his custom, with his hands behind his back, head bent forward, the two little Bancrofts and other children following him with pleased faces, and stooping every now and then with broad smiles, after which they would rise and run on again behind him. Puzzled at these manoeuvres, I watched closely, and found that although he hardly moved a muscle except to walk, yet from time to time he dropped a penny, for which the children scrambled.

Among our regular visitors in that first year were: Emerson, who came occasionally to spend a day; Margaret Fuller, who passed weeks at a time with us; and Theodore Parker, who was a frequent caller. The last, a warm personal friend of Mr. Ripley, lived within walking distance, and we were often amused at the ceremonies of his leave-taking. When he took his departure, after spending two or three hours in close conversation with Mr. Ripley, the latter always started to accompany him part of the way; at the end of a mile or so, when Mr. Ripley turned back, Mr. Parker, in his turn, became escort, Mr. Ripley resuming the role when Brook Farm was reached. In this way, the two men, always absorbed in conversation, walked back and forth, until sometimes another couple of hours were added to the solid talk. . . . [398]

As our family soon grew too large for the Hive, two other houses were built while I was there. One, perched on a hill not far from the Hive, and built upon the rock, was named the Eyrie. In this was a good-sized room for our musical evenings and dancing; also a library, to which, on its completion, the books were removed from the hall in the Hive. At the Eyrie Mr. and Mrs. Ripley had their rooms; also my sister, who came a year after me, and myself, with several other young people; but we continued to go to the Hive for our meals and recitations. That the Eyrie was built on the Scriptural foundation I know, from having once seen the elegant Burrill Curtis, brother of George William Curtis, filling the oil lamps of the house on the cellar floor of solid rock.

Mr. and Mrs. Minot Pratt took charge of the Hive, and there all the cooking and washing were done. Mr. Bradford continued to keep his room there until he left, I believe.

One of the houses was a cottage built in the form of a cross, by a cousin of Mrs. Wendell Phillips, a wealthy lady, who lived in it herself. Charles A. Dana and other young people also had rooms there . . . [399]

. . . .

[400] The arrival of George William Curtis, then a youth of eighteen, and his brother Burrill, two years his senior, was a noteworthy event in the annals of Brook Farm, at least in the estimation of the younger members. I shall never forget the flutter of excitement caused by Mr. Ripley's announcing their expected coming in these words: "Now we're going to have two young Greek gods among us." Nor have I forgotten their first appearance at the gate at the bottom of the hill leading to the Eyrie. This was the gate by which I had stood, at Mr. Bradford's request, to study the expressions on the faces of the cows as they came through. After we moved up to the Eyrie, this gate always seemed to separate the two different lives led at Brook Farm: on one side, the rest and recreation of the Eyrie; on the other, the busy, active, happy life of the Hive, where sweeping, dusting, lessons with Mrs. Ripley, and pleasant chitchat filled the morning hours. On a bright morning in May, 1842, soon after Mr. Ripley's announcement, as I was coming down from the Eyrie to the Hive, I saw Charles A. Dana with two strange young men approaching my "magic gate" from the direction of the Hive. Arriving at the gate before me, Mr. Dana threw it open with the flourish peculiar to his manner, and stood holding it back. His companions stood beside him, and all three waited for me to pass through. I saw at a glance that these must be the [401] "two young Greek gods." They stood disclosed, not, like Virgil's Venus, by their step, but by their beauty and bearing. Burrill Curtis was at that time the more beautiful. He had a

Greek face, of great purity of expression, and curling hair. George too was very handsome,—not so remarkably as in later life, but already with a man's virile expression.

Burrill, whom I soon came to know very well, was quite unconscious of himself, and interested in all about him. He talked of the Greek philosophers as if he had sat at their feet. He carried this high philosophy into his daily life, helping the young people in their studies, and ready at any time to take his share of the meanest and commonest work. He had that thoroughgoing truthfulness that made him feel that every mood *must* be lived through. One result of this was that he gave himself up so completely to the person in whom he was for the moment interested as to create false impressions, and sometimes cause disappointment. But he was so much more attuned to another life than to anything here, so entirely fine in thought, manner, and deed, that one could not resolve to pain him by speaking of this. He was unworldly and wholly indifferent to what others thought of him, as also to their laughter when he changed his opinions, which he often did. Burrill's influence must have been of value to George in keeping him from caring too much for the admiration showered upon him later in life, the pleasures of this world being in many ways more enticing to him than to his brother. . . .

About George William Curtis there was a peculiar personal elegance, and an air of great deference in listening to one whom he admired or looked up to. There was a certain remoteness (at times almost amounting to indifference) about him, but he was always courteous. His friends were all older than himself, and he appeared much older in manners and conversation than he was in years; more like a man of twenty-five than a youth of eighteen. I, being a year younger and quite immature, did not then know him so well as a few years later, from which time the privilege of calling him my friend became one of the greatest pleasures of my life. As time passed he grew more genial, but he was always more sociable with some of the older men and women—George P. Bradford, Caroline Sturgis, and Mrs. Shaw, the last two being our near neighbors—than with any of the younger people at that time, excepting Charles A. Dana, with whom he and his brother used to take long walks. . . .

I passed a happy year and a half as a scholar at Brook Farm; but for the following three years, until I left New England, I was in the habit of making frequent visits there, and was always received as one of their own,—"a child of the farm," as it were. In the course of these visits I made the acquaintance and in some cases the friendship, of later comers. Among these I must not omit to mention Abby Morton

(Mrs. Diaz), who became very dear to me, and whose peculiar combination of liveliness and dignity, together with her beautiful singing, made her a favorite with all the members, old and new. [402]

Another whom I first met at the farm, and whose friendship I prized, was Isaac Hecker. It was on one of my earliest visits after leaving the school that I went out to the kitchen to see some of my friends, and there beheld, on one side of the chimney, a strange young man with the regulation baker's cap on his head. His face attracted me. It was pockmarked and not handsome, but it was earnest, high-minded, and truthful. Circumstances—among other things the friendship then existing between him and Georgiana Bruce—led to a somewhat intimate acquaintance and frequent correspondence between him and myself, the latter continuing after Mr. Hecker went to the Catholic college at Worcester. Young as we both were, our correspondence was yet on high, spiritual themes, and his persuasive powers almost made me too a Roman Catholic. Undoubtedly, Isaac Hecker's influence had much to do with Mrs. Ripley's conversion to the church in which his restless mind finally found "surcease of doubt." My dear young friend Sarah Stearns became not only a Catholic, but a nun. . . . [403]

That many of the Brook Farmers went to church I know; for I remember well the hot walk with them two miles and back on summer Sundays. Most of them fulfilled their duty as citizens by voting, although a few refrained on the ground taken by Garrison and Samuel J. May, that the United States Constitution was a pro-slavery document.

Not long after the burning of the Phalanstery, Brook Farm closed its six years of existence. I cannot regard it as a failure. The influence of the fine, magnanimous living there must have carried blessing to all parts of our land, as its members scattered and planted in distant communities the seeds of the harvest they had themselves gathered at Brook Farm. . . .

no. 126 ⌇

Passages from John Thomas Codman, *Brook Farm, Historic and Personal Memoirs* (Boston: Arena, 1894).

[Pages 46-52]

It was a pleasant afternoon in March, 1843, when I left Boston, in a small omnibus, that started from Brattle Street for West Roxbury Village and Brook Farm. My father's family of three had preceded me, he remaining behind to close his business; it was a question of but a few days when we should be all embarked in the new and untried life to which we were looking forward with pleasurable emotions.

The nine miles of interval was passed, riding through an undulating country, by pleasant farms surrounded with the stone walls so common in Massachusetts and the eastern states, and by pretty white houses, with green window blinds and little front flower gardens, with fruit and shade trees standing sentinels on their borders. Here and there a ledge of "pudding-stone" cropped out, and the scenery grew more primitive as we neared the vicinity of the farm. Slowly we rode on, leaving passengers and parcels by the way until it showed signs of deepening twilight, when we reached by a slight acclivity the door of the farmhouse that was at the entrance of the place, where I was soon joined by my relatives who took me in charge and made me presentable for supper; but I was too late to join with [47] the family, and took my first meal with them the following day.

Looking out of the window the next morning, I found it overlooked the farmyard and the broad meadow that lay south of the house. What awakened me was the sound of a trumpet or horn, blown by some one for rising or breakfast. I dressed leisurely, as I found it was the first or "rising horn," and went out of the front door for a survey. Before me was the driveway. A wooden fence, and a row of mulberry and spruce trees stood guarding the two embankments that were terraced down to the brook and meadow. On the embankments were shrubs and flower beds. A couple of rods to the right stood a graceful elm, beside a gateway that opened on a pathway to the garden and fields.

Passing by the front of the house I found that two wings had been added to it in the rear, leaving shed and carriage room beneath. Directly in front of me, and facing due east, was a large barn raised upon stone posts, which was open on the south side to the large barnyard, and between the barn and house was a driveway or road, leading over the premises.

In the kitchen, which was directly in the rear of the dining room, there was a clatter of dishes, and a few persons were going from place to place outside.

Some one was in the barn attending to the cattle. He had on a tarpaulin straw hat, and a farmer's frock of blue mixture that hung down below the tops of his cowhide boots. I looked sharply at the man, and found it was Mr. George Ripley. The "second horn" sounded; it aroused the dog, who howled pitifully [48] or musically—in bad unison with it. Soon the persons from the other houses came to breakfast, strolling leisurely along.

I found that all the people, unless ill, took their meals at the farm-house dining room. A little quaintness of dress, some picturesque costumes—such as the blue tunics with black belts of leather, that the men wore; the full beards, that were not common then as now; the broad hats and graceful, flowing hair of the young ladies; the varied style of garments of the students and the boarders—all interested me.

The long, low dining room had rows of tables, some six in number, seating on an average fourteen persons each. White painted benches supplied the place of chairs. The tables were neatly set in white ware; white mugs served for both cups and drinking glasses. There were white linen table cloths, and everything was scrupulously neat.

At the farther end of the room sat Mr. Ripley. The garments of the husbandman and farmer had all been laid aside, and, neatly dressed, he was smiling and laughing, his gleaming eyes seeming to reflect their brilliancy on the golden bows of his spectacles. At his right sat his wife, and nearby his sister, who poured the morning libation of tea or coffee. Most of the pupils were at this table. Mrs. Ripley, tall, graceful and slim, was, like her husband, near-sighted, but only on occasions would she raise a gold-bowed eye-glass to look at some distant object or person. The fare at the table was plain; good bread, butter and milk from the farm were present. It is hardly necessary to say that I looked around with peculiar interest on those who [49] were to be my new friends and companions. It was not a dismal or sober meal. There was a happy buzz that indicated to me a probability of great future happiness.

How well do I remember the old dining-room with its familiar forms and faces—too many to describe now! There were the young and pretty Misses Foord; the one a dimpled blonde, lovely, rosy-complexioned, with large, wonderful blue eyes; and her sister with her clear skin and dark hair and eyebrows, both wearing their contrasted and unbound tresses flowing over their graceful shoulders. And hark! 'tis Dolly, dear Dolly Hosmer, with her rollicking, noisy laugh. And pretty Mary Donnelly—oh, how pretty! with the dimples and the peach-bloom on her face, her white teeth and coal-black hair—ever pretty whether she was smiling at you or peeling potatoes. And Charles Newcomb, the mysterious and profound, with his long, dark, straight locks of hair, one of which was continually being brushed away from his forehead as it continually fell; with his gold-bowed eye-glass, his large nose and peculiar blue eyes, his spasmodic expressions of nervous horror, and his cachinnatious laugh. There were sturdy Teel, and heavy Eaton, and frisky Burnham, and bluff Rykman, with round-eyed Fanny Dwight and another graceful Fanny, and oh! so many more men and women, friends and workers striving for a sublime idea. I could describe very many of them and the minute details of all the houses and surroundings, but it would unwisely overcrowd these pages.

Mounting the central and highest portion of the farm I found it was beautifully situated in an amphitheatre [50] surrounded by hills on all sides, and formed a charming picture. There was a young orchard of apple trees, and here and there stood a few shade trees by the walls and roadside. There were fields, or rather patches, where corn and vegetables were grown for family use. Some of them were exposed on the southern faces of the hills, and some were in the hollows. In front was the broad, meadow, like a pleasant sea of green, stretching far away.

From the first house, the old farmhouse called now "the Hive"—a pretty and well-chosen name—the driveway led to the other houses. It descended nearly to the level of the meadow, and did not rise again until it neared the "Pilgrim House," the most distant one. From that it turned on itself on the high ground toward the "Cottage" and "Eyry," the remaining houses.

The "Pilgrim House," an oblong double house, occupying a commanding position, was plain and white, without ornamentation, and squarely built like most of the New England country houses of its date. There were no trees around it, and it was the least attractive house on the place.

The "Cottage" had four gables, and was also plain and unpretending; it had only some half-a-dozen rooms, and was painted a dark brown color. It was situated on a little knoll, with flower beds in the rear, and greensward all around it.

Beyond and nearer to the "Hive," in the centre of the domain, was the "Eyry" (this is the way Mr. Ripley spelled it; some spelled it "Eyrie" and some "Aerie"). It had for its base a ledge of Roxbury conglomerate called "pudding-stone," and it was banked [51] up with two greensward terraces. It had the highest and finest location, with a background of oak and maple woods, and looked out on the orchard, commanding a fine view. It was a square, smooth, wooden structure, painted a light gray, sandstone color. It was made of smooth, matched boards, and had a large, flat cornice or flange that surrounded it near the top, which saved it from extreme plainness. Yet it was pleasing to the eye, and it had low, French windows that open like doors out on to the upper terrace.

As I looked in it for the first time I saw that a few pictures adorned the walls: pressed fern leaves filled the mantel vases, and the bright remnants of last autumn's foliage were in some places fastened to the walls. There was also a piano, over which hung an oil painting, and in the opposite room was a large array of Mr. Ripley's books. It was "the library," and many of the works were in German. In particular, there was a set of fourteen volumes, "Specimens of Foreign Literature," edited by Mr. Ripley, that attracted my attention.

At the Cottage were the school-rooms principally for the younger children; and the Pilgrim House was used mostly for family lodgings.

For a time my sleeping apartment was with others in the upper room of the rear wing of the farmhouse, dignified by the name "Attica." My companions were all single men; good, reliable fellows who were working for a principle and would ordinarily have declined such a lodging-place, but under the circumstances were not apt to grumble, but made the best of it. It was like camping out, and all its mischances were turned into [52] fun. My roommates were called "the Admiral," "the Dutchman," "the General" and "the Parson,"—nicknames given each one of them for some personal peculiarity.

There were advantages as well as disadvantages in living in "Attica." It was nearest the centre of the life and business of the place. In the winter mornings there was no long walk to meals, as those had who lived at the other houses. We were near the warm kitchen; and when the house was still and work suspended—all save the baking of bread, which often proceeded in the evening in the range ovens—a group would gather around the fire and talk and gossip—for we were not beyond the last; speculation, theory and argument went pleasantly on until bed-time. . . .

[*Ibid.* pp. 66-67]

There was in the farming group a healthy-looking young man, of ruddy countenance and fair skin, with brown hair and beard that grew luxuriantly, who soon [67] made himself conspicuous by his individuality, his good nature and cheerfulness. There was a positive side to his character; he was in earnest, and he put himself by his earnestness into a positive way that to the superficial seemed to savor of the important, so that Irish John nicknamed him "John Almighty," and it stuck to him as an old simile says, "like a burdock to a boy's trousers." His devotion was rewarded by chances to lecture. He became one of the faithful, and faithful he has always remained. Amid all the changes of life that have come to him since, and notwithstanding the many persons indoctrinated with Fourier's ideas, he has been for years almost the only man among them broadly advocating them and directly working for the laboring man by endeavoring to organize societies and industrial unions of various sorts for their benefit. I sincerely honor the devotion of John Orvis, continued through so many years of his life.

[*Ibid.* pp. 73-74]

Mr. Albert Brisbane, of New York, was equally tall with Mr. Channing, but of a type of features that was ordinarily less pleasing; wearing a full beard closely trimmed, intellectual in forehead and face, with a voice one could hardly call musical; a rapid, earnest talker; the travelled son of a wealthy man, who had spent some years abroad and in France, where he became acquainted personally with Fourier and with his doctrines of association, which had deeply impressed him. On his return to America he advocated them in the New York *Tribune*, and by the publication of two or more volumes, by active interest in a society, and by various writings for papers and magazines.

I do not know whether Mr. Brisbane owned stock in the Brook Farm Association or not. Certainly he never gained any dividend by his labor there, but was an interested observer who boarded at the farm at intervals, sometimes passing a few days only, and finally residing some months, occupied in the study and translation of Fourier's works. [74]

He was an enthusiast, but his over enthusiastic moods influenced the Brook Farmers, it seemed to me, often-times unwisely. He saw the full-blown phalanstery coming like a comet and expected every moment. We shortly would be in a blaze of glory! He loved to talk of the good things to be—of social problems worked out by science and by harmonic modes; to flatter himself that without great self-sacrifice, devotion and untiring industry, the world was to be regenerated. It seemed to his mind, that it could be done all at once by organization and enthusiasm, and it was only necessary to create enough of them to carry everything before them as in a bayonet charge.

He labored hard with the society to change its name to Phalanx, and to push the movement as far as possible into the formulas and organization described by Fourier, which did not advance it a single step in material or spiritual progress, and acted, as in the case of the constitution, as a dead weight, owing to the burdensomeness of its details, which called for too much labor to keep the accounts of so complex an organization.

[*Ibid.* pp. 88-89]

The workshop, which was being built at the time of my arrival, was two stories in height, sixty by forty feet in size, with a pitched roof;

well lighted with windows, and situated some three hundred yards behind the Hive, in a northwesterly direction. At its further end, in the cellar, was placed a horse-mill, afterwards [89] exchanged for a steam-engine, that carried the machinery for all the departments of labor. Our engineer, Jean M. Pallisse, a worthy Swiss, a very intelligent man, had a calm face that fitted well with the quiet wreaths of smoke he sent up on the air, from his almost ever-present cigar. It was our delight to coax him to bring out his violin on dance nights, and give us a charming waltz or two. You would hardly associate his intelligent and pleasant face with the dull work of an engine room, but he was there day by day, faithful and regular as a clock, for he was in earnest. He had the sublime faith in him, and in later years held a responsible position in a wealthy importing house in New York City.

The shop was partitioned off, according to the needs of business, and in the time of our greatest numbers, when crowded with members and visitors, no other place being found to stow people in, beds were placed in its upper story.

[*Ibid*. pp. 105-106]

The paper was not local. It aimed high as a purely literary and critical as well as progressive journal, and I must ever consider it a fault that it did not chronicle more of Brook Farm life. We look almost in vain through its pages for one word of its situation, finding none except in some allusions to it in the correspondence from abroad. Occasionally the school was advertised in a corner, but for the rest it might as well have been published elsewhere as at Brook Farm. The leaders, feeling that the life there was an experiment, and perhaps a doubtful one, were not disposed to gratify [106] a curiosity which they probably considered morbid, by yielding to it. This was a mistake. It was a mistake, as much as it would be for us to leave out of our letters to our friends the petty incidents of daily life, and describe only grand principles and outside events. It is only to those loved most by us that we recite the trivial things, for we know that those trivialities link us closer than anything else, filling all the chinks in our friendship or love. It was a disappointment to those who desired to know often of the spirit of the workers, and of the little events that happened there, not to find more notices of them.

In many other respects the *Harbinger* was a grand success. In all that pertained to music, criticism, poetry and progress no journal stood higher. I cannot tell of it pecuniary success for I do not find any memorandum of its finances. The first number commenced with a story translated from the French of George Sand (Madame Dudevant) entitled "Consuelo"—in some respects the sweetest story she ever wrote. It was translated by our neighbor, Mr. Francis G. Shaw, who would oftentimes mount his horse, and, with his little boy, a tiny fellow, on a pony by his side, gallop over to see us. How hard it is for me to realize that afterward the same little fellow, as Col. Robert G. Shaw, led his colored regiment through fire and smoke and the whizzing bullets up to the cannon's mouth of bloody Fort Wagner, and there laid down his life for his country.

[*Ibid* p. 134]

In the matter of dress, the women who chose, had made for themselves a short gown with an under garment, bound at the ankles and of the same material. With this dress they could walk well and work well. It was somewhat similar to the dress worn by Mrs. Bloomer and called by her name years after this date.

no. 127 ～

From Arthur Sumner, "A Boy's Recollections of Brook Farm," *New England Magazine*, X, New Series (March-August, 1894), 309-313.

Let it be understood, at the outset, that I know very little about the origin or general scope of the famous Brook Farm enterprise. I only present my own life there, so far as I can recall it. I was about sixteen years old at the time. The impressions of my year at Brook Farm remain perfectly distinct in my mind, after a lapse of fifty years. But a great deal passed before me which I took little interest in, at the time; and so it would be unsafe for me to say much about the purpose which drew the people together. I know that when I first went there they repudiated the name of Fourierites; nor was it, at any time of my sojourn, a genuine socialist community. The elders formed an association, to which they contributed their labor, and their money, if they had any. But the principal income of the society or, as it was called, the Community, was derived from the boarders, who were not regular members of the association. There were many boarders; and most of them were young people, who received instruction from the members, though there was no regular school. I was one of the scholars; and very little did I learn. That was my own fault. I have never regretted my idleness. I was too busy in the fields and by the river to study. Plenty of time for that afterwards.

We Brook-Farmers were exceedingly happy people, and perfectly satisfied with our little isolated circle. We always spoke of the outer world of "civilization" (a term of contempt) as "outside barbarians." But by and by the "barbarians" [310] began to encroach. Towards the close of my year, Fourierism came to be discussed by the members. Meetings were held in the long dining-room of The Hive. We boys took very little interest in these proceedings; but we understood that the theories of Fourier were to be adopted. To what extent they were I did not know at the time, nor do I know now. Soon after this agitation began, some very unpleasant people appeared upon the scene. They seemed to us boys to be discontented mechanics. They soon fell into a group by themselves. After dinner they would collect together in the great barn, and grumble; and when the others passed through, the malcontents eyed them with suspicion, and muttered, "Aristocrats!" all because they knew themselves to be less cultivated and well-bred. Yet there was the kindest feeling of brotherhood among the members; and it did not need that a man should be a scholar or a gentleman to be received and absorbed.

I remember one sour-looking apostle, with scowling brows, whose whole talk was hate. He kept a glass shop in Boston, and but for this circumstance would have thrown stones at all the world; but he made a good living out of that established order which made him swear so.

About this time a famous Socialist, Albert Brisbane, used to visit the Community, and harangue the people, yet not in a way to secure the constant attendance of the youngsters. A story was told of him. He and others were lying out in the grass in the moonlight. "What a beautiful world! What a heavenly moon!" said one. "Miserable world! Damned bad moon!" was poor Brisbane's reply.

The outcome of this fermentation was the building of a huge frame-house, called the Phalanstery, which, being burned down before it was quite put up, the Community fell flat and soon dispersesd. There was not much capital, and very little business sense; and the soil was poor, though the landscape was beautiful.

This famous experiment, since known almost the world over, had a life of seven years. There were a hundred people present during my time; but I cannot remember more than three married couples, though there were several betrothals which afterwards led to marriage.

I don't believe anybody was ever hurt by being at Brook Farm. The life was pure, the company choice. There was a great deal of hard work, and plenty of fun,—music, dancing, reading, skating, moonlight walks, and some flirting in pairs. After the dispersal, the people went back to the world, and most of them prospered.

Mr. George Ripley was the head man. His sunny, beaming face, cheerful kindness, and elastic step are not to be forgotten. Yet he could look stern. I remember we had some *tableaux vivants*. He stood for a Suliote chief at bay, with his daughters clinging around him. The thing was taken from an annual. Mr. Ripley came in hastily from work, and made no change in his clothes, though he did take off his spectacles. He took a fine, heroic pose, and with a leopard-skin thrown over his breast, he and his Greek daughters looked fully equal to the occasion. It is perfectly certain that he would have faced a real danger with equal composure.

Mr. Ripley favored our going to church; so they used to rig up a two-horse hay wagon, of a Sunday morning, and ride over to Theodore Parker's meeting-house in West Roxbury, a pretty village two miles away. I think I went once. This was in the earlier part of Parker's ministry, before he had become obnoxious to "true believers." Many years after this ancient history, I used to visit a young lady in West Roxbury—a farmer's daughter—who told me that Mr. Parker had always been greatly interested in the young people of the village, and had thrown open his library and his study and himself to all the girls and boys who would come to see him. There were also several families of cultivated people. The effect was marked. As in Concord, there grew up a circle of studious, thoughtful, refined young people, reading books not commonly read in small towns by farmers and others of the working people.

The Rev. William Henry Channing, nephew of the famous Dr. Channing, came out several Sundays to preach to us at the Pilgrim House; so our religious wants [311] were not neglected. Yet the grown people were freethinkers. All that I remember of Mr. Channing is that his sermons were beautiful, and that he stood at the end of the parlor, with a high, white forehead in striking contrast with a sun-browned face.

Not all the people of the present day, who read the New York *Sun*, are aware that Mr. Charles A. Dana was a member of the Brook Farm Community, and the companion of those unworldly philosophers. He was Mr. Ripley's right-hand man, and between them there was a most affectionate and jovial friendship. I call to mind Dana's vigorous stride, hearty laugh, and belted blouse. Like the rest, he taught and worked and sang, and then worked again. He was the bass in a choir which sang *Kyrie Eleison*, night and day. It seemed to me they sang it rather too often; but I might have been mistaken.

I cannot forbear to speak of a young man who was at Brook Farm during the early part of my time. He would not recognize the description of himself, could he see it; but all the old Brook-Farmers would. His name and work are known wherever Americans are found. He was a comely youth of eighteen, and when I first saw him he was chopping fagots with a billhook behind the Erie all alone. His face and manners, his singing, and his general tone made him very attractive to women, and I think equally so to men. I know one boy who was almost as well pleased with him as any girl would be. I am what is left of that boy; and the young man was George William Curtis. I speak of his early years, because of the contrast between the guitar-playing, serenading, moonlight young fellow and the earnest reformer he soon grew to be.

Mr. John Dwight used to come in from his toil in the hot sun at noon, to give me a lesson on the piano; and after faithfully doing that job, he would lie down on the lounge and go to sleep, while I played to him. What a piece of nonsense it was, to have a man like that hoeing corn and stiffening his eloquent fingers! But the idea was (I think) that all kinds of labor must be made equally honorable, and that the poet, painter and philosopher must take their turn at the plough or in the ditch. Mr. Dwight had a quite feminine sweetness and delicacy of nature. I suppose only the non-musical need be told that he was afterwards the editor of Dwight's *Journal of Music*. Boston has only lately mourned his death.

To me this year of my youthful life stands out single and conspicuous. Simply as a happy memory, it is inestimable. I learned little or nothing from books, and only worked occasionally in the fields, just to amuse myself. But the regular members worked in the house, or out of doors, at general farm work, domestic duties, and in giving lessons to the pupils. The ladies used to go around from house to house, to do the chamber work in the morning; and in rainy weather they were sometimes escorted by us boys, who held our umbrellas over them. The washing and ironing were done at the Pilgrim House, by another "group." There it was that I first learned to iron towels. I think there were only two paid women servants, and they worked in the kitchen. The waiters at the table were selected from the regular members, under the direction of Mr. Dana as head waiter. They were skilful, assiduous and very gay. . . .

I remember a fancy-dress picnic in the woods, which might have furnished Mr. Hawthorne his scene in the "Blithedale Romance." The big dog and the Indian chief were there, and Silas Foster, but no Zenobia. I am glad to say that there [312] was never at Brook Farm anybody remotely resembling Zenobia; because if there had been, Hawthorne would never have presented that superb creature. I am often asked this question, so I make the answer. The Indian chief of our picnic was a young fellow,—George Wells,—a hero among us boys, tall, straight and handsome, with long, fair curls hanging down his shoulders (the fashion at the Farm). He was bright, kind and strong, and could do everything that a boy ought to do, and better than any of us. He afterwards became distinguished in the Massachusetts Legislature, in the ante-bellum days, where he contended successfully with the veteran Caleb Cushing about the stirring issues of that day. Wells was killed in Virginia, while colonel of the Thirty-fourth Massachusetts and commander of a brigade. I do not remember Silas Foster's name; but I recall his beautiful smile and white teeth. Across half a century, this plain, sun-browned farmer, who spoke little, but had a kind voice and pleasant ways, stands before me so clearly that I could paint his portrait. I do not say that Hawthorne had him in mind; but he was our head farmer, just as Silas Foster was in the "Romance." . . .

Margaret Fuller spent three days with us at Brook Farm in my year, and I had the honor of sitting alone with her in the library of the Erie for one hour. She was quite unconscious of my presence, though I sat near her, and could not take my eyes off her face. I have no idea why I did so look at her, but I did. Associated with Miss Fuller in my memory, because he shared her tragic fate, was Horace, youngest brother of Charles Sumner. Horace was living at the Farm when I first came there.

We had a great deal of company,—curious tourists from abroad, artistic people, and socialists. It became necessary to charge a moderate price for their accommodation. The houses were, first, The Hive, largest and oldest. It was an old farmhouse, standing near the quiet country road, the land sloping down in front to a pretty brook which ran through the farm to join the river. Close by was a magnificent elm. The Hive contained the kitchen and dining-room, and thither flocked the whole Community, summoned three times a day by a bugle horn, which set the black dog a-howling. The other houses were about a quarter of a mile away, and a few hundred yards from each other. One of them was built by Mr. Morton of Plymouth, and was called the Pilgrim House. Mr. Morton was the father of Mrs. Abby Morton Diaz, who was at one time a member. She was a pretty girl. Near by

was a brown house called The Cottage. The first time I slept at the
Farm I was put into a room in this house, and, the night being cool, I
got up and laid a light table upside down on the bedspread as a blanket.
I do not recommend the expedient, but I slept well that night. Next
to The Cottage was The Erie, a square, frail house, standing on some
high terraces, and looking over a wide prospect of meadow and hill.
Back of it, within a few rods, a pine forest stretched away, I don't
know how far.

Many years afterwards I went to view the old scenes, and found the
Second Massachusetts Regiment encamped on the grounds, and ready
to go to the front. The Erie had gone,—nothing left but the cellar, in
the middle of which stood a tall pine-tree. But this was not my first
return. Once I rode out from Boston on horseback, and found, attached
to the Pilgrim House, the scene of so many merry dances, a great yard,
surrounded by a high, open fence, which corralled a pack of screaming
urchins belonging to the Roxbury poorhouse. [313] As I rode by they
ran along the fence after me, with such remarks as naturally suggest
themselves to persons of their condition. I went on, and came to a high
knoll in sight of the river, crowned with a clump of ash-trees. I was
looking for the grave of the old cook, whom I shall call Hannah. She
was lame and suffered much pain, and was therefore cross; but I remember she sometimes spoke pleasantly to me, and I have pleasant
memories of her. Indeed, she had a perfect right to be cross; she was
quite alone in the world. Hannah died while I was there, and was
buried on this lonely, breezy knoll. Her grave had been protected by
a fence of two rails, and shaded by the beautiful summer trees; but I
could not now find her grave, nor any vestige of it.

I must tell who "we boys" were. During my year there were not
many. There were two Spanish boys from Manila, who had been con-
signed by their father to a Boston merchant, to be sent to school; so
they were kept at Brook Farm for several years. They learned very
little; but that was just as well, for one was dull, and the other was a
leper, and died at sea on his voyage homeward. There might have been
a dozen more boys. For a little while there was a crowd of Cuban boys,
—most unpleasant fellows, haughty, jealous, quarrelsome and suspicious.
There was one, however, Ramon Lacuna, who had none of these
traits. The other boys and girls came mostly from Boston and its
neighborhood. A tall, fair-haired stripling from Virginia was my crony.
If young Booth is yet alive, and should see this, it may interest him to
know that I remember him perfectly and can see his blue eyes to-day.

Lucas, the Spanish leper, had a broad, good-humored face, was an

244

exquisite waltzer. Poor fellow, he grew worse before the Community broke up; and his father, a Manila lawyer, abandoned him, stopped the supplies, and cast him off! But the Boston merchant took care of him, and finally put him on board a ship bound to Manila. He died and was buried at sea.

A queer character was a man named John Cheever. He came over to this country as valet to an English baronet, who spent a day at Brook Farm and died suddenly the day after. What John's means of subsistence were I do not know; but long after I left, I was told that he wandered away and was never heard of again. He had droll, quaint ways of talking; and though treated on terms of perfect equality, being a general favorite, he never abandoned the deferential, formal manner of a well-trained English servant. He wrote to me after I left; and you would have thought he was addressing a duke. I wish I had that letter. I kept it until five years ago; and the old yellow leaves, with the queer style and formal speech, were the only relic I had of Brook Farm.

It is often asked, "Why has no one written a complete history of this queer little Community, giving its bearings and results upon the social problems, and describing the extent to which Fourierism was adopted?" Perhaps the reason is that it never had any result, except upon the individual lives of those who dwelt there. And perhaps the best way to give an idea of Brook Farm is to simply sketch what one saw and did there. It was a beautiful idyllic life which we led, with plenty of work and play and transcendentalism; and it gave place to the Roxbury poorhouse.

no. 128 ❧

Passages from John Van Der Zee Sears, *My Friends at Brook Farm* (New York: Desmond Fitzgerald, 1912).

[From Ch. III, "A Stranger in a Strange Land," pp. 36-41.]

Racial prejudice was cherished as a virtue in the Old Colonie and the real, solid Dutch families found it anything but creditable that Van Der Zee children—we had the honor of being regarded as Van Der Zees in Beaver street—should be sent to an English school in far off Boston town. Massachusetts was, to them, an English colony, and the people there were English, that is to say, foreigners, strangers, and not to be trusted. However, when it was learned that we were actually going, and mother set about making the elaborate preparations considered necessary for so formidable an undertaking, kind friends came in bringing gifts deemed suitable for the occasion, knitted mittens and mufflers, pies and cakes, apples and cider, and choice stores of the cellar and pantry [37] enough to provision a ship for a long cruise. My nearest boy friend, Gratz Van Rensselaer, gave me his knife. How close were our relations may be understood from the fact that we had a private signal, a peculiar whistle of our own which we used to call each other, as boys are wont to do when on terms of exclusive intimacy. To quote Mr. Peggotty, "A man can't say fairer nor that, now, can he?"

When Gratz went down into his pockets and handed me that knife in solemn silence, I fully realized that he was making a sacrifice on the altar of friendship. Any critic of this writing will be justified in objecting that I did not probably formulate the idea in just these terms, but this is about the size of it, all the same.

Whether my schoolmate ever afterward used our call, I do not know, as our parting was a finality, but for my part, I took it with me to Brook Farm where my new mates adopted it forthwith. Later, the elders took it up, and eventually it became widely known over the face of the earth [38] as "the Brook Farm call." It went to California with a young married couple in the early fifties, to China with one of our boys who became the Captain of a Pacific steamer; to Spain and to Russia with another in the United States diplomatic service; to Italy with two girls whose father was an artist; to the Philippines with students returning to their home in Manila, and to all quarters where Brook Farmers found their way, as they seem always to have remembered it.

A peculiarity which may have helped keep it in mind was that it consisted of two parts, the summons, and the response; the first part differing slightly from the second, to distinguish friend answering friend from the stranger merely imitating sounds accidentally or incidentally heard. Just what the difference was may be learned from the notation here given.

Another peculiarity of the call was that it had the quality of taking character from the person uttering it. For example, Annie Page was the girl I most devotedly [39] admired, and when "she gaed me her answer true" in response to my signal, her musical little trill sounded to me like the voice of the thrush that sang down in the pine woods. Per contra, there was Frank Barlow, whom we used to call "Crazy Barlow" because of his headlong rush at whatever object he had in view, and he could make the call shrill and thrill like a fife.

THE BROOK FARM CALL

I met Frank one morning in the later days of the Civil War when he was striding along Pennsylvania Avenue in Washington at his usual breakneck pace. He [40] was Major General Barlow, then, one of the great generals of the Union Army, but he was, first, last and always, a Brook Farmer, so I signaled to him with the same old call. He came to an abrupt halt, answered my greeting and dashed across the Avenue with both hands extended. Neither of us had more than a short allowance of time, but we could do no less than adjourn to a convenient resort for a good hearty talk about the old days in West Roxbury.

Other experiences with the call have come to me since then but none that I remember with more pleasure. Today there are few or none to answer, no matter how earnestly I might sound the old appeal. As may be seen above, the little succession of notes is very simple, but they convey a world meaning to my old ear. . . .

[*Ibid.* Ch. IV. "A Bad Beginning," pp. 49-65.]

Mr. Jonas Gerrish, or familiarly, just plain Gerrish, was the United States Mail, the Express, the Freight Line and the rapid transit system for Brook Farm. He made two trips daily between the Hive and Scollay's Square, covering the distance, six miles, in about an hour and a half, going out of his way to accommodate his patrons, as occasion required. We found Gerrish waiting at the depot when we arrived in Boston, half-an-hour late. He was a little impatient, as he said there was snow coming and he feared delay in getting back to the city. Gerrish was apt to be impatient, but that was all on the surface as he was really very kind-hearted and obliging. The snow began to fall before we were beyond the streets, and we reached our [50] destination in the midst of a driving storm.

Father decided to return at once with Gerrish, having business in Boston which might go amiss if he should be storm-stayed in West

Roxbury. His apprehensions were only too well founded, the Brook Farm community being snowbound in the Hive during the next three days. He hastily left us in charge of good Mrs. Rykeman, the house-mother at the Hive, promising to come out on Saturday for the week-end at the Farm—though I don't know, come to think of it, that the weekend of our present day outings was known to us at that period.

Mrs. Rykeman had two forlorn, cold and tired children on her hands, one of whom at most was a very miserable youngster, indeed, far from mother and home and everything that makes life worth living. Our hostess took us to her own room and made us comfortable as she could, and, presently, as the bell rang for supper, conducted us to the dining-room. This [51] was a long, bare room, containing ten or twelve square tables, also bare, save for the napkin, knife and spoon and bowl at each place. As we entered at one end of the room, a group of girls came in at the other end bringing pitchers of milk and piles of Boston brown bread. There was also Graham bread or, as we now call it, whole-wheat bread, and apple-sauce, but the meal consisted mainly of brown bread and milk. I then and there learned that the foreign milk was poor and thin because it was skimmed. The idea of putting skimmed milk on the table was unknown in the Old Colonie.

I could not or would not touch the abominable brown bread, and, while waiting for the girls to serve the eggs or chops or whatever there was for supper, passed the time in trying to make out the meaning of the chatter and laughter that filled the room with merriment. There seemed to be a gleam of sense discoverable now and then, but, on the whole, it was impossible to catch the significance of the rapid- [52] fire talk volleying from table to table. Indeed, it was always difficult for a stranger to swing into the current of general conversation at Brook Farm. The bright young enthusiasts there were all of one mind, in a way; in close sympathy and quick to understand each other. A word, a look, a gesture expressed a thought. An allusion, a memory, an apt quotation suggested an idea which was clearly apprehended by ready listeners; and a flash of wit was instantly followed by a peal of mirth, echoed to the limit.

It goes without saying that these reflections were not in my young noddle at the moment, but being of later date, are the findings of longer observation. I must have been in a sort of maze, wondering at the fun going on which I could see and hear but could not comprehend, and wondering too when supper was coming. I was about to ask Mrs. Rykeman how long we would have to wait, when, whiz! the whole business of the meal was over and done with. Everybody sprang

up at [53] once, and away they all flew like a flock of birds, leaving
an astonished little boy looking for something to eat. Althea took
flight with the others, presently returning to look after her forlorn
brother, but, finding I had been taken to the kitchen for something that
might at least alleviate the pangs of hunger, she rejoined the girls in
the parlor, where there was already a dance under way. Althea was
a bright-spirited girl, vivacious, alert, appreciative and companionable.
She forthwith took her place in the Brook Farm community with the
best grace. She readily made friends with Abby Ford and her sister,
with Annie and Mary Page, with the Barlow brothers and with the
Spanish students of about her own age. Of these latter, Ramon Cita
or Little Raymond became subsequently her particular cavalier. Ramon
was the youngest and smallest of the Spaniards, besides being the best
looking according to our standards, and a very charming little gentleman he was, too. There were eight [54] of these boys and young
men, and they were all courteous and polite to a degree that we
American youngsters could admire, but to which we could hardly
attain. They must have been members of distinguished families, as they
more than once received visits from high officials of the Spanish lega-
tion in Washington.

It may as well be said here that these students were sent from
Manila to prepare for Harvard in Dr. Ripley's school in Boston; a
school which was of the first repute in the early forties. The Doctor
transferred it with several of the teachers to West Roxbury, where it
became the nucleus of the Brook Farm school. The Ford girls, with
their aunt, Miss Russell, the Barlow boys and their mother, and the
Manila youths were, I believe, among those migrating from the Boston
school.

We all liked the young Spaniards very much, and I have ever since
liked the people of their nationality I have met at home and abroad.
They can teach us good manners every day in the week; but [55]
they have one peculiarity that must strike the average American as
certainly rather strange. This is their common and familiar use of
words and names which we regard as sacred and hardly to be spoken
outside of the meeting-house. As an example, it may be allowable, at
this late day to mention without giving family names, that one of our
students was baptized Jesus Mary, and another by the same rite was
designated Joseph Holy Spirit.

Before bedtime the snowstorm had risen to the height of a terrific
tempest, the heaviest and hardest of the winter, and what the New
England winter can do when it tries can only be known by experience.

as no description can convey any adequate idea of the fierce blasts, the drive of hard-frozen snow and the terrible cold forced straight through clothes and flesh and bones by the piercing spears and pounding hammers of the Northeast gale fiends. Three days and three nights the raiding powers of the arctics raged about us and [56] blockaded all but the hardiest and strongest of us in the close quarters of the Hive. To venture out of the house was to risk life and limb. No one was allowed to run such risks alone, as, in case of a fall, the chances would be against getting up again without help, but parties of twos and threes of the young men went to the barns to look after the cattle or up to the Eyrie, the Cottage and Pilgrim Hall to see that all was right and to bring down a sled-load of bedding for the shut-ins. In their services, the vegetarians matched themselves against the "cannibals" as they disdainfully called those who were still in bonds to the flesh-pots of Egypt, but I do not believe there was beef enough eaten on the place to warrant any comparisons being made, and, at any rate, they all came out alike, pretty much exhausted.

Next morning I awoke on a sofa in the upper hall, where I had stretched out, along toward midnight, for a moment's rest. Althea had carefully taken off my [57] shoes, and had covered me over with cloaks and shawls, without my knowing it. The swarm in the Hive had exemplified the poet's idea of the tumultuous privacy of storm fairly well as to the tumult, but as to the privacy, that was what could be had in a house overcrowded with excited young folk. Frolic and fun were to the fore, and everybody bore the troubles of that tempestuous evening with high good humor; one weary, cross and fretful little chap being left out of the account. Left out he was, for sure. Always at Brook Farm, anyone not strictly in it, to use a phrase of later date, was absolutely out of it. One had to be aboard the train or find himself standing alone on the platform.

I was in better case after what had to serve as a morning toilet, as Mrs. Rykeman had promised to make up for a scanty supper by a treat of good hot brewis. Brewis was a new word and I was more than ready to test the merits of the unknown aliment, as, in my experience, anything commended as good to eat, was sure [58] to prove palatable. The dining-room was occupied as a shake-down dormitory for women and girls, and breakfast was taken standing in the parlor or hall or anywhere places could be found outside of the kitchen where work was going on. When my bowl was handed me it was filled with the everlasting brown bread boiled in milk. That was brewis. I was just mad!

Wednesday and Thursday of that first week at Brook Farm were sad days indeed. I made a bad beginning! Shut up indoors by the most violent tempest of the year, I sulked in corners, alone in a crowd, the loneliest kind of solitude. The teachers did their best to keep classes going in the bedrooms, but, in the irregularity of the sessions, I was allowed to be absent without remark. Althea and some others tried to draw me into the continuous picnic performance going on all over the house only to learn there was nothing doing in brother's retreat. At meal time the exasperating brown bread was invariably offered for my delectation, and that [59] I regarded as a personal affront. Resorting to alliteration's artful aid, it may be said I seemed bound to be bothered by Boston brown bread. I brooded morning, noon and night over the one idea that when my father came, I would beseech him to take me back home.

It appeared, later, that I was not being altogether neglected by the authorities during this trying period, as they had kept their eyes on the new boy and were seriously considering this same idea, thinking it would perhaps be better to advise his father to take him away. The dour youker was plainly enough so unhappily out of place that they were inclined not to try to keep him. Truly, a bad beginning!

This was not a decision adopted to meet the special case in hand, but rather an unwritten rule of the community. Brook Farm was a solidarity, a company united to put in practice certain principles and to accomplish certain results, and only those were wanted who could enter into the spirit of the movement and aid in [60] carrying on the great work. Those who did not help, hindered, and to hinder the task of reforming society could not be permitted. As with the community, so also with the school. The school was an independent organization, but it was likewise an experimental organization, being, practically, a first attempt to inaugurate industrial education, and only pupils suited for such an education were wanted. It was not a place for the feeble-minded, the deficient or the intractable, but for bright children capable of responding to instruction directed to certain ends. The teachers, earnestly devoted to these selected courses of instruction, could not afford to give time and attention to incompetents. . . . [61]

On Friday the storm abated and things began to mend all around as the skies cleared. In the afternoon Dr. Ripley and Charles Hosmer made their way home from Boston, hailed with rejoicings by everyone except Master Grumpus, who should have been more than thankful for their timely arrival, had he only known it. Saturday morning regular lessons were resumed in the classroom, but I held aloof in out-of-the-way coverts; one hiding place being the cow-stable. Here Charles Hosmer happened to find me, just incidentally, as it seemed, but really by kindly [62] design no doubt, and gave me a hearty greeting which I couldn't be so churlish as not to return.

"Are you the boy who came from Albany?" he asked.

"From the Old Colonie, in Albany," I replied.

"I suppose," he continued, "you have not yet been assigned to your classes?"

I accepted this account of what was in fact absence without leave, and he then suggested that if I had nothing else on hand I might help him in making a toboggan-slide. Never having heard of such a thing I accepted the invitation. Securing a couple of shovels we cleared a path to the knoll; and, on the way, Mr. Hosmer explained that Angus Cameron, another new pupil, hailing from Canada, had brought to the school a toboggan, a kind of sled, and we were to make a smooth path or slide for it, so the boys and girls could try it in the afternoon when there were no lessons.

We went to work with a will, spanking [63] the snow down with the shovels, leveling uneven places and forming a clear, hard track from the top of the Knoll to the brook. On the edge of the bank we piled up an inclined plane, wetting down the snow and building a mound perhaps five feet high. From this elevation, Mr. Hosmer stated, the toboggan, flying down the slide, would shoot upward and forward and land on the far side of the brook. That seemed to me a very desirable thing to do, and, while I finished up the shovel-work, my companion went back to the Hive and brought out the toboggan.

This conveniency, well enough known to-day, was new to us, and we did not quite know how to manage it. However, we got onto the thing somehow, and away we went down the slide. The slide was all right and the inclined plane was all right, so we made the descent and the ascent all right, soaring over the brook like a bird, but the landing on the far side was all wrong. We hit the snowbank like a battering ram, the snow piling up in front of [64] us as hard as stone; the shock was terrific! Mr. Hosmer got the worst of it as he catapulted into the drift, while I alighted in a heap on his shoulders. He scrambled out of the drift on all fours, concerned only with learning whether I was badly hurt. On my assurance that unless his back and legs and arms were broken, there was no damage done, he straightened up and declared he was unhurt but dreadfully humiliated. "How could a man be such a condemned idiot as to plunge head-first against a barricade like that?" This was the question suggested to his mind, only he did not say "condemned idiot" exactly, but he apologized for the emphatic words he did use, and as they do not look well in print, they need not be repeated.

Despite his bluff I saw he was in pain and wanted him to return to the Hive, but he insisted on finishing our job. Under his direction I wallowed through the snowdrift, back and forth, trampling down a passage, and then pressed the snow hard and flat, using the toboggan [65] like a plank. Meanwhile Mr. Hosmer had turned very white and now dropped onto the toboggan, limp and sick. The shock had upset his digestion. How to get him home? Borrowing rails from the roadside fence I laid them across the streak of open water in the middle of the brook, piled snow over them, and dragged my patient across on the toboggan. I attempted to haul him up the Knoll, but he protested, asserting that he was much better and fully able to walk. He managed to crawl up the hill and left me with directions to find Angus Cameron and join him in taking charge of the slide in the afternoon.

After making half-a-dozen or more flying leaps over the brook on the new conveyance, with as many jolts and tumbles in the snow, I managed to get the hang of the thing, and could steer it over the course with delightful ease, suggesting the flight of a bird.

[*Ibid.* Ch. V. "A Good Ending," pp. 66-71.]

Saturday's dinner dispelled all fears of starvation from Brook Farm's meager fare, the table being abundantly supplied with boiled beef, vegetables, Graham bread and good, sweet butter like home, and, best of all, baked Indian pudding, a real luxury. Mr. Hosmer did not appear, being confined to his room in the cottage. Learning that Dr. Ripley intended calling there, I asked leave to go with him, and was told to be in the library, which was also the President's office, at four o'clock.

Not being accustomed to Brook Farm's quick changes, my little talk with Dr. Ripley made me a few minutes late at the Knoll, where I found two-score or so of children and half as many grownups engaged in a snowball scrimmage. Inquiring for Angus, I turned over the toboggan [67] to him for the first ride. He asked if the slide was all right, if I had made the jump over the brook, and if Mr. Hosmer was badly hurt. As he was a little backward about coming forward, so to speak, I took the initiative, inviting any girl to join me who had courage enough to face the music. Urged by my sister Althea, Annie Page took the offered seat, and down the slide we plunged like a shot, all the company watching our venture with intense interest and not a little anxiety. The flight took the breath away, but we sailed over the brook and out to the thin snow on the meadow in one grand swoop, without a bump or a break on the way. Annie was delighted and thanked me, over and over for giving her such a surprising pleasure.

Under the circumstances I thought Althea might be the next girl to make the trip, and, on the way up the hill, I gave the Old Colonie call, which she recognized and answered. Annie noticed the whistle and the reply, and asked what it meant, [68] and when I explained the signal, she said, "I would like to learn that." I immediately repeated it until she caught the notes, and presently the strain was echoed all over the Knoll, and from that moment it became the call of the school. From that moment, too, Annie Page became the one girl of the place for me. She held that position in my regard until three years later, when she and her sister went to live with their parents in Italy. She was a year and a month and a day younger than myself, but was far my senior in the school. That was an advantage to me, as it had the effect of driving me ahead in my studies in order to reach her classes. We were together a good deal out of school hours, taking the same work to do, when that was practicable, as feeding the rabbits in the warren back of the Eyrie, and cultivating the herb-garden where we raised mint, anise and cummin, sage, marjoram and saffron for the Boston market.

One other incident occurred on the Knoll perhaps worth recording, as it gave [69] me a name. Annie insisted on helping me pull the toboggan up the slide, and, on the way, she remarked, "I did not know boys liked perfumery."

"That," said I, "is from the cedar chest our clothes are packed in."

Just as we reached the group at the top of the hill she answered, "Oh, cedar! So it is."

As she spoke, a little toddlekins, three or four years old, came running to me, exclaiming, "Cedar, can't I ride on the 'boggan?"

That settled it! My Brook Farm name was thenceforth Cedar, and would be Cedar, still, were there any of my companions left to remember it. . . .

At four o'clock my sister and I trudged up to pay our call at the Eyrie. This was a square house of the surburban villa type, two-and-a-half stories high, and the hand-[70]somest building on the place, though plain enough, as compared with villas in the neighbor-hood to-day. Doctor and Mrs. Ripley received us very kindly and gave us a most cordial welcome to Brook Farm. Mrs. Ripley, born Sophia Dana, was a slender, graceful lady, belonging to what Dr.

Oliver Wendell Holmes calls the Brahmin class of Boston; charming in manner, animated and blithe, but profoundly serious in her religious devotion to what she regarded as the true Christian life. She had, informally, the general charge of the girls in the school, and she at once made Althea feel at home under her motherly care.

Dr. Ripley gained my confidence by claiming old acquaintance, recalling a former meeting that I had quite forgotten. Several years previous, when I was a very small boy indeed, my father had taken me with him on a flying trip from New York to Boston, deciding to do so, I suppose rather than to leave mother in a strange city with two children on her hands. [71] During that brief visit Dr. Ripley had taken father to call on an illustrious artist, and he now recalled the circumstances to my mind. With his prompting I could remember riding in a carriage; seeing a tall silvery old gentleman wearing a black velvet robe lined with red, and tasting white grapes for the first time; but I could not think of the silvery gentleman's name.

"Well," said my mentor, "perhaps you will be glad sometime to know that the gentleman you saw was Washington Alston."

no. 129 ∿

From a Note on Anna Q. T. Parsons, by Helen Dwight Orvis, Wellesley, Massachusetts, March, 1928. Here reprinted from Marianne Dwight, *Letters from Brook Farm 1844-1847*, edited by Amy L. Reed (Poughkeepsie, N. Y.: Vassar College, 1928), pp. xiii-xv.

[xiv] . . . Miss Parsons was a frequent visitor at Brook Farm and some of her letters written from there are headed "Heaven." She longed to become a member but was prevented by [xv] family obligations. She was one of its most earnest well-wishers and to her "combined home" on Pinckney Street, a cooperative house run somewhat on Brook Farm principles, some of the people went after the Farm was given up. Here John Dwight and Mary Bullard were married and here Anna Parsons started her Union or Woman's Exchange.

The day before the sale of Brook Farm at auction was Fast Day and some of the young folk of the Religious Union had a picnic at Bussey Hill woods. William Henry Channing and Anna Parsons attended it, and then went on to Brook Farm to spend the night with Miss Macdaniel, who was living all alone at the Eyrie. She and the Codman family at the Hive were all that were left of the remarkable group who had formerly made their home there. In the evening, after a picnic supper to which all contributed, Mr. Channing read aloud, from a volume he had brought out in his pocket, Browning's new poem, *Paracelsus*. The next morning, when none of the party could bear to be present during the sale, they went into the Pine Woods, where Mr. Channing finished reading the poem and they spent the day on the spot so endeared to them, where their Sunday services had sometimes been held. After all was over and the people gone, they returned and all had supper with the Codmans at the Hive.

Some time before this when there had been talk of disbanding, Anna Parsons had said, "If Brook Farm is given up, I will go to its funeral," and Rebecca Codman added, "And I will stay behind and sweep it up." And this they literally did.

HELEN DWIGHT ORVIS

Wellesley, Massachusetts.
March, 1928.

Exercises

Exercises for Part One

Write one page, carefully annotated, in answer to one of the following groups of questions:

1. How was Emerson invited to join Ripley at Brook Farm? What was his response?

2. What did George Ripley expect to accomplish at Brook Farm? Were his expectations based on religious ideas? Economic ideas? Political ideas? Personal hopes and plans?

3. To what extent were the first Articles of Association designed to direct and control daily life at Brook Farm? What particular concerns of the founders are most clearly reflected in the Articles?

4. What persons lived at Brook Farm at the time when the first Articles of Association were signed? What persons who had lived there as members of Ripley's community had by this time departed? What persons then planned to depart?

Exercises for Part Two

Write an annotated theme on one of the following groups of questions:

1. How does the entry for October 22, 1841 in Hawthorne's *Notebooks* compare with his entry (see Part One) for September 27 of the same year? In what important ways do they differ? Do intermediate entries show a fairly consistent change in his general attitude toward life on the Farm? How do you account for the fact that his notebook entries begin as late as September? How does the intonation of his notebook entries compare with that of his letters to Sophia Peabody? If you find the two different, how do you account for the difference?

2. What are the important differences between the "Constitution" of 1844 and the "Articles of Association" of 1841? In what important ways are the two documents alike?

3. On the basis of evidence in Parts One and Two, define the following terms in the sense which they came to be used at Brook Farm: "association," "Phalanx," "social science."

4. To what extent are the ideas expressed in Elizabeth Peabody's "Plan of the West Roxbury Community" reflected in the Constitution of

1844? In Brisbane's and Macdaniel's "What is Association?" In Charles Lane's "Brook Farm"?

5. In his letter to Emerson dated December 17, 1841, what was Ripley's purpose? Do Emerson's entries in his *Journal* during this period indicate that Ripley might reasonably have expected an affirmative response?

Exercises for Part Three

Write an annotated theme on one of the following groups of questions:

1. Study the following readings carefully: John Sullivan Dwight, "Association . . . with Education" (February 29, 1844); G. W. Curtis, letter to Dwight on March 3, 1844; John Sullivan Dwight, "Individuality in Association" (October 4, 1845); and "Oliver Cromwell's Letters and Speeches . . ." (January 3, 1846). What central issue are the two men debating? What position does each man assume? What is your own opinion on the question?

2. How would you describe the personality of Marianne Dwight? What individuals among the group at the Farm interested her most? How trustworthy was her judgment in appraising the worth of other persons? What were her contributions to the "industrial" activities of the Farm? How well did she behave during the crisis of the smallpox epidemic? What were her relations with George Ripley? What was her relation to the "R. L. S. G."? (See her letter of March 2, 1845.) How does her career at the Farm compare with that of Hawthorne?

3. What was the plan of the Phalanstery? When was its construction begun? How was it financed? On what grounds might the Farmers have differed on the question whether it should be built? Did they in fact differ?

4. In what important ways had life at the Farm changed from the beginning in 1841 to the fire in 1846? To what causes do you attribute the changes?

5. Choose one day in the year 1845 and describe the events which did happen, and which probably may have happened, on that day at Brook Farm. If you wish, you may pretend that you were there and write in the first person. You may even write a letter to some imaginary friend describing a day's experience there.—But though the form of your essay be imaginative, you are responsible for the facts. Don't contradict the record as we have it. Presumably, since this is an annotated essay, your letter will be presented in a thoroughly edited form, as though for publication in 1945.

Exercise for Part Four

Write in no more than two hundred words a concise prospectus, or plan, for a long essay on some aspect of the general history of Brook Farm. No annotation is required.

Suggested Titles for Final Papers

The following titles for extensive papers on Brook Farm are no more than suggestions. Students may use them, or they may devise their own.

Brook Farm: The Plan Compared with Its Fulfillment
The Economics of Brook Farm
Why Brook Farm Failed
Why Brook Farm Succeeded
A Narrative History of Brook Farm: 1841-1847
The Friendly Phalanx
The Middle Years at Brook Farm
Two Extremes: Nathaniel Hawthorne and Marianne Dwight
The First Year at Brook Farm
The Women of Brook Farm
Brook Farm: Patron of the Arts
Brook Farm and Emerson

Index

Index